1994

Piers Plowman

A GUIDE TO THE QUOTATIONS

medieval & renaissance texts & studies

Volume 77

Piers Plowman

A GUIDE

TO THE QUOTATIONS

John A. Alford

medieval & Renaissance texts & studies
Binghamton, New York
1992

Library of Congress Cataloging-in-Publication Data

Alford, John A., 1938–
    Piers Plowman : a guide to the quotations / John A. Alford.
    cm. — (Medieval & Renaissance texts & studies : v. 77.)
    Includes bibliographical references and index.
    ISBN 0-86698-088-1
    1. Langland, William, 1330?-1400? Piers the Plowman.
2. Langland, William, 1330?-1400?—Knowledge and learning.
3. Quotations in literature. I. Title. II. Series.
PR2017.Q67A44 1992
821'.1—dc20   91-31220
                                                              CIP

This book is made to last.
It is set in Antiqua, smythe-sewn
and printed on acid-free paper
to library specifications

Printed in the United States of America

Contents

Acknowledgments

I WOULD LIKE TO THANK the following persons for their help in this guide: Stephen A. Barney, Andrew Galloway, Ralph Hanna III, Traugott Lawler, and M. Teresa Tavormina, for their suggestions; Kathleen Blumreich Moore and Margaret Wesseling, for checking the accuracy of the citations; Joseph S. Wittig, for providing a computer printout of the Athlone edition of the C version; and above all, George Russell and George Kane, for giving me permission to cite it before publication.

Abbreviations

Alford 1972	John A. Alford, "*Piers Plowman* B.xviii.390: 'Til Parce It Hote.' " *MP* 69 (1972): 323–25.
Alford 1975	——, "Some Unidentified Quotations in *Piers Plowman*." *MP* 72 (1975): 390–99.
Alford 1977	——, "The Role of the Quotations in *Piers Plowman*." *Speculum* 52 (1977): 80–99.
Alford 1984	——, "More Unidentified Quotations in *Piers Plowman*." *MP* 81 (1984): 146–49.
Alford 1988a	——, ed., *A Companion to Piers Plowman*. Berkeley: Univ. of California Press, 1988.
Alford 1988b	——, *Piers Plowman: A Glossary of Legal Diction*. Cambridge: D. S. Brewer, 1988.
Auctores Octo	*Auctores Octo cum Commento*. London: Jacobus Myt, 1514.
AV	Authorized Version
Bennett	J. A. W. Bennett, ed., *Piers Plowman: The Prologue and Passus I–VII of the B text as found in Bodleian MS. Laud 581*. Oxford: Clarendon Press, 1972.
Brev.	*Breviarium ad Usum Insignis Ecclesiae Sarum*, ed. Francis Procter and Christopher Wordsworth. 3 vols. Cambridge: Cambridge Univ. Press, 1879.
Brinton	*The Sermons of Thomas Brinton, Bishop of Rochester (1373–1389)*, ed. M. A. Devlin. 2 vols. Camden Society, 3d ser., vols 85 and 86. London: Royal Historical Society, 1954.
Bromyard	John Bromyard, *Summa Praedicantium*. 2 vols. Venice, 1586. Cited by volume, folio, and column (e.g., 1:201/2).

x

Cato	*Disticha Catonis. Recensuit et Apparatu Critico Instruxit*, ed. Marcus Boas and Henricus Johannes Botschuyer. Amsterdam: North-Holland, 1952 (cited by book and number); also *Dicta Catonis* (*Disticha Catonis*), ed. J. Wright Duff and Arnold M. Duff, *Minor Latin Poets*, 585–633. Loeb Classical Library. Cambridge, Mass.: Harvard Univ. Press, 1934.
CIC	*Corpus Iuris Canonici*, ed. Aemilius Friedberg. 2 vols. Graz: Akademische Druck u. Verlagsanstalt, 1955.
CT	Geoffrey Chaucer, *The Canterbury Tales*, in *The Riverside Chaucer*, gen. ed. Larry D. Benson. Boston: Houghton-Mifflin, 1987.
EETS	Early English Text Society. Oxford and London. Cited by title and volume.
ELH	*English Literary History*
es	extra series (Early English Text Society)
Foedera	*Foedera, Conventiones, Literae, et cuiuscunque Generis Acta Publica, inter Reges Angliae*, ed. Thomas Rymer. 2d ed. London: Tonson, 1728.
FM	*Fasciculus Morum: A Fourteenth-Century Preacher's Handbook*, ed. and trans. Siegfried Wenzel. University Park: The Pennsylvania State Univ. Press, 1989.
Graces	*Latin Graces*. Ed. F. J. Furnivall in *The Babees Book*, 382–96. EETS 32 (1868).
Glunz	Hans Glunz, *History of the Vulgate in England*. Cambridge: Cambridge Univ. Press, 1933.
Gratian	*Decretum Magistri Gratiani* or *Concordia Discordantium Canonum*. Vol. 1 of *Corpus Iuris Canonici* (*CIC*).
Gray	Nick Gray, "Langland's Quotations from the Penitential Tradition." *MP* 84 (1986): 53–60.
Horstman	Carl Horstman, ed., *Yorkshire Writers: Richard Rolle of Hampole ... and His Followers*. 2 vols. London: Sonnenschein, 1895.
Hort	Greta Hort, *Piers Plowman and Contemporary Religious Thought*. New York: Macmillan, 1938.
Hugh	Hugh of St. Cher, *Postillae in Universa Biblia*. 7 vols. Lyons, 1667.
JEGP	*Journal of English and Germanic Philology*

Kane	George Kane, ed., *Piers Plowman: The A Version.* London: Athlone Press, 1960.
Kane-Donaldson	George Kane and E. Talbot Donaldson, eds., *Piers Plowman: The B Version.* London: Athlone Press, 1975.
Legenda Aurea	Jacobus a Voragine, *Legenda Aurea,* ed. Th. Graesse. 3d ed., 1890; repr. Osnabrück, 1969.
Lindemann	Erika Lindemann, "Analogues for Latin Quotations in Langland's *Piers Plowman.*" *NM* 78 (1977): 359–61.
Lyndwood	William Lyndwood, *Provinciale.* Oxford: Hall, 1679.
MAE	*Medium Aevum*
Manly	John M. Manly, ed., *Specimens of the Pre-Shaksperean Drama.* 2 vols. Boston: Ginn, 1897.
MED	*Middle English Dictionary,* ed. Hans Kurath, Sherman Kuhn, John Reidy, Robert Lewis, et al. Ann Arbor, Mich.: Univ. of Michigan Press, 1952–.
Menot	*Sermons choisis de Michel Menot,* ed. J. Nève. Paris: Champion, 1924.
ME Sermons	*Middle English Sermons . . . from British Museum MS. Royal 18 B. xxiii,* ed. Woodburn O. Ross. EETS 209 (1940).
Missale	*Missale ad Usum Sarum,* ed. F. H. Dickinson. Oxford: Clarendon Press, 1861–83; repr. Farnborough, Hants.: Gregg, 1969.
NM	*Neuphilologische Mitteilungen*
MP	*Modern Philology*
MS	*Mediaeval Studies*
MS(S)	Manuscript(s)
N&Q	*Notes and Queries*
Nico.	*The Gospel of Nicodemus,* ed. H. C. Kim. Toronto Medieval Latin Texts 2. Toronto: Pontifical Institute of Medieval Studies, 1973.
ns	new series
om.	omitted
Pearsall	Derek Pearsall, ed., *Piers Plowman by William Langland: An Edition of the C-Text.* Berkeley and Los Angeles: Univ. of California Press, 1979.
Pennafort	Raymond of Pennafort, *Summa de Poenitentia et Matrimonio.* Rome, 1603; repr. Farnborough, Hants.: Gregg, 1967.

PG	J.-P. Migne, ed., *Patrologiae Cursus Completus. Series Graeca*. 161 vols. Paris, 1857 ff.
PL	J.-P. Migne, ed., *Patrologiae Cursus Completus. Series Latina*. 221 vols. Paris, 1857 ff.
Prick of Cons.	Richard Morris, ed., *The Pricke of Conscience*. Berlin. Asher, 1863.
PQ	*Philological Quarterly*
P. R. O.	Public Record Office, London
Ps. iuxta Heb.	Jerome's third translation of the Psalms, from the Hebrew (printed in *Vetus Italica*)
Rigg and Brewer	A. G. Rigg and Charlotte Brewer, eds. *William Langland. Piers Plowman: The Z Version*. Toronto: Pontifical Institute of Mediaeval Studies, 1983.
Robertson and Huppé	D. W. Robertson, Jr., and Bernard F. Huppé, *Piers Plowman and Scriptural Tradition*. Princeton: Princeton Univ. Press, 1951.
Scase	Wendy Scase, *'Piers Plowman' and the New Anticlericalism*. Cambridge: Cambridge Univ. Press, 1989.
Schmidt	A. V. C. Schmidt, ed., *The Vision of Piers Plowman: A Complete Edition of the B-Text*. New York: Dutton, 1978.
Skeat	W. W. Skeat, ed., *The Vision of William concerning Piers the Plowman in Three Parallel Texts together with Richard the Redeless*. 2 vols. London: Oxford Univ. Press, 1886; repr. 1968.
SP	*Studies in Philology*
Spec. Sacer.	*Speculum Sacerdotale*, ed. Edward Weatherly. EETS 200 (1936).
Summa Virtutum	*Summa Virtutum de Remediis Anime*, ed. Siegfried Wenzel. The Chaucer Library. Athens: Univ. of Georgia Press, 1984.
Szittya	Penn Szittya, *The Antifraternal Tradition in Medieval Literature*. Princeton: Princeton Univ. Press, 1986.
Thomson	David Thomson, *A Descriptive Catalogue of Middle English Grammatical Texts*. New York: Garland, 1979.
Ullmann	Walter Ullmann, *The Medieval Idea of Law, as Represented by Lucas de Penna*. London: Methuen, 1946.
Upland	*Jack Upland, Friar Daw's Reply, and Upland's Re-*

joinder, ed. P. L. Heyworth. Oxford: Oxford Univ. Press, 1968.

var.   variant

VL   *Bibliorum Sacrorum Latinae Versiones Antiquae, seu Vetus Italica*, ed. Pierre Sabatier. 3 vols. Rheims, 1743–51. (*Vetus Latina*)

Voragine   Jacobus de Voragine, *Sermones Dominicales per Totum Annum*. Venice, 1579.

Vulg.   Latin Vulgate Bible (Clementine version), ed. A. Colunga and L. Turrado. 4th ed. Madrid: Biblioteca de Autores Cristianos, 1965.

Walther   Hans Walther, *Proverbia Sententiaeque Latinitatis Medii Aevi*. Göttingen: Vandenhoeck & Ruprecht, 1963–69. Vols. 1–5 (items 1–34283); *Proverbia Sententiaque Latinitatis Medii ac Recentioris Aevi*. Nova series. Göttingen: Vandenhoeck & Ruprecht, 1982. Vols. 6–8 (items 34284–44470).

Weber   Robert Weber, Boniface Fischer, et al., eds., *Biblia Sacra juxta Vulgatem Versionem*. 3d ed. Stuttgart: Deutsche Bibelgesellshaft, 1985.

Whiting   B. J. Whiting, *Proverbs, Sentences and Proverbial Phrases from English Writings Mainly before 1500*. Cambridge, Mass.: Harvard Univ. Press, 1968.

Wordsworth   John Wordsworth and Henry White, eds., *Novum Testamentum Latine*. Editio minor. Oxford: Clarendon Press, 1920.

Wright   Thomas Wright, ed., *The Political Songs of England*. London: Camden Society, 1859.

YLS   *The Yearbook of Langland Studies*. East Lansing, Mich.: Colleagues Press, 1987–.

Introduction

THE FEATURE THAT MOST OBVIOUSLY SETS *Piers Plowman* apart from other Middle English poems is its extensive use of quotations. "Anyone familiar with medieval vernacular literature," Greta Hort observed in 1938, "must at some time have been struck by the extraordinarily large number of Latin quotations found in *Piers Plowman*. In this respect alone Langland's poem differs from all other vernacular books that have come down to us."[1] More precisely, the three versions of *Piers Plowman* contain nearly 600 different tags or quotations in Latin and French or, counting repeated instances, nearly 1,200 in all.[2] Impressive as they are, however, these statistics

---

[1] *Piers Plowman and Contemporary Religious Thought*, 43. Similarly Sister Carmeline Sullivan observes, "No work, whether literary production or dogmatic treatise, is so interlarded with Latin Scriptural quotations and patristic *excerpta*" (*The Latin Insertions and the Macaronic Verse in Piers Plowman* [Washington, DC: Catholic Univ. of America, 1932], vii).

[2] These figures are based on the alphabetical index below. To give more precise figures would be misleading. For one thing, the number of quotations varies according to manuscript and edition; Kane and Donaldson reject several from their edition of the B text as scribal additions (see their introduction, 221–24). For another, agreement is lacking in many cases on what constitutes a Latin or French borrowing; editors are inconsistent in their italicization of words felt to be non-English. For example, Kane and Donaldson italicize *Magi* (B.19.85), regarding it, apparently, as a single-word quotation from Matt. 2:1; so does Pearsall (C.21.85); Russell does not. Such statements as the following, then, should be treated with skepticism: "There are in *Piers Plowman* 422 Latin quotations in all, and of these 422 quotations no less than 301 are of biblical origin" (Hort, 43–44); "There are 619 Latin passages (514 of which are quotations from the Bible)" (Peter Nolan, "Beyond Macaronic: Embedded Latin in Dante and Langland," *Acta Conventus Neo-Latini Bononiensis*, Proceedings of the Fourth International Congress of Neo-Latin Studies, ed. R. J. Schoeck, Medieval & Renaissance Texts & Studies, vol. 37 [Binghamton, NY,

do not fully indicate the importance of the quotations to Langland's art. Since most of them are followed by translations or extended commentary, they could be said to account for nearly half the poem's substance and, if some critics are right, for much of its form as well.

A comprehensive guide to the quotations in *Piers Plowman*, together with their sources and analogues, has long been a desideratum of Langland scholarship. W. W. Skeat's list of the quotations in his Early English Text Society edition (1867–84) and the notes in his parallel-text edition (1886) are incomplete and inaccurate. The expansion of Skeat's list by Dorothy Chadwick (1922) and Anne Havens Fuller (1961) is limited to biblical allusions; that by Greta Hort (1938), to liturgical borrowings and echoes.[3] The picture provided by modern editions of the poem also remains incomplete. Thomas Knott and David Fowler's edition of the A version (1952) lacks notes on the quotations; J. A. W. Bennett's edition of the B version (1972) stops at passus 7; though well annotated, A. V. C. Schmidt's edition of the B version (1978) and D. A. Pearsall's edition of the C version (1979) do not provide cross references to other versions. The Athlone editions upon which this guide is based contain no historical or literary notes of any kind.[4]

This book attempts to consolidate—and add to—what is known about the Latin and French quotations in the several versions of *Piers Plowman*. The information is organized in three ways. Index 1 records and identifies the quotations in their natural order. Index 2 lists the quotations from the Bible in biblical order. Index 3 arranges all the quotations in alphabetical order.

1985], 539). The fact that these figures are at such variance with each other, and with my own, raises a number of unanswered questions. Which version or versions of the poem are the figures based on? Do they include repeated instances? Are single-word allusions counted? What criteria were used to determine the "biblical" origin of certain problematical quotations?

[3] Chadwick, Appendix to *Social Life in the Days of Piers Plowman* (Cambridge: Cambridge Univ. Press, 1922); Fuller, "Scripture in 'Piers Plowman' B," *Mediaeval Studies* 23 (1961): 352–62; Hort, Appendix to *Piers Plowman and Contemporary Religious Thought*.

[4] A team of scholars, led by Stephen Barney, is working currently on a volume of notes keyed to the Athlone texts.

Editorial Treatment of the Quotations

The guide is based on the Athlone editions of the poem: *Piers Plowman: The A Version*, ed. George Kane (London: Athlone, 1960), *Piers Plowman: The B Version*, ed. George Kane and E. Talbot Donaldson (London: Athlone, 1975), and *Piers Plowman: The C Version*, ed. George Russell (in press).[5] Other editions, though excellent in themselves, are less useful for the present purpose. Only the Athlone editions provide both a full listing of variants and a consistent treatment of the quotations across all three versions. Nevertheless, a comparison of the Athlone and other editions, with respect to their treatment of the quotations, raises several questions that go to the heart of the poet's craft. These concern the assigning of line numbers, the italicizing of Latin and French words, and the establishing of the text.

Line Numbers

In her book *The Latin Insertions and the Macaronic Verse in Piers Plowman*, Sister Carmeline Sullivan distinguishes three categories of quotations: (1) "quotations extraneous to the text," such as B.14.212a ("The hei3e wey to heuenwarde ofte Richesse letteþ: / *Ita inpossibile diuiti &c.*"); (2) "quotations syntactically articulated with the text," such as B.5.55 ("For whoso contrarieþ truþe, he telleþ in þe gospel, *Amen dico vobis nescio vos*"); and (3) "macaronic lines," such as B.Prol.30 ("*Qui loquitur turpiloquium* is luciferes hyne"). This scheme lies beneath most editorial systems of line-numbering. George Kane explains in his edition of the A version: "When Latin lines contain English words [Sullivan's "macaronic lines"] or are evidently part of the syntactical structure [Sullivan's "quotations syntactically articulated with the text"], they are numbered like the English lines; when they are detachable (and might have made their way into the text by way of the margin) [Sullivan's "quotations extraneous to the text"], they are referred to by the number of the preceding English line followed by a Greek letter" (167). Derek Pearsall adopts the same system in his edition of the C version: "The practice here is to number Latin lines which contain any word of English or which are integral to the syntax of the surrounding English lines. The remain-

---

[5] The editions of the A version and B version were reissued jointly by the Athlone Press and the Univ. of California Press in 1989 as "revised editions." On the extent of such revisions, see Kathleen Hewett-Smith, *YLS* 4 (1990):151–54.

der, mostly biblical quotations, are unnumbered and indented" (23). In short, the categories identified by Sullivan govern the line numbering of virtually every edition (and translation) of *Piers Plowman* from Skeat to Russell.[6]

These categories are less distinct than they look, however; as Pearsall himself acknowledges, "No two editors will agree on the treatment of the Latin" (23). Kane and Donaldson number the following lines (thus implying that they are "part of the syntactical structure"): B.Prol.196, 1.119, 2.39, 3.96, 3.249, 3.330, 3.336; Skeat does not (implying that they are "extraneous"). Russell numbers C.2.40, 2.42, 2.81, 2.124, 3.483, 3.488; Pearsall does not. Thus, the numbering of lines, though intended primarily for ease of reference, is unavoidably an interpretative act.

A few examples of lines that fail the test will show how arbitrary, if not irrelevant, the criterion of syntactic relation can be. The first is from Will's argument against a friar:

> Ac a barn wiþouten bapteme may noȝt be saued:
> *Nisi quis renatus fuerit.*
> Loke, ye lettred men, wheiþer I lye or noȝt.
>
> (B.11.82–83)

According to Kane and Donaldson's line numbering, the quotation belongs to the category of "extraneous" and "detachable." But does it? If the Latin is extraneous, then what are the "lettred men"— Langland's habitual phrase for those learned *in Latin*—being admonished to "loke" at? As Schmidt observes, "Here the quotation, while syntactically free-standing, forms part both of Will's diatribe against the friar for failing to baptize and also part of the written 'text' of the poem, referred to the clerks among his readers for their judgement as to its intrinsic truth and its argumentative weight."[7] A second example comes from Imaginatif's speech to the dreamer:

> Clergie and kynde wit comeþ of siȝte and techyng

---

[6] A notable exception is A. G. Rigg and Charlotte Brewer, eds., *Piers Plowman: The Z Version* (Toronto: Pontifical Institute of Mediaeval Studies, 1983), which numbers all lines without regard to their possible originality. Of course, in saying that the categories identified by Sullivan govern the line numbering of other *Piers* editions, I do not mean to impute any indebtedness to Sullivan's work. The categories are already implicit in Skeat's edition, which appeared nearly fifty years earlier.

[7] *The Clerkly Maker: Langland's Poetic Art* (Cambridge: Brewer, 1987), 89.

As þe book bereþ witnesse to burnes þat kan rede:
Quod scimus loquimur, quod vidimus testamur.
Of *quod scimus* comeþ Clergie, a konnynge of heuene,
And of *quod vidimus* comeþ kynde wit, of siȝte of diuerse
peple.

(B.12.64–67)

Though classified as extraneous, the Latin line is closely connected to the English on both sides: the first two lines look ahead to the quotation as the "witnesse to burnes þat kan rede," and the last two lines look back to it as the source of the excerpts *quod scimus* and *quod vidimus*. To be sure, the quotation is not absolutely essential to our comprehension of the passage, but the dividing line between extraneous and non-extraneous should not be that point at which our ingenuity is no longer adequate to fill in the missing pieces. Indeed, tested by this criterion, half the *English* in the poem might lose its line numbers.

If any Latin quotations are extraneous, it would seem to be those that are repeated in English translation. Yet even in these cases—and they are numerous—the classification is problematic. Take, for example, Conscience's use of Scripture in his speech before the king:

Ther are two manere of Medes, my lord, bi youre leue.
That oon god of his grace gyueþ in his blisse
To hem þat werchen wel while þei ben here.
The prophete precheþ it and putte it in þe Sauter:
Domine, quis habitabit in tabernaculo tuo?
Lord, who shal wonye in þi wones wiþ þyne holy seintes,
Or resten in þyne holy hilles; þis askeþ Dauid.
And Dauid assoileþ it hymself as þe Sauter telleþ:
Qui ingreditur sine macula & operatur Iusticiam.
Tho þat entren of o colour and of one wille
And han ywroght werkes wiþ right and wiþ reson,
And he þat vseþ noȝt þe lyf of vsurie,
And enformeþ pouere peple and pursueþ truþe:
Qui pecuniam suam non dedit ad vsuram et munera super innocentem &c,
And alle þat helpen þe Innocent and holden with þe
riȝtfulle,
Wiþouten Mede doþ hem good and þe truþe helpeþ,
Swiche manere men, my lord, shul haue þis firste Mede
Of god at a gret nede whan þei gon hennes.

(B.3.231–45)

In no edition are the Latin lines in this passage numbered. They are not "syntactically articulated with the text." But syntax is not the only or even the closest way in which the quotations may be articulated with the text. Because Conscience's speech is largely an exegesis of Psalm 14, it is difficult to say which is the "text"—the Latin being glossed or the English that glosses it. Each exists for the sake of the other. Insofar as the English expands upon the quotations, it is in the service of the Latin; insofar as the choice of quotations was determined by the need to explicate *mede*, the Latin is in the service of the English.

Although Conscience's quotations are meant primarily to clarify the nature of *mede*, they also shed light on other words in the passage. What, for example, is the meaning of the phrase "of o colour" (line 238)? The definition given by the *Middle English Dictionary*, "of one and the same kind," seems not to apply; and the context provides little or no help. In Talbot Donaldson's translation of the B version, the phrase is glossed, correctly I believe, as "without spot."[8] The warrant for this singular definition is in the preceding quotation, *sine maculo*. "Paradoxical as it may sound," A. V. C. Schmidt writes concerning a different passage, "the *Latin* is needed to 'gloss' the English."[9] The final clause of the same sentence, "And he þat . . . enformeþ pouere peple and pursueþ truþe," also raises questions. If

---

[8] *Will's Vision of Piers Plowman: An Alliterative Verse Translation*, ed. Elizabeth D. Kirk and Judith H. Anderson (New York: Norton, 1990), 29.

[9] *The Clerkly Maker*, 91. Why Langland did not render the psalmist's words more literally is a further and more difficult question. In my view he was led both by the representation of *mede* as an obstacle to justice and by the dramatic setting of the speech, a law court, to narrow the general moral signification of *sine maculo* to the specifically legal sense of *unicolor*, "of one color." Gower's use of the term in *Confessio Amantis* is instructive:

> Legibus vnicolor tunc temporis aura refulsit,
> Iusticie plane tuncque fuere vie. (Prol. ii)
> [The air of that age shone, one-hued, with laws;
> The paths of justice then were plain and smooth.]

As noted by Siân Echard and Claire Fanger in their translation *The Latin Verses in the Confessio Amantis* (East Lansing, Mich.: Colleagues Press, 1991), "The single color of law in the golden age contrasts with the particolor of the modern age, represented [a few lines later] by the variegated and ever-changing chameleon" (5n). In Langland's translation of Psalm 14, therefore, the metaphorical associations of *unicolor* merge with those of *sine maculo*: "of o colour" means not only "without spot" but more precisely "without the spot of hypocrisy or duplicity." As if to confirm this meaning, Langland expands the phrase pleonastically: "of o colour and *of one wille*."

to "enform pouere peple" is to "helpen þe Innocent"—that is, those in need of but unable to pay for justice—how does one go about it? To "train, educate, or instruct" them (*MED*) is hardly the kind of help they would most welcome under the circumstances. What they need is legal assistance. Again, the quotations provide a gloss, this time not in a single word but rather in the meaning they had acquired through repeated use as rhetorical *topoi*. Whenever Langland inveighs against meed and the sale of justice, he routinely discovers his *argumentum* in the words of Psalm 14. In passus 7 (the pardon scene), he returns to the problem:

> Men of lawe leest pardon hadde, leue þow noon ooþer,
> For þe Sauter saueþ hem noȝt, swiche as take ȝiftes,
> And nameliche of Innocentȝ þat noon yuel konneþ:
> *Super innocentem munera non accipies.*
> Pledours sholde peynen hem to plede for swiche and helpe;
> . . . .
> Ac he þat spendeþ his speche and spekeþ for þe pouere
> That is Innocent and nedy and no man apeireþ,
> Conforteþ hym in þat caas, coueiteþ noȝt hise ȝiftes,
> Ac for oure lordes loue lawe for hym sheweþ,
> Shal no deuel at his deeþ day deren hym a myte
> That he ne worþ saaf sikerly; þe Sauter bereþ witnesse:
> *Domine, quis habitabit in tabernaculo tuo.*
>
> (B.7.40-52a)

Using this passage to illuminate the earlier one, we can say with some confidence that to "inform poor people" means not to educate the economically deprived but rather (addressing a more immediate need) to *advise* "þe pouere / That is Innocent," to give legal counsel, to "shewe lawe."[10]

The topical significance of Psalm 14:1-5 can be inferred from its

---

[10] Although Langland shows no reluctance to bend the language to his own purposes, his use of *enforme* is not entirely without precedent. The *OED* gives "to advise" as a meaning of the word (*inform*, III.4.a) in Brunne's *Chronicle* (ca. 1330).

repeated use in the poem. To appreciate the meaning of other quotations, however, it is often necessary to go outside the poem. This fact is brought home again and again by critics who make use of patristic exegesis. T. P. Dunning was the first to argue that Langland's biblical quotations must be interpreted "in accordance with the tradition of the Church" as that tradition is recorded in the writings of the Fathers and then in medieval commentaries on the Bible.[11] Dunning's rather flexible approach hardens into critical doctrine in Robertson and Huppé's *Piers Plowman and Scriptural Tradition*. They view the scriptural quotations in the poem as "a key to the ultimate source of its allegorical meaning," and their first approach to any section is "always to consult a variety of interpretations of the passages from the Vulgate quoted in the poem" (15). *Piers Plowman* is thus assimilated to scriptural tradition. It is seen to exist partly as the fragmentary expression of a larger argument, to which the quotations provide access. In varying degrees this perspective governs all "exegetical" criticism of the poem.

With respect to the quotations, there is little difference between the uses of exegetical tradition and the so-called antifraternal tradition in interpretations of the poem. Rabanus Maurus and Bruno Astensis simply give way to William of St. Amour and Richard Fitzralph. Penn Szittya in *The Antifraternal Tradition in Medieval Literature* glosses a number of Langland's quotations by reference to the meanings they had accumulated in polemical writings against the friars;[12] and Wendy Scase provides a virtual lexicon of such meanings in *"Piers Plowman" and the New Anticlericalism*.[13] In contrast to Robertson and Huppé's somewhat static view of the poet's relation to exegetical tradition, Szittya and Scase emphasize his dynamic interaction with his inherited material, that is, his participation in a tradition, himself an exegete. What they share with these critics, however, is a high appreciation of the work's intertextuality, a tendency to view Langland's quotations primarily as *incipits* whose full meaning can be determined or completed only within a context outside the poem.

---

[11] *Piers Plowman: An Interpretation of the A Text*, 2d ed., revised and edited by T. P. Dolan (Oxford: Clarendon Press, 1980), 3.

[12] (Princeton: Princeton Univ. Press, 1986). See, for example, his comments on B.20.340 *Penetrans domos* and C.13.44a *Necessitas non habet legem*, 3, 270–76, 285.

[13] Her discussion of the linked texts *Si vis perfectus esse* (B.11.274a) and *Diuicias nec paupertates* (B.11.271) is typical (57).

Without considering other uses of the quotations—for example, their authoritative value,[14] or their role within the poem's intricate pattern of verbal concordance,[15] or the metaphorical significance of the Latin[16]—enough has been said to raise doubts about such classifications as "extraneous" and "detachable." The editorial practice of excluding from the line numbering those quotations that are not "syntactically articulated with the text" devalues them (and, at the same time, every kind of relation that is not syntactic). It suggests that these quotations are less important than numbered quotations, dispensable, perhaps not even authorial. To be sure, as Kane observes, some of these "might have made their way into the text by way of the margin."[17] But it is nearly impossible to tell. Precisely because they are quotations and not the poet's own words, their authorial status cannot be judged by the usual criteria (imperfect alliteration, inferior style, and so forth).

The numbering of lines is a modern practice, imposed for the convenience of modern scholarship; and, as a sign of the editor's evaluation (extraneous or integral, scribal or authorial), it reflects a modern conception of the "text." If medieval scribes inserted any of the quotations, they probably saw their action not as *adding* to the poem but rather as making explicit what was already in it.

The Use of Italics

The question of whether to give a quotation its own line number, based on its syntactic relation to the surrounding English, does not arise in the case of macaronic lines. The Latin (or French) is an essential part not only of the meaning but also of the alliteration, as

---

[14] For a view of their use as authorities, see Siegfried Wenzel, "Medieval Sermons," in Alford 1988a, 159–60.

[15] See Alford 1977; Jill Mann, "Eating and Drinking in *Piers Plowman*," *Essays and Studies* 32 (1987): 1–30; Judson B. Allen, "Langland's Reading and Writing: *Detractor* and the Pardon Passus," *Speculum* 59 (1984): 342–62.

[16] Peter Nolan, "Beyond Macaronic: Embedded Latin in Dante and Langland," *Acta Conventus Neo-Latini Bononiensis*, Proceedings of the Fourth International Congress of Neo-Latin Studies, ed. R. J. Schoeck, Medieval & Renaissance Texts & Studies, vol. 37 (Binghamton, NY, 1985), 539–47; Helen Barr, "The Use of Latin Quotations in *Piers Plowman* with Special Reference to Passus XVIII of the 'B' Text," *Notes and Queries* ns 33 (1986): 440–48.

[17] *Piers Plowman: The A Version,* 167. In their edition of the B version, Kane and Donaldson append a list of the lines deemed unoriginal (221–24). These lines include ten Latin quotations.

illustrated by the very first quotation in the poem, "*Qui loquitur turpiloquium* is luciferes hyne" (B.Prol.39). Nevertheless, such lines are also subject to editorial classification. The process merely shifts from whole lines (numbered versus unnumbered) to words within lines (roman versus italics). In the introduction to his edition of the A version, George Kane explains that all Latin words and "unmistakably French" words are printed in italic type (167), and this explanation holds for the Athlone series in general.

The convention raises a number of questions that must be addressed here, since italicized words form the basis of this guide. What is an editor's purpose in distinguishing between the different languages in *Piers Plowman*? Is it to highlight the "macaronic" quality of the verse? As apprehended by whom—readers of the fourteenth or of the present century? To put the question another way, does Kane's phrase "unmistakably French" refer to those words that would fail subsequently to establish themselves in modern English (a fact no medieval reader could have known) or does it refer to those words that had not yet been assimilated into Middle English (a fact no modern editor can know)? Into which category does the word *parentrelynarie* fall?

> If fals latyn be in þat lettre þe lawe it impugneþ,
> Or peynted parentrelynarie, parcelles ouerskipped.
>
> (B.11.304–5)

Since Kane and Donaldson do not italicize *parentrelynarie*, we are led to assume that this word is not "unmistakably French." Yet neither the *Oxford English Dictionary* nor the *Middle English Dictionary* cites any other instances of its use, and the only record of its use outside *Piers Plowman* is in documents written in French (for example, the *Yearbooks of Edward 2*: "Migg' chalengea le fet pur entrelinarie"[18]). Little wonder that Schmidt, though he follows Kane and Donaldson in not italicizing the word, should ask if it ought to be, "the line then being classified as a simple isolate macaronic" (*The Clerkly Maker*, 103). Similar examples abound. In fact, a comparison of editions of *Piers Plowman* reveals some disagreement on the extent to which certain loanwords had become anglicized. Russell italicizes *beau fitз* (C.9.312), an affectionate form of address, while Pearsall does not. Wherever the polite expression *pur charite* appears, Russell italicizes it (C.8.169, C.8.265, C.10.11, C.15.32); Pearsall never does.

---

[18] Alford 1988b, 109–10.

The same problem arises in the treatment of individual Latin words. Russell prints C.2.190 as "Sommnours and sodenes þat supersedias taketh"; Pearsall regards the manuscript spelling as a scribal error rather than an anglicization, and emends it, with italics, to *supersedeas*. Concerning J. A. W. Bennett's use of italics in B.5.450 (B.5.442 in Kane and Donaldson), "Til *Vigilate* þe veille fette water at his ey3en," N. F. Blake writes:

> Here *Vigilate* is both given an initial capital and put in ital-
> ics. . . . It is assumed to represent an echo of the passage in
> Matthew 26:41 *Vigilate et orate* . . . ; and *Vigilate* is hence a per-
> sonification of watchfulness. However, the use of italics implies
> that the medieval reader would also understand this as a Latin
> word which occurred in a particular biblical context rather than
> a word which had been anglicized and extended to a more
> general frame of reference. . . . Because of the absence of any
> real sense of English and foreign words, I find this view unlike-
> ly.[19]

Blake makes an important point. At a period when the language was rapidly assimilating loanwords from both French and Latin, many speakers themselves might have been hard pressed to say what was properly "English." Yet it is difficult to accept the generalization that they lacked "any real sense of English and foreign words." Then, as now, people's sense of the language must have varied according to their education and social status. Although clerkly Conscience is perfectly at home with grammatical terminology, his listener the king wants to know "What is relacion rect and indirect aftur, / Thenne adiectyf and sustantyf, for englisch was it neuere" (C.3.342-43). Langland repeatedly calls attention to individual Latin words and even inflects them according to their grammatical function in the line; for example, "a lippe of *caritatis*" (B.2.35), "Ac vnkyndenesse *caristiam* makeþ amonges cristen peple" (B.14.73), "*ingrati* ben manye" (B.14.169), and "be *ingratus* to þi kynde" (B.17.257). In B.18.392, the verb *parco* is personified as the agent of a command and is thus given in the imperative form: "They shul be clensed . . . / In my prisone Purgatorie til *parce* it hote." Such care cannot have been lost upon the clerks in Langland's audience. They knew a Latin ending when they saw one.[20]

---

[19] *The English Language in Medieval Literature* (London: Dent, 1977), 76.

[20] Further instances of Langland's concern for syntactic agreement be-

The real question is not whether Langland's readers could recognize Latin words, but whether they would have seen any point in marking them. Evidently, despite Blake's misplaced criticism of Bennett, they did. The scribe of Bodleian MS Laud 581 (the base manuscript for both Bennett and Skeat) distinguishes *vigilate* from the surrounding English by means of rubrication; so does the scribe of Trinity College Cambridge MS B.15.17 (the base manuscript for Kane-Donaldson and Schmidt); so apparently does the scribe of the lost manuscript that underlies Robert Crowley's first edition in 1550.[21] The use of such print devices as italics (Bennett, Skeat, Schmidt, Kane and Donaldson) or smaller typeface (Crowley, fol. xxvii^v) accurately reflects the scribal intention. Occasionally, as indicated already by the example of *supersedeas*, editors will treat individual cases differently. However, what must strike anyone who bothers to read a printed text of *Piers Plowman* alongside the manuscripts is not how often the use of italics is arbitrary but rather how often it is faithful to scribal practice.

Why the scribes of *Piers Plowman*, if not the poet himself, chose to highlight certain words is a more interesting problem than the vagaries of modern editors. Although the rubrication (sometimes boxing or underlining) is confined mostly to Latin and French, it does not follow that the purpose is to distinguish foreign words as such. The rubrication of individual words, like strings of words (quotations), announces among other things that these words are to be taken at more than face value.

To cite an obvious example, when the workers on Piers's half-acre demand that their food be served "*chaud* and *plus chaud*" (B.6.311), their upstart behavior is indicated less by the literal meaning of their words than by their imitation of upper class speech. Similarly, to say that Dives lived "in *douce vie*" (B.14.123) is to convey more than the idea that he led a soft life. Here the French updates the biblical parable of the rich man in hell. It reinforces his role as a type for "lordes and hir ladies [that] also lyuede hir lif in murþe" and, at the same time, defines such soft living in terms of French modes of behavior, cuisine, fashion—best epitomizing, for a moralist like Langland, the sin of luxury.

---

tween the Latin and English of his poem include the following: "*Filius* by þe fader wille and frenesse of *spiritus sancti*" (B.16.88); "And þanne spak *spiritus sanctus* in Gabrielis mouþe" (B.16.90). See also 15 below.

[21] Facsimile edition by Bennett (London: Paradine, 1976).

Latin words are used as well to evoke different systems of discourse: *contra, ergo, quodlibet* and probably *in genere* take us immediately into scholastic disputation; *fornicatores* and *infamis* into canon law; *licitum, pateat,* and *si* into the common law; *caritas, consummatus deus, deus homo, filius,* and *ymago dei* into theology.

The rubrication (and hence italicization) of such words is appropriate and helpful. Like punctuation, it guides our understanding of the text; perhaps more precisely, it can be explained as the visual equivalent of a suprasegmental phoneme (for example, pitch or intonation). Rubrication of a word signals a shift in register, the addition of extra-lexical meaning, an enlargement of the context in which the word should be read and interpreted.

The identification of specific contexts is, of course, an important aim of this book. Indeed, sources have been found for nearly all of the poet's quotations. But it is often possible to identify the sources of single words as well. There can be no doubt that *multi* and *pauci* (B.11.112, 114) are from Matt. 22:14; *crucifige* (B.18.39) from John 19:6; or *dirige* and *placebo* from Psalms 5:9 and 114:9 (by way of the Office of the Dead). Where certitude is not possible, as in the confession of Sloth, the circumstantial evidence may still be considerable:

> "Repentestow noȝt?" quod Repentaunce, and riȝt wiþ þat
> he swowned
> Til *vigilate* þe veille fette water at hise eiȝen
> And flatte it on his face and faste on hym cryde
> And seide, "ware þee, for wanhope wol þee bitraye."
> (B.5.441–44)

As noted earlier, Blake is skeptical about Bennett's tracing the word *vigilate* to Matt. 26:41 or, indeed, to any "particular biblical context" (76). However, the number of possibilities is limited. The form occurs only sixteen times in the Vulgate. Several of these examples are clustered around the same incident in the garden of Gethsemane, Jesus's warning to his disciples on the eve of his betrayal (Matt. 26); and *vigilate*'s own explication of his name—"ware þee, for wanhope wol þee bitraye"— echoes the language of the warning. Most convincing, however, is the traditional interpretation of Matt. 26:41 as a call to repentance and, more specifically, as a warning against the sin of sloth.

> In the Gospels *acedia* is most impressively illustrated in the sleeping Apostles in Gethsemane and the Lord's warning words, "Vigilate et orate" (Matt. 26:36ff). "By the sleeping disciples are indicated the *accidiosi*, whose inner eyes are heavy with the

sleep of indolence" [Petrus de Limoges]. And Peraldus explains
that "to wake in the Lord means, following His example, to
guard against the sleep of *accidia*."[22]

Whatever the path by which "*vigilate* þe veille" entered the poem,
there can be little doubt that his birth was in Matt. 26:41.

Not every isolated French and Latin word in the poem can be
given a context. But I have included them all—that is, all that are
italicized in the Athlone editions—on the grounds that to exclude any
of them would diminish the value of this guide. I cannot anticipate
every use to which the guide might be put, and the possibility always
remains that further research will identify the external frame of
reference to which these words belong.

The Text

Central to the editorial treatment of the quotations—far more
important than the numbering of lines or the italicization of words—
is the establishment of the text. What is the correct reading at
A.10.90: *intencio indicat hominem* or *intencio iudicat hominem*? Editors
of *Piers Plowman* (and of other vernacular works as well) have been
remarkably reticent about the criteria used to answer such questions.
Presumably, the editorial objective, as in the case of the English, is to
recover the authorial text. As noted already, however, the usual
criteria do not apply. The quotations cannot be judged (normally) on
the basis of such features as meter, alliteration, and style. But there
are other tests of originality.

Unlike the poet's words, which survive only in the fifty-two manuscripts of the poem, the quotations can be checked against a vast
body of external evidence. For example, given the fact that *intencio
iudicat hominem* appears in numerous treatises and commentaries on
canon law, while *intencio indicat hominem* (Skeat, Kane) is nowhere
attested, *iudicat* is more likely the correct reading. Even so, the
external evidence must be used with caution. To emend or even to
choose a manuscript reading on the basis of external evidence is not
necessarily to recover Langland's own words. No doubt he was
capable of misquoting as well as deliberately modifying his borrowings to fit new contexts.

---

[22] Siegfried Wenzel, *The Sin of Sloth: Acedia in Medieval Thought and
Literature* (Chapel Hill: Univ. of North Carolina Press, 1967), 102.

The caveat is especially applicable to Langland's scriptural borrowings, which illustrate a broad range of possibilities. When Dame Study quotes Matt. 7:6 against men in general in C.11.7–8 ("*Nolite mittere*, ȝe men ... "), she uses the plural form of the verb *nolo*; when she cites the same Scripture against the dreamer in particular in B.10.9 ("*Noli mittere*, man ... "), she uses the singular form. The alteration of the biblical text from *nolite* to *noli* to fit the audience being addressed is further evidence of the poet's concern to preserve syntactic agreement between Latin and English. (Why Kane and Donaldson thought it necessary to emend B.10.9 to "*Noli[te] mittere*, man ... " is unclear.) That Langland might have modified a few borrowings for alliterative reasons is also possible. One of the happier emendations proposed by the Athlone editors is in the line "*Christus [rex] resurgens*, and it aroos after" (B.19.152, C.21.152), where the Vulgate reads simply "Christus resurgens" (Rom. 6:9).

In general, however, editors' emendations depart only rarely from the Vulgate text. In fact, where the quotations are at variance with the Vulgate, the temptation is to "correct" them. At B.6.236 the manuscripts read *Piger pro frigore* (and so also Skeat, Bennett, and Schmidt); Kane and Donaldson emend to *Piger [propter frigus]*, attested by C and closer to the Vulgate's *propter frigus piger* (Prov. 20:4). At B.17.200a the majority reading *qui peccat in spiritu sancto*, though grammatically defensible, is emended by all editors to *qui peccat in spiritum sanctum*. Where the manuscripts consistently show the form *eice* (for example, B.7.143a, A.8.125a, B.10.270a)—attested as well in the *Fasciculus Morum* (530)—Kane and Kane-Donaldson emend to the Vulgate *ejice*.[23]

---

[23] Although it was originally my plan to record all editorial emendations in the indexes, this proved to be impracticable. It would have inflated the entries greatly: instead of quoting from one version, with cross-referencing to other versions, I would have had to reproduce in full the quotations from all three (or four) versions. Moreover, it soon became apparent that such information in itself would have little value unless accompanied by further interpretative commentary; some of the emendations are conjectural, others are made in conformity with repeated quotations in the same passage, and still others are based on well-attested variants. Not surprisingly, emended forms in the Athlone editions and unemended forms in other editions based on different manuscripts (e.g., Skeat, Bennett) are sometimes in agreement. It is not the purpose of this guide to argue for particular readings as "authorial"–in effect, to present an edition of the quotations–or to eliminate the necessity of consulting the Athlone editions, where the relevant facts are set forth in great amplitude.

Whatever authority the Vulgate may enjoy as a standard in the editing of *Piers Plowman*, any determination of its weight in individual cases (including those above) is difficult because of the presence of other relevant factors. But the *obiter dicta* of editors in notes and elsewhere reveal misconceptions about the biblical text that have almost certainly affected editorial decisions. These misconceptions will be examined at length in the next section.

The Question of Sources

Many of the Latin passages in *Piers Plowman*, including those from the Bible, were derived from secondary sources.[24] The evidence is manifold. As noted already, the quotations often bring with them an acquired meaning or context. Langland is more likely to have found Sir Penetrans-Domos (B.20.340) in the polemical literature that linked 2 Timothy 3:6 with friars than in the Bible itself; he is more likely to have taken the words *Spera in deo* (B.11.287) from the liturgy, where they are applied explicitly to priests, than from Psalm 42:5. The quotations do not come into the poem naked but as liveried servants. Neither do they come alone. The pairing of Psalms 22:4 and 41:4 in the pardon scene (B.7.120–21 and 128a) argues that the Mass of the Dead, where these two verses occur together, figured in the composition of the passage; the network of biblical texts used to dramatize the Harrowing of Hell (B.18, C.20) suggests the influence of the pseudo-gospel of *Nicodemus*. Other telltale signs include verbal changes for which there are precedents (such as the alteration of Juvenal's *Cantabit vacuus* to *Cantabit paupertas*) and significant misattributions (for example, "þe apostel saide: *Non oderis fratrem*" [C.2.34], words actually said in Leviticus 19:17 but cited by commentators as the *meaning* of St. Paul's words in 1 Timothy 5:20).[25] Finally, it is well to remember the means by which knowledge was often transmitted in the Middle Ages, that is, by florilegia, encyclopedias, commentaries, alphabetical reference books, and other compilations: such were the probable channels through which a number of quota-

---

[24] Most of the quotations for which Skeat's parallel-text edition cites no sources or analogues have been traced in a series of notes over the past decade and a half (listed in the table of abbreviations as Alford 1972, 1975, 1984, 1988b; Gray 1986; Lindemann 1977) and in the notes to the editions by J. A. W. Bennett (1972), A. V. C. Schmidt (1978), and Derek Pearsall (1979).

[25] E.g., Hugh of St. Cher.

tions reached Langland, most notably those of a proverbial nature.

The distinction between original and intermediate sources, fundamental to any theories about the poem's composition or the poet's intellectual background, is developed further in the following analysis of the quotations by category—first the scriptural and then the non-scriptural examples.

The Scriptural Quotations

The caveat against assuming an original source for Langland's borrowings is especially necessary in the case of his scriptural quotations. His deviations from the Vulgate text have led many critics to question the accuracy of his scriptural quotations, his knowledge of the Bible, even his ability to read it. Skeat finds fault with a number of quotations (for example, B.1.119, B.5.283a, B.5.506, B.6.226a, B.8.20a, C.14.134a, B.12.281, B.15.212, C.17.40a); Bennett says that Piers quotes Prov. 22:10 "inexactly" (B.7.143a); Pearsall gives the poet's quotation of Matt. 6:3 as it should "properly" be (C.3.74a).

Actually we have little basis for judging the "accuracy" of Langland's quotations. For one thing we do not know what the original text of the poem looked like. The wording of scriptural citations varies from one manuscript to another. Consider the example of Prov. 22:10 cited above: if Bennett had based his edition of the B *Visio* not on MS Laud Misc. 581 but on MS Corpus Christi College Oxford 201 (in which the quotation more nearly coincides with the Vulgate), he would have had no occasion to remark on the apparent discrepancy. Neither do we know what Langland's Bible looked like. There was no fixed text. Beneath the notices of Langland's "misquotations" from Scripture, however, lies the assumption that there was only one correct reading during the Middle Ages and that we can find it simply by consulting a printed Vulgate. When Skeat remarks that the quotation at C.14.134a (Ezekiel 33:11) is "inexact," what he really means is that it differs from the Clementine edition of the Vulgate published two centuries later.

During the Middle Ages the biblical text existed in a variety of forms. Chief among them was the Latin translation attributed to St. Jerome (ca. 346–420), now referred to as the Vulgate (meaning the "commonly accepted" version). It was not the only translation, however. The Old Latin Bible or *Vetus Latina*, which Jerome's translation was intended to replace, still circulated in whole or in part;[26]

---

[26] *Bibliorum Sacrorum Latinae Versiones Antiquae, seu Vetus Italica*, ed. Pierre

moreover, many of its readings were preserved and transmitted in the writings of the early church fathers, such as Ambrose and Augustine. Gregory the Great states explicitly in the preface to his commentary on Job: "Now it is the new Translation [i.e., Jerome's] that I comment on; but when a case to be proved requires it, I take now the new and now the old for testimony, that as the Apostolic See, over which I preside by ordinance of God, uses both, the labours of my undertaking may have the support of both."[27] In medieval expositions of Scripture, the use of Old Latin forms, along with other *ad hoc* translations, was common practice, and the fact that these eventually insinuated themselves into the textual tradition of the Vulgate itself is hardly surprising. Medieval scholars were not unaware of what had happened. Indeed, Roger Bacon seems to have observed that the text of glossed Bibles deviated more from the ancient manuscripts than non-glossed Bibles.[28] During the thirteenth century several efforts were made to clear the Vulgate text of scribal corruptions. The work carried out by theologians at the University of Paris about 1226 was the most important, for the so-called "Paris text" later served as the basis of the official Latin Bible of the Roman Catholic church, commissioned by the Council of Trent in 1546 and issued by Pope Clement VIII in 1592.[29] "Unfortunately, as a text," according to the preface of the Vulgate edition recently issued by the Württemberg Bible Society, the Clementine "left much to be desired."[30] Even this new edition, the editors frankly acknowledge, should be regarded in some areas as "provisional" until the completion of the big edition being prepared by the Benedictines of St. Jerome's monastery in Rome.[31]

In the light of history, then, the use of words like "inexact" and "inaccurate" to describe Langland's quotations from Scripture is hardly appropriate. The poem simply reflects the instability of the medieval Latin text. Variant readings from the pre-Vulgate, the Vulgate, and later translations (e.g., from commentaries) stand side

---

Sabatier, 3 vols. (Rheims, 1743–51).

[27] Gregory the Great, *Morals on the Book of Job*, trans. by members of the English Church, 3 vols. (Oxford: Parker, 1844), 1:1.

[28] Glunz, 281.

[29] Glunz, 293; Bruce Metzger, *The Early Versions of the New Testament* (Oxford: Oxford Univ. Press, 1977), 348.

[30] Weber, 1: 20.

[31] On which edition, see Metzger, 351–52.

by side. Illustrations of this are plentiful. For Psalm 144:9 the Clementine edition reads, *Suavis Dominus universis; et miserationes eius super omnia opera eius*, which shows up in *Piers* as *Misericordia eius super omnia opera eius &c.* (B.5.281a); although Skeat remarks, "The Latin quotation is not quite exact," the substitution of *misericordia* for *miserationes* actually restores the original Vulgate reading (ed. Weber). Similarly the quotation of Rom. 12:19 as *Michi vindictam* (B.6.226), "though the Vulgate has *Mihi vindicta*" (Skeat), is attested by the earliest Vulgate manuscripts. The B manuscripts' quotation of John 10:11 as *Bonus pastor animam suam ponit* (B.15.497a)—where for *ponit* the Vulgate has *dat*—preserves the Old Latin reading, a reading which Gregory the Great seems consciously to have adopted in his *Moralia* since the "case to be proved requires it."[32] Another Old Latin form appears in B.Prol.39, *Qui loquitur turpiloquium*, apparently a reminiscence of what "Poul precheþ" in Col. 3:8, *Nunc autem deponite et vos . . . turpem sermonem de ore vestro*. Although the word *turpiloquium* appears nowhere in the Vulgate, it is given for *turpem sermonem* in the *Vetus Latina* and in quotations of the verse by early Christian writers, such as Tertullian, Ambrose, Ambrosiaster, and Vigilius.

Numerous additional examples could be cited. But whether Langland took any of them directly from the Bible itself is problematical. Most of the above variants, for example, can be found also in biblical commentaries. That Langland read the Bible with the help of a commentary is beyond doubt. He cites "the gloss" in support of his own interpretations of Scripture (e.g., B.5.276, B.12.294, B.15.82), he uses repeatedly the telltale formula *id est* (e.g., C.11.49a, B.15.212, B.19.273), and many of his quotations bear the marks of exegetical revision. To explain a biblical passage, to reveal the hidden *res* beneath the *verba*, often required that it be reworded. Hans Glunz cites hundreds of examples in *The Vulgate in England*. These rewordings in the service of interpretation typically assume one of three forms—expansion, substitution, and conflation. All are well represented in *Piers Plowman*.[33]

---

[32] Glunz, 21.

[33] In the most common form of expansion, an implied, and hence potentially ambiguous, referent is made explicit. The following quotations are a sampling (with insertions into the Vulgate text indicated by brackets): C.11.4–9a, *Ecce audiuimus eam [i.e. caritatem] in effrata* (Ps. 131:6); B.10.252a, *Ego in patre et pater in me est, et qui videt me videt et patrem [meum]* (John 14:9–10); B.13.61a, *Ve [vobis] qui potentes estis ad bibendum vinum* (Isa. 5:22); B.14.46a,

Besides the Vulgate and the commentaries on it, the service books of the liturgy must also be considered an important source of Langland's scriptural citations. Hort was the first to make a detailed comparison of these books and the poem. "The Latin quotations in *Piers Plowman*," she concluded, "show that its author had an intimate knowledge of the Breviary [and] that he was familiar with the Missal" (55). She displayed the evidence in a ten-page appendix citing liturgi-

---

Quodcumque pecieritis [a patre] in nomine meo (John 14:13, Oxford ed.); B.15.200a, *Et vidit [deus] cogitaciones eorum* (Luke 11:17); B.15.318, *Numquid, dicit [Iob], rugiet onager...* (Job 6:5); B.15.500, *Ite vos in vineam [meam]* (Matt. 20:4, Oxford ed.). Other expansions are more boldly interpretative: B.8.20a, *Sepcies [in die] cadit Iustus* (Prov. 24:16); B.12.281, *Saluabitur vix Iustus [in die Iudicij]* (1 Pet. 4:18); B.16.25a, *Cum ceciderit [iustus] non collidetur...* (Ps. 36:24); B.17.293a, *Vindica sanguinem [iustorum]* (Apoc. 6:10). All of these readings find support in the commentaries.

Substitutions include the following: B.11.88, *Non oderis fratres* [Vulg.: *fratrem*] *secrete in corde tuo...* (Lev. 19:17); C.14.134a, *Nolo mortem peccatoris* [Vulg.: *impii*] (Ezek. 33:11); B.14.212, *Ita inpossibile* [Vulg.: *difficile*] *diviti &c.* (Matt. 19:23); B.16.47, *Videatis qui peccat in* [Vulg.: *dixerit contra*] *spiritum sanctum numquam remittetur* (Matt. 12:32); B.16.252 (var.), *Ecce agnus dei qui tollit peccata* [Vulg.: *peccatum*] *mundi* (John 1:29, 36). Substitutions like these are usually explicable and often have their own individual histories. The pluralizing of *fratrem* in Lev. 19:17 reflects the anti-mendicant practice, beginning in the thirteenth century, of reading into Scripture prophetic warnings against the friars (see Szittya, 6 ff. and passim). The substitution of *peccatoris* for *impii* is sanctioned by the formulaic equation of the two elsewhere in the Bible (e.g., Prov. 11:31, Ecclus. 12:4, 12:7, 39:32, 1 Tim. 1:9, and 1 Peter 4:18, which Langland quotes just seventy lines later). The replacement of *dixerit contra* by *peccat in* summarizes the gloss, "quod aliquid *fit peccatum in* Spiritum sanctum" (Hugh of St. Cher, 6:47a). The reading *peccata* for John 1:29, adopted by the short-lived Sixtine Vulgate (1590) and rejected by the Clementine (1592), may owe something to Alcuin's interpretation of the verse (see Glunz, 94).

Finally, conflation was used as an exegetical device where two verses, though different in wording, were thought to have the same meaning. Thus Luke 6:20, *Beati pauperes, quia vestrum est regnum Dei*, was often conflated with Matt. 5:3, *Beati pauperes spiritu...*, for the reference in both cases is to spiritual poverty (although at B.14.215a, where the concern is with material poverty as well, Langland drops the word *spiritu*) (Glunz, 188). Other examples from *Piers* include B.10.25a (Job 21:7 and Jer. 12:1), B.15.428a (John 16:24 and Matt. 7:7), B.16.110a (Matt. 9:12 and Mark 2:17 or Luke 5:31), and B.19.161 (Luke 24:46 and Luke 24:26). As these examples suggest, conflation occurred most frequently in quotations from the gospels, a result not only of their close verbal similarities but also of the belief in the absolute harmony of their separate accounts: four versions, one truth (cf. Chaucer's prologue to *The Tale of Melibee*: the words of the four evangelists differ, "but doutelees hir sentence is al oon" [VII 952]).

cal sources for most of the biblical quotations. Thereafter it was widely accepted that Langland had drawn largely on the Roman liturgy for the composition of his poem. Robert Adams opened up a fresh inquiry into the matter, however, in his article "Langland and the Liturgy Revisited."[34] His examination of Hort's tables revealed that "there is scarcely any form of error (with the exception of deliberate misrepresentation) which cannot be found in them." But the larger issue is methodological. The mere appearance of a large number of Langland's biblical quotations in the Missal and Breviary does not prove that they came from these books rather than from the Vulgate or its commentaries (where, after all, the entire number can be found). It is necessary to show either coincident variation (that is, agreement between the poem and the Breviary against the Vulgate) or liturgical "encrustation" (for example, the borrowing of both the quotation and some part of its original setting).

A number of Langland's biblical quotations meet these criteria. Hort herself, far more rigorous in her discussion of specific examples than in her tabular display of the evidence, notes that the loose rendering of Daniel 9:24 at B.15.600 and B.18.109a (*Cum sanctus sanctorum* ...) occurs "word for word" in the Breviary; and she shows that the verse quoted against covetous priests at B.11.286a (*Iudica me, deus*) has brought with it its liturgical context: "The full force of the quotation from Psalm xlii is missed here, unless we realize ... that it occurs in the Ordinary of the Mass, and is said by the priest while going up to the altar" (51). Other scholars have uncovered additional instances. The appropriateness of Ps. 84:7, *Deus tu conuersus viuificabis nos*, following the confession of the folk on the field (B.5.506), is derived from its use as a prayer following the *Confiteor* of the Mass (*Breviarium* 2:53). At B.18.392 the force of Langland's allusion to Job 7:16, "In my prisone Purgatorie til *parce* it hote," depends on our knowing that the verse begins the first *lectio* of the *Dirige*, said for the benefit of the souls in purgatory.[35] At C.17.66a Langland's citation of Ps. 111:9 as proof of the heavenly reward given "Laurence for his largenesse" was prompted by the use of this verse as the opening line of the Introit and the Gradual for the Vigil-Mass of St. Lawrence.[36]

---

[34] *SP* 73 (1976): 266–84.

[35] See Alford 1972, 323–25.

[36] See M. Teresa Tavormina, "*Piers Plowman* and the Liturgy of St. Lawrence: Composition and Revision in Langland's Poetry," *SP* 84 (1987): 245–71.

Although the biblical text, its commentaries, and the liturgy certainly account for the vast majority of Langland's quotations, a wide range of other sources remains. Besides the anti-friar literature mentioned already, these include narratives based on the Bible (for example, the apocryphal *Gospel of Nicodemus* and Peter Comestor's *Historia Scholastica*), canon law and penitential manuals (often overlapping), and vernacular works such as plays and popular sermons. Space will permit no more than a brief illustration of each.

The *Gospel of Nicodemus*, extremely popular in the Middle Ages (though never accepted as canonical), is the source, whether direct or indirect, of Langland's account of the Harrowing of Hell. To say, "In *Piers Plowman* (B-Text, Pass. 18) there is a more or less complete *Gospel of Nicodemus*,"[37] is to exaggerate; but the work did furnish the basic story line of the passus and many of the scriptural texts in it. Clearly the following quotations were not assembled by the poet from their various locations in the Bible or liturgy but were taken as part and parcel of the pseudo-gospel itself, where their dramatic and prophetic significance is exploited to the fullest: C.20.259a, *Non visurum se mortem* (Luke 2:26; cf. Nico. 18:2); B.18.262a, *Attollite portas* (Ps. 23:7; cf. Nico. 21:1, 3); B.18.316a–18a, *Quis est iste? . . . Rex glorie . . . Dominus virtutum* (Ps. 23:10; cf. Nico. 21:3); B.18.323, *populus in tenebris* (Isa. 9:2, Matt. 4:16; cf. Nico. 18:1); B.18.324, *Ecce agnus dei* (John 1:29; cf. Nico. 18:3).

Canon law, a major influence on Langland's thought, contributed its share of biblical quotations. Several of these have retained their legal significance in the poem. Luke 10:7, *Dignus est operarius mercede sua*, quoted at B.2.123, was "traditionally used by canonists and legists to justify the acceptance by lawyers of moderate fees from those who could afford to pay."[38] Levit. 19:13, *Non morabitur opus mersenarii etc.*, invoked at C.3.308a, is cited routinely by canon lawyers in support of the right to an adequate wage.[39] Deut. 23:25, rendered maximally as *Nolite mittere falsem in messem alienam* (B.15. 530a), serves as "the *auctoritas* prohibiting confessors from hearing the confessions of those who come under another's jurisdiction."[40]

---

[37] H. C. Kim, ed., *The Gospel of Nicodemus* (Toronto: Pontifical Institute of Medieval Studies, 1973), 7.

[38] Beverly Brian Gilbert, " 'Civil' and the Notaries in *Piers Plowman*," *MAE* 50 (1981): 56.

[39] Ullmann, 184.

[40] Gray, 57.

Finally, a word must be said about the role of vernacular literature in Langland's quotations from Scripture. David Fowler is the main proponent of the view that readers of *Piers Plowman* must be acquainted "with scriptural influence in literary tradition," that is, "the Bible as it is employed in the drama, poetry, and prose of the period in which our poet is practicing his art."[41] Langland's debt to specific literary works has not been argued convincingly, but "literary tradition" tends to confirm that he handled Scripture in thoroughly traditional ways. At B.20.44–47, for example, he attributes the following speech to Christ "on þe selue roode": "The foxes have holes, and the birds of the air nests: but the son of man hath not where to lay his head" (Matt. 8:20). Skeat comments: "A singular mistake; the saying belongs to a much earlier period of our Lord's life" (2:276). The anachronism, however, is neither singular nor a mistake. Its basis is the liturgy for Passion Sunday, and it occurs in both the Towneley and York plays of the Crucifixion.[42]

> All creatoures that kynde may kest,
> Beestys, byrdys, all haue thay rest,
>   when thay ar wo begon;
> Bot godys son, that shuld be best,
> hase not where apon his hede to rest,
>   Bot on his shuder bone.
>   (255–60)[43]
>
> For, foxis ther dennys have they,
> Birdis hase ther nestis to paye,
> But the sone of man this daye
> Hase noght on his heed for to reste.
>   (192–95)[44]

---

[41] *Piers the Plowman: Literary Relations of the A and B Texts* (Seattle: Univ. of Washington, 1961), 45; see also *The Bible in Middle English Literature* (Seattle: Univ. of Washington Press, 1984).

[42] How it began is not difficult to understand: just three verses earlier, Matthew quotes the prophet Isaiah, "He took our infirmities, and bore our diseases," a saying that medieval exegetes almost unanimously interpreted as a reference to the Crucifixion.

[43] *The Towneley Plays*, ed. George England, with notes and introduction by Alfred W. Pollard, EETS 71 (Oxford: Oxford Univ. Press, 1897), 266.

[44] David Bevington, ed., *Medieval Drama* (Boston: Houghton Mifflin, 1975), 586.

The Non-Scriptural Quotations

One of the most striking features about Langland's non-scriptural
quotations, especially to anyone who has just come from Chaucer or
Gower, is the almost total absence of classical examples. There is
only one (from Juvenal's *Satires*), and even that, as noted above,
seems to have been derived from an intermediate source.[45] We
must not conclude, however, that the poet was unfamiliar with
auctores such as Cicero or Ovid or Statius, who were, after all, fix-
tures in the school curriculum. More probably he excluded them as
rhetorically inappropriate. Outside the Bible itself, Langland found
the most powerful endorsement for his point of view in three kinds
of authority, namely, the authority of grammar, of law, and of the
church (through its official creeds, prayers, and hymns).

Like other writers on the subject, Langland regarded grammar as
the foundation of learning, "þe ground of al" (B.15.372). Instruction
began with the eight parts of speech. The introductory textbook was
the fourth-century *Ars Minor* of Donatus, the standard for so long
that "Donatus" became a common term for primers in general:
"Thanne drouȝ I me among drapiers my donet to lerne" (B.5.207).
More advanced study focused on syntax and agreement, the basis of
the notorious grammatical metaphor beginning in C.3.332, where the
concept of "acordaunce" is explored not only in the grammatical
terms proper to it (kynde, case, nombre, rect relacion, adiectif,
sustantif, *Quia antelate rei recordatiuum est, hic & hec homo*) but also in
the language of the Bible and the liturgy (*Retribuere dignare domine
deus, verbum caro factum est, credere in ecclesia, deus homo, qui in caritate
manet, trinitas vnus deus, nominatiuo, pater & filius & spiritus sanctus*).
Because of the overlap with grammatical terminology (*retribuere,
verbum, nominatiuo*), the latter group of quotations might have been
grammarbook examples, as, in fact, scriptural verses often were; and
even Langland's reference to 1 Kings as *regum* in lines 408 and 413
(where elsewhere he refers to this book simply as "holy writ"
[C.Prol.104] and "the bible" [B.10.285]) might have been intended to
evoke the grammatical theory of *regimen*. From such standard text-
books as Thomas of Hanney's *Memoriale Iuniorum* and John Leylond's

---

[45] Langland attributes other quotations to classical authors, however; he
names Seneca as the author of the quotation in B.14.309, and he says in
B.11.37, " '*Homo proponit*,' quod a poete, and Plato he hiȝte." Where these
attributions might have come from (if they are not the merest caprice) is
unclear.

De Regimine Casuum, students learned the ways in which the inflection of a word is governed (*regitur*) by the power (*ex vi*) of another word in the same sentence.[46] The doctrine of *regimen* also underlies the metaphor in B.13.151, "Wiþ half a laumpe lyne in latyn, *Ex vi transicionis,* / I bere þer in a bouste ybounde, dowel"; the wordplay in B.14.181, "Thus *in genere* of gentries Iesu crist seide [*conuertimini ad me*]"; and possibly the saying in A.10.108a, *Qui circuit omne genus in nullo genere est.* Despite the confusion and even impatience of earlier critics (viz. Skeat's reaction to C.3.332 ff.: "The reader must puzzle out this passage for himself if he cares to read it"),[47] more recent research has not only solved these riddles but also shown their language to have been commonplace in the grammar schools of late fourteenth-century England.[48]

The understanding of grammatical concepts like *regimen* was furthered by exercises in "construing," that is, the analysis of a text at one or more levels in order to reveal its meaning or *culorum* (C.3.433, B.10.415, etc.). Of "þise newe clerkes," Langland complains, there is "nauȝt oon among an hundred þat an Auctor kan construwe" (B.15.375). The *auctores* set for this purpose varied from school to school,[49] but the collection most widely used between 1300 and 1500 was the so-called *Auctores Octo*, chosen as much for their moral content as for their grammatical usefulness. In manuscripts and early printed editions, these are normally bound together in the following order: the third-century *Distichs of Cato*; the ninth-century *Eclogues of Theodulus;* a social primer or "rules of living" called *Facetis* (of which there were several versions); an anonymous *De Contemptu Mundi* of the twelfth or thirteenth century (also known as *Cartula* from its opening word); the twelfth-century *Liber Parabo-*

---

[46] Thomson, 37; for a detailed explanation of *regimen* theory, see Cynthia Bland, *The Teaching of Grammar in Late Medieval England* (East Lansing, Mich.: Colleagues Press, 1991).

[47] Skeat, 2: 250.

[48] See Coleman's discussion of the grammatical metaphor in *Piers Plowman and the Moderni* (Rome: Edizioni di Storia e Letteratura, 1981), 85–99. She observes, "Langland is explaining the elements of the process of salvation in the only language he was likely to know: that of his contemporaries" (94). On the ordinariness of *ex vi* terminology at the time, see Cynthia Bland, "Langland's Use of the Term *Ex vi transicionis*," *YLS* 2 (1988): 125–35. For a general study of grammatical metaphor, see my article, "The Grammatical Metaphor: A Survey of Its Use in the Middle Ages," *Speculum* 57 (1982): 728–60.

[49] Thomson, 25. *14 9, 5·18*

larum (ascribed to Alan of Lille); the versified *Tobias* of Matthew of Vendome; the *Fables* of Aesop; and *Floretus*, a religious poem on faith, virtue, sin, the sacraments, and so forth.[50]

Although no connection between the *Auctores Octo* and *Piers Plowman* has ever been argued, it deserves to be explored. I can only touch upon the matter here. The *auctor* cited most frequently in the poem is the pseudo-Cato. Langland portrays him as Reason's own "knave" or servant (A.4.17), pairs him with "canonistres" as an authority on dreams (B.7.155), and makes him the standard of literacy in complaining of priests that "can nat construe catoun ne clergialiche reden" (C.7.34). There are ten different quotations from the *Distichs* in the poem.[51] The *Liber Parabolarum* furnishes two quotations (C.9.265a, B.18.408a–b [C.20.451a–b]). The verses beginning "Si quis amat christum" (B.14.60a [C.15.259a]), identified here for the first time, come from the *Cartula*.

Many additional quotations from the Bible and classical sources might have come to Langland through the *Auctores Octo* and its commentaries. For example, the proem to the *Distichs* quotes and glosses Isa. 55:1, *Omnes sitientes venite ad aquas, id est ad sapientiam vel ad doctrinam suscipiendam* (cf. B.11.120a, C.12.55a); and the interlinear commentary includes the texts *Honora patrem & matrem* (B.5.567), *Parce lauda vitupera parcius* (B.11.106), and *Parce mihi domine* (B.19.295).[52] In the *Eclogues of Theodulus*, we read *Non plus sapere quam oportet sapere* (B.10.121 etc.) and learn that Nebuchadnezzar is another name for Lucifer, *qui sedem suam voluit ponere in aquilone & esse similis altissimo* (B.1.119, B.15.51a, etc.).[53] Some of Langland's quotations from Tobit might have come by way of Matthew of Vendome's paraphrase.

Besides providing a rich store of familiar quotations, the *Auctores Octo* might have influenced the invention of Langland's poem in other ways. The scope of this introduction does not permit more than a few illustrations. The *Floretus* author's pun on *ingratus / gratus* (*Non sis ingratus domino si vis fore gratus*)[54] anticipates Langland's

---

[50] The *Auctores Octo* is discussed in Nicholas Orme, *English Schools in the Middle Ages* (London: Methuen, 1973), 103–4, 126. The edition used for this study was *Auctores Octo cum Commento* (1514).

[51] B.6.315, B.7.73, B.7.156, A.10.98, B.10.195–96, B.10.343a, B.11.404, C.13.224a, B.12.22a, B.19.296a.

[52] *Auctores* (1514 ed.): fols. 1ʳ, C2ᵛ, C6ʳ (twice).

[53] *Auctores* (1514 ed.): fol. Fʳ.

[54] Fol. T2ᵛ.

still richer wordplay in B.14.169-70, "Of þe good þat þow hem gyuest *ingrati* ben manye; / Ac god, of þi goodnesse gyue hem grace to amende." A line in *Cartula, Fac bene dum vivis post mortem vivere si vis*,[55] combines two phrases from Langland's satire of the gluttonous friar, "Do well" and "*post mortem*" (B.13.44, 103 ff.). The proem to the *Distichs* derives the "cardinal" virtues from *cardo* (hinge), as does *Piers* B.Prol.103-4; and, more, it identifies these four virtues as "the material cause" of the work, just as *truth*, sown from the four "seeds" of the cardinal virtues by Piers the Plowman (B.19.274 ff.), is the material cause of Langland's poem.[56]

The *Auctores Octo* represent only one group of grammatical texts that Langland would have known. Alexander of Villa Dei's versified *Doctrinale*, one of the most popular grammars during the thirteenth and fourteenth centuries and a source for other grammars as well,[57] provided the verse *Pauper ego ludo dum tu diues meditaris* (B.11.269a). Many of the manuscripts listed in David Thomson's *Descriptive Catalogue of Middle English Grammatical Texts* contain *latinitates* or "translation sentences," intended to illustrate grammatically interesting problems, such as the biblical verses *Michi vindictam & ego retribuam* (B.6.226a etc.) and *Saluabitur vix iustus in die iudicii* (B.12.281 etc.). It is impossible to say how many of the quotations in *Piers Plowman* might have come from "the general riot of verses and scribbles which fills up the pages of these manuscripts" (29). What Thomson writes about two later poets seems even more relevant to Langland: "The presence of this sort of material in the schoolroom may help to explain why, amongst the schoolmaster poets of the fifteenth century, Dunbar relishes the Latin tag or Lydgate the moralisation which seems trite to a modern reader" (30).

Like grammar, law held a special place in the poet's thinking. If grammar was the *ars recte loquendi*, then law was the *ars recte vivendi*, and both derived their exceptional authority from being "a recorde of treuthe."[58] In the terms and concepts of law, Langland found a

---

[55] *Auctores*, fol. H8ᵛ.

[56] *Auctores*, fol. 1ʳ.

[57] Thomson, 33.

[58] See my article, "The Grammatical Metaphor": "Truth, we learn, is not only the political virtue *par excellence*—governing the relation between king and subject, master and servant, and the like—but it is also the fundamental principle of grammar. Like society, speech depends upon *fidelitas*, each constituent part observing its proper relation to others: adjectives much be governed by nouns; pronouns must be ruled by their antecedents; there must

form of expression that was naturally suited to his purpose. Yet one
senses that it was personal experience, and not theme alone, that
disposed him to invoke the law so frequently. He knew it well.
Possibly his clerkly duties involved the copying of legal documents,
as implied by A.8.42–44:

> Þanne were marchauntis merye; many wepe for joye,
> And ȝaf wille for his writyng wollene cloþis;
> For he copiede þus here clause þei couden hym gret
> mede.

Whether this passage has any autobiographical value or not, Langland's extensive use of the law suggests a firsthand acquaintance. To
the conventional parody of a charter, he brings the technical phrase
"þe fyn is arerid" (A.2.48). To the usual opening of a letter patent,
he adds the apparently original phrase *per passionem domini* in imitation of the warrants (*per regem, per concilium*, etc.) actually found at
the bottom of such documents. The wording of the writ *capias* by
which Lady Meed is taken (C.4.164) is specific to the circumstances.
Langland's use of legal diction and metaphor is far from conventional, even in the midst of a literature given to such devices. Of the
seven or eight hundred legal terms in the poem—a remarkable figure
in itself—more than a hundred have no precedent in English.[59]

The Latin terms and phrases cover the gamut of the law of the
period. Several are broadly philosophical, such as the maxims *Audiatis alteram partem* (C.4.188) and *Necessitas non habet legem* (C.13.44a;
cf. also B.Prol.132, B.Prol.141, C.5.60a, C.9.213, B.15.88). A large
number are drawn from the instruments of English common law,
such as writs (C.2.190, C.4.164, C.4.190), petitions (B.7.46, B.19.416),
letters patent (B.14.190a), laws and statutes (C.3.300, B.11.96,
B.14.73, B.15.215), deeds, wills, and charters (B.2.74a, C.3.327,
B.6.86, B.13.44). A few reflect the influence, possibly, of civil or
Roman law (B.Prol.145, B.5.168, B.14.169), the study of which served
as an introduction to canon law. Most of the Latin identified here
with the canon law appears also in a variety of sources outside the
Corpus Iuris Canonici and its commentaries. This is hardly surprising.

---

be agreement in number, gender, and case. Social and linguistic order meet
in the grammatical concept of 'relacion rect,' which Langland says, 'ys a
recorde of treuthe' " (756).

[59] Langland's use of legal diction and concepts is explored in my *Piers
Plowman: A Glossary of Legal Diction* (Alford 1988b).

The law of the church is based on Scripture, the writings of the fathers, papal letters, and so forth; and much of this material, after the Fourth Lateran Council of 1215, was recycled in penitential treatises and popular manuals of instruction. It is difficult, therefore, to judge Langland's knowledge of ecclesiastical law with any precision. Nevertheless, of the nineteen quotations that fall into this category, a fair number are accompanied in the poem by their interpretations in canon law sources.[60]

The liturgy of the Roman Catholic church was both the original and intermediate source of a large number of quotations. Besides an indefinite number of embedded scriptural verses, such as those discussed already, the liturgy contributed more than four dozen examples of its own. The antiphons and hymns account for twenty-one; the various creeds for seventeen; lessons and responses for five; the ordinary and canon of the mass for five; and formulas connected with the sacrament of confession for three.[61] In addition, but closely related, are borrowings from the Lord's Prayer, said communally during the service, and the traditional graces that belonged to each individual's daily worship.[62]

Finally, for the sake of completeness, mention should be made of the four dozen or so miscellaneous quotations in the poem. These include sayings of the Fathers and others (Jerome, Augustine, Chrysostom, Isidore, Peter Cantor, Bernard),[63] largely unidentified scraps,[64] and a number of proverbs, including four in French.[65]

---

[60] The nineteen examples are B.2.123, B.3.241, C.3.308, B.4.143, B.5.168, C.6.257, A.10.90, A.10.94a, B.10.325, B.11.58a, B.11.81a, B.11.316, B.13.426a, B.14.17a, B.14.92, C.16.29, B.15.41, B.15.530a, B.20.279.

[61] These are as follows: (hymns and antiphons) B.3.311, B.3.328, B.5.483a, B.5.603a, B.12.150, B.12.286a, C.18.241a, B.17.114a, B.17.170a, C.19.140a, B.18.7, B.18.8, B.18.162a, B.18.407a, B.18.422, B.19.80a, B.19.152, B.19.187, B.19.201, B.19.210; (Athanasian creed) B.2.27a, C.3.402a, C.3.406, B.7.113, B.10.246a, B.16.223a; (Apostles' creed) C.3.357, C.3.481, B.10.473, B.15.608, B.17.151a, C.19.125a, B.18.111; (Nicene creed) C.3.356, B.5.58, B.18.112, B. 18.370; (lessons and responses) B.15.327, C.17.66a, B.19.295, B.18.149a, B.18. 392; (mass) B.5.412, C.17.238, B.16.242a, B.16.252a, B.18.421; (confession) C. 6.64, B.5.390, B.7.3.

[62] Quotations from the Lord's Prayer include C.5.46, B.10.468, B.13.396 (C.6.283), C.16.323; C.5.88, C.11.153a, B.14.50 (C.15.249), B.15.179 (C.16. 321), C.16.323, C.16.374a, B.19.394a (C.21.394a); parts of traditional graces occur at B.1.86 (A.1.84, C.1.82), C.3.340a, C.3.403a, C.9.125a, B.10.85a (C.11. 65a), B.10.359, B.14.63a (C.15.262a), C.16.320, C.17.66a.

[63] B.5.283a, C.7.118a, B.7.75, B.7.77, B.9.94, B.10.261, B.10.461, B.11.3, B.12.50a, B.14.144a, B.14.276, B.15.39a, B.15.60, B.15.63, B.15.118, B.15.343a.

[64] For example, B.5.269a, B.5.474, B.5.476, B.7.44, A.10.50, C.11.18a-b,

All of these could have come from the kinds of sources described already—florilegia, grammatical miscellanies, commentaries on law and on Scripture.

Janet Coleman introduces the final chapter of her study of Langland with the following statement:

> If we assume that his readers understood his poem and that he was writing with an audience in mind, it seems clear that we must close by trying to establish what kind of grammatical, legal and theological education such men were likely to receive in the second half of the fourteenth century.[66]

Coleman's emphases—"grammatical, legal and theological"—are mirrored in the poet's choice of quotations. Thus, the quotations direct us not only to the poem's beginning but also to its end. In the process of composition, they served as *topoi*, generating hundreds of lines in the form of translation, commentary, and narrative; in the finished work, they served as *confirmationes*, compelling assent from readers nourished by grammar, law, and the language of holy church. That *Piers Plowman* is more than the sum of its borrowings hardly needs stating. But no study of the poem—whether of its author, its audience, or its art—can afford to ignore them.

B.12.216a, B.13.45a, B.13.50, B.15.318, C.17.140a, B.16.47a, C.18.117, C.19.73, B.17.200a, B.18.23, B.18.24, B.18.26, B.18.216.

[65] The French quotations are B.Prol.225, B.10.445, B.11.385–86, C.17.163–64; words and phrases specifically identified as French in the manuscripts (that is, by rubrication) include *douce vie* (B.14.123), *bele paroles* (B.15.115), *beau fit3* (C.9.312), *pur charite* (C.10.11, C.15.32), *chaud* and *plus chaud* (B.6.311), *treys encountre treys* (C.18.238). Langland's use of anglicized loanwords is, of course, another matter. Schmidt treats the question briefly in *The Clerkly Maker*, 102–7.

[66] *Piers Plowman and the Moderni*, 172.

Indexes

I
The Latin and French Quotations

THIS INDEX LISTS ALL INSTANCES OF Latin and French in the poem—including single words, which are often allusions to larger contexts—as these appear in the following editions:

MS Bodley 851 ("Z version"), ed. A. G. Rigg and Charlotte Brewer
A version, ed. George Kane
B version, ed. George Kane and E. Talbot Donaldson
C version, ed. George Russell

Citations from Oxford, MS Bodley 851 are given here as a convenience to the reader; their inclusion is not meant to endorse the editors' claim that this manuscript represents the earliest distinct version of the poem. The order of the index is that of the B version. Where the order of C is significantly different from that of B due to wholesale revision (for example, the shift of a large block of B.13 to C.7), the cross references should provide adequate guidance.

Because the rationale behind incomplete scriptural quotations is often unclear, many of those below have been expanded in brackets. Also in brackets are a large number of variant readings from other *Piers* manuscripts that bring the text more in line with the Vulgate Bible. For example:

B.13.39a (C.15.44a) *Edentes & bibentes que apud eos* [*illos* Vulg., B var.] *sunt.* Lk. 10:7. [B.2.123 (A.2.86a)]

This is to be read as follows: at B.13.39a (and correspondingly at C.15.44a) occurs the quotation *Edentes & bibentes que apud eos sunt* from Luke 10:7; however, the pronoun *eos* appears in the Vulgate and in one or more manuscripts of the B version as *illos*; the same scriptural verse is also quoted at B.2.123 (and correspondingly at A.2.86a).

The Bible used here is the Clementine edition (A. Colunga and L. Turrado, Biblioteca de Autores Cristianos, 4th ed. [Madrid, 1965]), but variant readings attested by other sources (such as the *Vetus Latina*, biblical commentaries, and liturgical books) are also noted.

Although I have drawn on the excellent notes in the editions by Skeat, Bennett, Schmidt, and Pearsall, I have tried to supplement rather than merely reproduce their comments. Many references appear here for the first time, and earlier inaccuracies have been silently corrected. Because repeated quotations are cross-indexed, source information is given only once (normally at the first occurrence in B).

Prologue

B.Prol.39 (A.Prol.39, C.Prol.40) That Poul precheþ of hem I dar nat preue it here; / *Qui loquitur turpiloquium* is luciferes hyne. Cf. Eph. 5:4, "Fornicatio autem, et omnis immunditia, aut avaritia, nec nominetur in vobis, … aut turpitudo, aut stultiloquium, aut scurrilitas" (summarized by Bromyard 1:459/1 as "de turpiloquio et scurrilitate"), and Col. 3:8, "Nunc autem deponite et vos … turpem sermonem de ore vestro" (to which Peter Lombard adds the gloss "vel turpiloquium" [*PL* 192:281]). For "turpem sermonem," the *Vetus Latina* has "turpiloquium"; thus also citations of the verse by Ambrose, Ambrosiaster, Tertullian, and Vigilius (see R. W. Muncey, *The New Testament Text of Saint Ambrose* [Cambridge: Cambridge Univ. Press, 1959], xxxii, 95). The line as a whole probably reflects a gloss on John 8:34, "Qui facit peccatum, servus est peccati" ("Id est, diaboli," Hugh of St. Cher). *Turpiloquia* is Latin for the rhetorical figure *aeschrologia*. [B.13.456 (C.7. 116); cf. B.11.204a (C.12.112a)]

—**C.Prol.108, 112** Thei were discomfited in batayle and losten *Archa domini* [*Archa dei* in some MSS]. 1 Reg. 4:6, "Et cognoverunt quod arca Domini venisset in castra"; 1 Reg. 4:11: "Et arca Dei capta est. …" [cf. B.10.288, B.12.113, 119 (C.14.58)]

B.Prol.132–38 (C.Prol.150–56)

> *Sum Rex, sum princeps; neutrum fortasse deinceps.*
> *O qui iura regis christi specialia regis,*
> *Hoc quod [vt C] agas melius, iustus es, esto pius!*
> *Nudum ius a te vestiri vult pietate.*
> *Qualia vis metere, talia grana sere.*
> *Si ius nudatur nudo de iure metatur* [line om. C]
> *Si seritur pietas de pietate metas.*

The verses are found also in Lambeth MS 61, fol. 147ᵛ, where they were added by a scribe to the text of a sermon preached in 1315 by Henry Harclay, Chancellor of Oxford; for minor variants see J. A. W. Bennett, "Sum Rex, Sum Princeps, etc." *N&Q* 205 (1960): 364, and the reply by Barbara Strang, *N&Q* 205 (1960): 436. A later version is found in Bibliothèque Nationale MS lat 5178, fol. 69 (Bennett 99).

B.Prol.141–42

> *Dum rex a regere dicatur nomen habere*
> *Nomen habet sine re nisi studet iura tenere.*

Variant of a commonplace verse, "O rex, si rex es, rege te, vel eris sine re rex / Et sine re regnas, te nisi rite regas" (Walther 19575).

The etymology is standard following Isidore of Seville (*Sententiae* 3.48, "De prelatis: Reges a recte agendo vocati sunt ideoque recte faciendo regis nomen tenentur"; *Etym.* 9:3, "Sicut enim sacerdos a sacrificando, ita et rex a regendo. Non autem regit, qui non corrigit. Recte igitur faciendo regis nomen tenetur, peccando comittitur. Unde et apud veteres tale erat proverbium: 'Rex eris, si recte facias; si non facias, non eris' "). Cf. Brinton 1:46 ("Dicit Ysidorus . . . Rex dicitur regendo . . .") and Gratian, *CIC* 1:68 ("rex a regendo"). Other analogues are noted in Bennett 100, Alford 1975. A brief history of the doctrine—"the *Rex* is so called *a recte agendo*"—can be found in Otto Gierke, *Political Theories of the Middle Age*, trans. Frederic William Maitland (Cambridge: Cambridge Univ. Press, 1913), 141–42. Classical precedents are cited in Jozsef Balogh, "Rex a Recte Regendo," *Speculum* 3 (1928): 580–82.

B.Prol.145 *Precepta Regis sunt nobis vincula legis*. Metrical variant of a maxim of Roman law, the so-called *Lex regia*: "Quod principi placuit legis habet vigorem" (*The Institutes of Justinian* 1.2.6, ed. T. C. Sandars [London: Longmans, 1962], 10); cf. Bromyard 1:22/3, "Quicquid principibus habet, legis habet vigorem"; Paris, Bibliothèque Nationale MS Latin 11867, "Precepto regis mihi subdita sanctio legis" (Walther 22136f). An index of medieval glosses on the *lex regia* can be found in Gierke (cited above) 147.

B.Prol.196 (C.Prol.206) *Ve terre vbi puer Rex est* [*est Rex* C] *&c.* Proverbial (Walther 32852c), based on Eccles. 10:16, "Vae tibi, terra, cuius rex puer est." Brunne's *Handlyng Synne* reads: "But how seyþ Salamon yn hys spellyng, / 'wo þe land, þere chylde ys kyng!' " (EETS 123 [1901], 340); see Whiting W436 for additional examples in English. The proverb is applied specifically to Richard II by Adam of Usk (Bennett 102).

B.Prol.225 (Z.Prol.92, A.Prol.103, C.Prol.226) And dryueþ forþ þe longe day with *"Dieu saue dame Emme."* "Evidently the refrain of a traditional song, perhaps about Emma wife of Canute" (Bennett 103) or Emma of Shoreditch in B.13.339 (Pearsall 41).

Passus 1

B.1.31a (C.1.30a) *Inebriemus eum vino dormiamusque cum eo / Vt seruare possimus de patre nostro semen*. Gen. 19:32, "Veni, inebriemus eum vino, dormiamusque cum eo, ut servare possimus ex patre nostro semen"; *VL* reads ". . . ut suscitemus *de patre* nostro semen."

B.1.52–53 (Z.Prol. 139–40, A.1.50–51, C.1.48–49) *"Reddite Cesari,"* quod god, "þat *Cesari* bifalleþ, / *Et que sunt dei deo* or ellis ye don ille." Matt. 22:21, Lk. 20:25, "Reddite ergo quae sunt Caesaris, Caesari: et quae sunt Dei, Deo."

B.1.86 (Z.1.31, A.1.84, C.1.82) I do it on *Deus caritas* to deme þe soþe. 1 Jn. 4:8, 16, "Deus charitas est"; part of a daily grace (*Graces* 382).

B.1.96 (Z.1.42, A.1.94, C.1.92) And taken *transgressores* [*trespassours* A] and tyen hem faste. Cf. James 2:8–9, which identifies *transgressores* as those who violate the law of love ("Diliges proximum tuum"). Hugh's comment distinguishes *transgressores* (of positive law) from *prevaricatores* (of natural law). See Alford 1975, 1988b. Cf. C.10.95 (*prevaricatores legis*).

B.1.119 (C.1.111a) *Ponam pedem* [*sedem meam* B var., *pedem meum* C] *in aquilone & similis ero altissimo.* Augustine, *Ennarationes in Psalmos* (*PL* 36:69 [Ps. 1:4], 534 [Ps. 47:2]), "Ponam sedem meam ad Aquilonem, et ero similis Altissimo"; a compression of Isa. 14:13–14 (*VL*), "In coelum ascendam, super stellas Dei ponam sedem meam, sedebo in monte alto, super montes altos in Aquilonem. Ascendam super nubes, ero similis Altissimo." The source was first identified by Robertson and Huppé, *Piers Plowman and Scriptural Tradition* (Princeton: Princeton Univ. Press, 1951), 44n52; they note a later example as well from Alanus de Insulis (*PL* 210:705). R. G. Risse argues that the quotation reached L through an intermediary such as the commentary on the *Fables* of Avianus ("The Augustinian Paraphrase of Isaiah 14.13–14 in *Piers Plowman*...," *PQ* 45 [1966]: 712–17). For L's substitution of *pedem* for *sedem*, see A. L. Kellogg, "Langland and Two Scriptural Texts," *Traditio* 14 (1958): 385–98. [B.15.51a (C.16.213a)]

—C.1.113 *In lateribus Aquilonis.* Isa. 14:13, continued from above.

—C.1.122a *Dixit dominus domino meo, sede a dextris meis.* Ps. 109:1, quoted in Matt. 22:44, Mk. 12:36, Lk. 20:42, Acts 2:34.

B.1.141a (C.1.140a) *Heu michi quia* [*quod* C] *sterilem duxi vitam Iuuenilem.* Proverbial (Walther 6232, 10736b). See John Rylands Library, Latin MS 394 (fol. 15): "Hu michi quod sterilem vitam duxi iuvenilem, de ocio iuventutis." For a description of the contents of this manuscript, see W. A. Pantin, "A Medieval Collection of Latin and English Proverbs and Riddles, from the Rylands Latin MS. 394," *Bulletin of the John Rylands Library* 14 (1930): 81–114. For the importance of this manuscript to *Piers Plowman*, see the letter by A. H. Bright in the *Times Literary Supplement*, April 24, 1930, and that by Bernard Hall, ibid., May 1, 1930. The same manuscript also contains the quotation at B.10.266a. [B.5.440a (C.7. 54a)]

—**C.1.143a (cf. C.7.209–210)** *Melius est mori quam male viuere.* Proverbial, perhaps from Tobias 3:6, "Expedit enim mihi mori magis quam vivere." Cf. Walther 14594, 38182d, and esp. 38183, "Melius est mori quam vivere moleste," and 38190, "Melius mori quam inquinari"; Innocent III, *De Contemptu Mundi* 1.24, "Melius est ergo mori vitae quam vivere morti" (noted in Skeat 2:27); also B. Hauréau, *Notices et extraits de quelques manuscrits latins de la Bibliothèque Nationale* (Paris, 1892), 5:177, "Melior est mors quam vita amara et requies aeterna quam languor perseverans." The proverb is translated at C.7.209–10, "That is to sey sothly ȝe sholde rather deye / Thenne eny dedly synne do," and, as noted by Pearsall (50), in Thomas Usk's *Testament of Love* (*Chaucerian and Other Pieces*, ed. W. W. Skeat [Oxford, 1897], 32). It occurs also in an English translation of Robert de Gretham's *Mirror* (Bodley Library, MS Holkham Misc. 40, fol. 56ᵛ): "þat is to seye, he schal ... raþere for to dye þan he schulde don a dedliche synne" (ed. Kathleen Blumreich Moore, Ph.D. dissertation, Michigan State Univ., 1991). [C.6.290a, C.17.40a]

B.1.178a (C.1.174a) *Eadem [quippe] mensura qua mensi fueritis remecietur vobis.* Lk. 6:38; cf. Matt. 7:2, Mk. 4:24. Bromyard also omits *quippe* (1:201/2, 231/4). [C.11.232a, B.11.228]

B.1.187a (C.1.183a) *Fides sine operibus mortua est &c.* James 2:26.

B.1.201 (Z.1.124, A.1.175, C.1.196) *Date & dabitur vobis,* for I deele yow alle. Lk. 6:38. [B.12.54a]

Passus 2

B.2.27a (C.2.27a) *Qualis pater talis filius.* From the Athanasian Creed, "Qualis Pater talis Filius: talis Spiritus Sanctus," *Brev.* 2:46; further discussion in Alford 1975. Also proverbial: Walther 840a15d, Whiting F80.

B.2.27b (C.2.29a) *Bona arbor bonum fructum facit.* Matt. 7:17, "Sic omnis arbor bona fructus bonos facit"; cf. Lk. 6:43. Walther 216: "Bona arbor generat bonum fructum." [C.10.244b]

—**C.2.31** The fader þat me forth brouhte *filius dei* he hoteth. Specific source unidentified. Cf. the centurion's pronouncement at the death of Christ—conterminous with the "birth" of Holy Church— "Vere Filius Dei erat iste" (Matt. 27:54). [B.10.246a, B.18.68 (C.20.70a)]

B.2.35 That he shal lese for hire loue a lippe of *Caritatis.* The use of

Latin suggests something more specific or technical than merely
"charity." Janet Coleman argues that in the context of fourteenth-
century theology, the term includes the notion of grace (cf.
C.11.224 "a lyppe of goddes grace"). She comments on C.17.122–
36: "While the Saracens may have a kind of charity similar to
Christian *caritas*, being the kind of natural love that attends natural law and which is a natural thing for a creature to bear towards
his Creator, yet there is a flaw in the direction or intention of
their *caritas*. . . . They are living by the law of nature alone, not by
the law of grace" (*Piers Plowman and the Moderni* [Rome: Edizioni
di Storia e Letteratura, 1981], 142). [C.14.14, C.18.14, C.18.32,
C.18.39]

B.2.39 (C.2.40) *Domine quis habitabit in tabernaculo tuo &c.* Ps. 14:1.
On the association of this verse with the theme of justice, see
above, p. 7. [B.3.234a, B.7.52a, B.13.127 (C.15.134)]

—C.2.42 *Et super Innocentem munera non accepit.* Ps. 14:5. [B.3.241a
(A.3.221a), B.7.42a (Z.8.47, A.8.46a)]

B.2.74a (C.2.81) *Sciant presentes & futuri &c.* Formula for the opening of a charter and other kinds of legal documents; see Thomas
Madox, *Formulare Anglicanum*, 355, 368, 371, 376, 378, 379, 398,
and passim. Cf. *The Charter of the Abbey of the Holy Ghost*, in Horstman 2:338: "Here begynniþ þe forseyd chartre. *Sciant presentes &
futuri &c.*: Wetiþ ȝe þat ben now here, & þei þat schulen comen
after ȝou" (Alford 1988b).

B.2.123 (Z.2.95, A.2.86a) For *Dignus est operarius* his hire to haue. Lk.
10:7, ". . . dignus est enim operarius mercede sua" (*VL:* "dignus
est operarius mercede sua"), quoted in 1 Tim. 5:18 (cf. Matt.
10:10). The text was "traditionally used by canonists and legists
[viz. Pennafort 212] to justify the acceptance by lawyers of moderate fees from those who could afford to pay" (Beverly Brian
Gilbert, "'Civil' and the Notaries in *Piers Plowman*," *MAE* 50
[1981]: 56). It was also used to support mendicancy: "And so to
his prechours Crist also þus seide . . . : *Dignus est enim operarius
mercede sua*" (*Friar Daw's Reply*, in *Upland* 92; see also 104). The
verse is apparently the origin of Langland's definition of "good"
meed as "mercede" in C.3.291 ff.

—C.2.187 Wol Ryde vppon Rectores and ryche men deuoutours.
Perhaps an allusion to Ecclus. 33:19 ff., in which *rectores ecclesiae*
are admonished to manage their goods wisely, for "fodder, and a
wand, and a burden are for an ass."

—C.2.190 Sommnours and sodenes þat supersedias taketh. *Supersedeas*, a writ that stayed or put an end to a proceeding; a large

number of writs of *supersedeas* contemporary with Langland may
be found in P.R.O. C264, the "stool bundle" (Alford 1988b).
[C.4.190, C.9.264]

B.2.181 (C.2.194) And fecchen oure vitailles at *Fornicatores*. One of
the main concerns of the ecclesiastical courts was the punishment
of fornicators (a jurisdiction recognized by the statute *Circumspecte
agatis* [1285]); the taking of bribes by church officials in such cases
is a common theme (see Alford 1988b, 62).

Passus 3

B.3.72a (A.3.54, C.3.74a) *Nesciat sinistra* [*sinistra tua* Vulg., B var.;
sinistra manus B var.] *quid faciat dextra* [*tua ut sit eleemosyna tua in
abscondito*]. Matt. 6:3–4; antiphon, Friday after Ash Wednesday,
Brev. 1:dlxi.

—**A.3.64a** *Amen, Amen* [*dico vobis, receperunt mercedem suam*]. Matt. 6:2,
5, 16. [B.3.254a (A.3.233a, C.3.312)]

—**C.3.118a** *In quorum manibus iniquitates sunt* [*dextera eorum repleta est
muneribus*]. Ps. 25:10. [B.3.249 (A.3.228)]

B.3.96 (A.3.85, C.3.124) *Ignis deuorabit tabernacula eorum qui libenter
accipiunt munera &c.* Job 15:34, "Et ignis devorabit tabernacula
eorum qui munera libenter accipiunt."

—**C.3.190a** *Sunt infelices quia matres sunt meretrices.* Unidentified.

B.3.234a *Domine, quis habitabit in tabernaculo tuo?* Ps. 14:1. [B.2.39,
(C.2.40), B.7.52a, B.13.127 (C.15.134)]

B.3.237a *Qui ingreditur sine macula & operatur Iusticiam.* Ps. 14:2.

—**C.3.300** That *pre manibus* is paied or his pay asketh. "Before-hand,"
a contractual term applied to payments in advance, often associated with usurious or unethical agreements; see the discussion,
along with other examples of the phrase, in Alford 1988b. [C.9.45]

B.3.241a (A.3.221a) *Qui pecuniam suam non dedit ad vsuram et munera
super innocentem* [*non accepit*]. Ps. 14:5, a proof-text commonly
cited against usury and excessive legal fees (e.g., Pennafort 236,
Vices and Virtues [EETS 89], 76). See Alford 1988b, 124. [C.2.42,
B.7.42a (Z.8.47, A.8.46a)]

—**C.3.308a** *Non morabitur opus mersenarii &c* [*tui apud te usque mane*].
Lev. 19:13. A commonplace in canon law, enjoining the prompt
payment of wages (e.g., Brinton 2:364); delayed payment was
regarded as a form of usury. See Walter Ullmann, *The Medieval
Idea of Law* (1946; repr. New York: Barnes and Noble, 1969), 184;
Raymond A. De Roover, *San Bernardino of Siena and Sant' Antoni-
no of Florence* (Boston: Baker Library, Harvard Univ. Graduate

School of Business Administration, 1967), 26. [cf. B.5.552]

B.3.249 (A.3.228) *In quorum manibus iniquitates sunt; dextra eorum repleta est muneribus.* Ps. 25:10, part of the *Lavabo* prayer of the mass (Bennett 140). [C.3.118a]

B.3.254a (A.3.233a, C.3.312) *Amen amen* [*Amen dico vobis* Vulg.] *Receperunt mercedem suam* [*Amen, Amen . . . Mercedem suam receperunt* C]. Matt. 6:2, 6:5. [A.3.64a]

—C.3.329 So god gyveth no grace þat *si* ne is the glose. The allusion is to the language of grants, deeds, contracts, etc. Cf. *Fleta* 3.15, "The word *ut* . . . denotes a mode, *si* a condition, *quia* a cause" (ed. H. G. Richardson and G. O. Sayles, Selden Society 89 [London: Quaritch, 1972]). Further discussion in Alford 1988b, 144.

—C.3.340a *Retribuere dignare domine deus &c.* Part of a Latin grace said after dinner: "Oremus: Retribuere dignare, domine deus, omnibus nobis bona facientibus, propter nomen sanctum tuum, vitam eternam" (*Graces* 383). Other graces are quoted at B.1.86 (A.1.84, C.1.82), C.3.403a, C.9.125a, B.10.85a (C.11.65a), B.10.359a, B.14.63a (C.15.262a), C.16.320, C.17.66a.

—C.3.344a *Quia antelate rei recordatiuum est.* In Latin grammars, a common formula used to explain grammatical relation, e.g., that of a relative pronoun to its antecedent. Margaret Amassian and James Sadowsky quote examples from Peter of Spain ("Relativum est duplex . . . aliud est relativum quod est ante latae rei recordativum, quia, ut vult Priscianus in maiori suo volumine, relatio est ante latae rei recordatio, ut 'Sortes currit qui movetur.' Ibi hoc relativum 'qui' facit recordationem sive relationem de Sorte qui est res ante lata") and from Thomas of Erfurt ("Recordatio . . . est, quam cognitio secunda, ut si aliquid sit primo cognitum, postea oblitum, et iterum ad memorian reductum; unde dicitur *relatio*, quasi *ante latae rei recordatio*") ("Mede and Mercede: A Study of the Grammatical Metaphor in *Piers Plowman*" C:IV: 335–409 *NM* 72 [1971], 466). For additional examples see L. M. deRijk, *Logica Modernorum* (Assen: Van Gorcum, 1967), 2:480; John of Genoa, *Catholicon* (Mainz, 1460; repr. Farnborough, Hants.: Gregg, 1971), 18ʳ; Gregorius Reisch, *Margarita Philosophica* (Basel, 1508), 81; Middle English translation quoted in Thomson, "How knowest a relatife? For it maketh mencion of a thinge seide bifore" (80).

—C.3.356 He acordeth with crist in kynde, *verbum caro factum est.* Jn. 1:14, repeated often during Advent, e.g., *Brev.* 1:clxxi, clxxxvi; the verse stands here for an article ("Et homo factus est") of the Nicene Creed, recited in the Ordinary of the Mass (*Missale* 591, *Brev.* 2:483), which lies behind Langland's development of the grammatical metaphor (cf. the next several quotations). [B.5.500a (C.7.140a)]

—**C.3.357** In case, *credere in ecclesia*, in holy kyrke to bileue. Cf. the Apostles' creed ("Credo in ... sanctam ecclesiam catholicam"), *Brev.* 2:2, and the Nicene creed ("Credo in ... unam sanctam catholicam: et apostolicam Ecclesiam"), *Missale* 592, *Brev.* 2:484. [cf. C.3.481, B.10.473, C.16.322, B.15.608 (C.17.316)]

—**C.3.402a** *Deus homo.* Echo of the Athanasian creed ("Ita Deus et homo unus est Christus"), *Brev.* 2:48.

—**C.3.403a** *Qui in caritate manet in deo manet et deus in eo.* [B.5.486b, B.9.65a]

—**C.3.405** As *hic & hec homo* askyng an adiectyf. For discussion of L's grammatical metaphor here, see Amassian and Sadowsky (cited above, C.3.344a), 473–74. The Latin suggests a grammatical exercise in the various kinds of noun. For example, "Genera nominum sunt quattuor, masculinum femininum neutrum et commune. ... Commune est quod simul masculinum femininumque significat, ut hic et haec sacerdos," *Commentum Sedulii Scotti in Maiorem Donatum Grammaticum,* ed. Denis Brearley (Toronto: Pontifical Institute of Mediaeval Studies, 1975), 82; "A nown substantyf ... ys clynud wit on artecul or to at þo most; wit on artycul as *hic uir,* wit to articuls as *hic & hec sacerdos,*" *Accedence,* ed. Cynthia Bland, in her *Teaching of Grammar in Late Medieval England* (East Lansing, Mich.: Colleagues Press, 1991), 149.

—**C.3.406** Of thre trewe termisonus, *trinitas vnus deus.* Cf. the Athanasian creed, *Brev.* 2:46–48.

—**C.3.406a** *Nominatiuo, pater & filius & spiritus sanctus.* From the formula "In nomine Patris et Filii et Spiritus Sanctus" (e.g., *Missale* 578, 581, 593; *Brev.* 2:480, 483, 497), with a pun on *nominativo* (possibly a grammarbook example); see Amassian and Sadowsky 474 (cited above at C.3.344a). [cf. C.2.31, B.10.246a, B.16.223a, C.18.51, B.18.68a (C.20.70a)]

—**C.3.407** Ac hoso rat of *regum* rede me may of mede. The books of Regum (Kings), specifically 2 Regum 14–18 (Absalom's conspiracy). [C.3.413]

B.3.259 (A.3.238, C.3.413) Ac reddestow neuere *Regum,* þow recrayed Mede. The allusion is to 1 Regum (1 Samuel AV) 15 and 16. [C.3.407]

B.3.280 (A.3.258, C.3.433) The *culorum* of þis cas kepe I noȝt to shewe. *Culorum* is glossed by most editors as "ending or conclusion," the Latin taken as an abbreviation of *in secula seculorum* (e.g., B.18.421), a common ending for prayers, psalms, anthems (e.g., *Brev.* 2:4, *Graces* 385). Whatever the origin of the term, the context in both *Piers* and *Richard the Redeless* is grammatical (cf. Skeat's edition of the latter, Prol. 72: "And constrewe ich clause with the *culorum*"). To "construe" a clause grammatically involved the analysis not only of its syntax, diction, and so forth, but also of its meaning or *culorum*. [B.10.415 (C.11.246)]

B.3.308a (C.3.461a) *Conflabunt gladios suos in vomeres* [*& lancias suas in falces* C] *&c.* Isa. 2:4, "Et iudicabit gentes, Et arguet populos multos; Et conflabunt gladios suos in vomeres, Et lanceas suas in falces. Non levabit gens contra gentem gladium, Nec exercebuntur ultra ad praelium," read in the first week of Advent (*Brev.* 1:lviii), continued at B.3.324a.

B.3.311 (C.3.464) Preestes and persons wiþ *Placebo* to hunte. First word of the antiphon ("Placebo Domino in regione vivorum") that begins the Office of the Dead at vespers, *Brev.* 2:271; based on Ps. 114:9. [C.5.46, B.15.125]

—C.3.464 Prestes and persones *placebo* and *dirige*. For *placebo* see above. *Dirige* is the first word of the antiphon ("Dirige Domine Deus meus in conspectu tuo viam meam") that begins the Office of the Dead at matins, *Brev.* 2:273; based on Ps. 5:9. Like Chaucer (The Merchant's Tale, *CT* IV 1476), Bishop Brinton plays on the words: "Plus timeo quod isti falsi consiliari qui tibi semper cantant 'placebo' et numquam 'dirige' per sua consilia te subuertent" (1:204).

B.3.324a (C.3.477a) *Non leuabit gens contra gentem gladium* [*nec excercebuntur vltra ad prelium* C] *&c.* Isa. 2:4, continued from B.3.308a above.

B.3.328 (cf. below) And Sarȝynes for þat siȝte shul synge *Gloria in excelsis, etc.* Gloria of the Mass (*Missale* 583, passim) and antiphon (e.g., *Brev.* 1:clxxiv), based on Lk. 2:14. [B.12.150 (C.14.94), B.19. 74a (C.21.74a)]

—C.3.481 And saresines for þat syhte shal syng *Credo in spiritum sanctum.* Apostles' creed, *Brev.* 2:2. [cf. C.3.357, B.10.473, C.16.322, B.15.608 (C.17.316), C.18.120]

B.3.330 (C.3.483) For *Melius est bonum nomen* [*nomen bonum* B var.] *quam diuicie multe.* Prov. 22:1, "Melius est nomen bonum quam divitiae multae."

—C.3.485 "Loo what salamon sayth," quod she, "in *sapiense* in þe bible!" Langland's name for the book of Proverbs (cf. B.6.235), quoted immediately following. In other contexts it might refer to any of the *libri sapientiae* (Proverbs, Job, Ecclesiastes, Ecclesiasticus, Wisdom); see Mary Clemente Davlin, "*Piers Plowman* and the Books of Wisdom," *YLS* 2 (1988): 23–33. [C.3.496]

B.3.336 (C.3.488) *Honorem adquiret qui dat munera &c.* Prov. 22:9, "Victoriam et honorem acquiret qui dat munera; Animam autem aufert accipientium," continued below at B.3.350.

B.3.339–43 (C.3.491–95) *Omnia probate ... Quod bonum est tenete.* 1 Thess. 5:21; *capitulum* for Sunday at sext, *Brev.* 2:64. L's association of the verse with a "lesson" (*lectio*) in line 338 suggests the Breviary as the source. [A.12.50–52, 56–57, C.20.234a]

—C.3.496 So hoso secheth *sapience.* [C.3.485]

B.3.350 (C.3.498a) *Animam autem aufert accipientium &c.* Prov. 22:9, continued from B.3.336. The next few verses, possibly implied by the "&c.," are also pertinent to the scene: "Cast out the scoffer and contention shall go out with him, and quarrels and reproaches [*causae et contumeliae*] shall cease. He that loveth cleanness of heart, for the grace of his lips shall have the king for his friend."

Passus 4

B.4.36a (C.4.36a) *Contricio & infelicitas in viis eorum [et viam pacis non cognouerunt; non est timor dei ante oculos eorum* C]. Ps. 13:3, quoted in Rom. 3:16–18.

B.4.37a *Non est timor dei ante oculos eorum &c.* Continued from above.

B.4.120 And Religiouse Romeris *Recordare* in hir cloistres. *Recordare,* "to reminisce, to meditate upon" (Alford 1975); the Latin probably lies behind the expression "to recollect oneself," as in the statement that Thomas More liked his privacy "the better to recollect himselfe to god" (*The Lyfe of Syr Thomas More,* EETS 222 [1950, for 1945], 49).

B.4.143–44 (Z.4.141–42, A.4.126–27, C.4.140–41)
> For *Nullum malum* þe man mette wiþ *inpunitum*
> And bad *Nullum bonum* be *irremuneratum.*

Common maxim (Walther 39079c), especially in the penitential tradition. Skeat traces it to Innocent III, *De Contemptu Mundi,* 3:15, "Ipse est iudex iustus ... qui nullum malum praeterit impunitum, nullum bonum irremuneratum" (Skeat 2:59). Gray cites other examples from Paul of Hungary's *De Confessione,* Hostiensis' *Summa Aurea,* Peter the Cantor's *Summa,* Alan of Lille's *Liber Poenitentialis,* Robert Courson's *Summa,* and an anonymous text on confession in MS Cambridge University Library Gg.4.32. The saying is attributed to God (i.e., Scripture) in Caxton's *The Book of the Knight of the Tower* (EETS supp. ser. 2 [1971]), 158 [cf. B.18. 390a (C.20.443)]; see also *Vices and Virtues* (EETS 89), 102. The

earliest vernacular example of the maxim appears in the thir-
teenth-century lyric "Worldes Blis": "Ne wort ne god þer unfor-
gulde, / ne non uuel ne worth unboukt" (Carleton Brown, ed.,
English Lyrics of the XIIIth Century [Oxford: Clarendon Press, 1932],
82). [B.18.390a (C.20.433)]

—**C.4.164–65** ... *capias* ... *Et saluo custodias set non cum carceratis.*
Variation on a standard formula in writs of *capias* or attachment
(Alford 1988b); e.g., *Registrum Omnium Brevium* (London, 1634),
Judicial Writs section: "Rex vic' salutem. Praecipimus tibi quod
capias A. si inventus fuerit in balliva tua, & eum salvo custodias ..." (1b); "Capias L. de C ... & eum in prisona nostra salvo
custodiri facias" (82b). No precedent has been found for L's
substitution of the clause "set non cum carceratis" for the usual
"in prisona nostra"; nevertheless it would not be justified to
conclude that L himself modified the wording to fit the dramatic
situation of the poem. The wording of writs actually varied considerably according to the charge and court of issue (see introduction to P. R. O. Chancery Files C244).

—**C.4.188** *Audiatis alteram partem* amonges aldremen and comeneres.
Roman law maxim, quoted repeatedly as one of the self-evident
propositions of natural law (Alford 1975); e.g., Augustine, *De
duabus animabus contra manichaeos* (*PL* 42:110); Caxton's *History of
Reynard the Fox*, "Ther ben many that complayne on other and
ben in the defaute them self. *Audi alteram partem.* here that other
partye" (ed. N. F. Blake, EETS 263 [1970], 54); *Pilgrimage of the
Life of Man*, "Every Rightful Iuge Sholde ... Seke and enqueryn
out the ryght Off outher part" (EETS es 77 [1899], 66). A history
of the phrase may be found in H. H. Marshall, *Natural Justice*
(London, 1959), esp. 17–20 and 53–60. See also the long note by
Thomas Heffernan in *The Chaucer Review* 10 (1975): 184.

—**C.4.190** Ne no supersedias sende but y assente, quod resoun.
[C.2.190, C.9.264]

—**C.5.32a** *Reddet vnicuique iuxta opera sua.* [B.12.213a (C.14.152a)]

—**C.5.43a** *In eadem vocacione qua vocati estis &c.* Cf. 1 Cor. 7:20,
"Unusquisque in qua vocatione vocatus est, in ea permaneat" and
Eph. 4:1, "Obsecro itaque vos ego vinctus in Domino, ut digne
ambuletis vocatione, qua vocati estis." [A.10.112]

—**C.5.46** Is *paternoster* and my primer, *placebo* and *dirige*. *Paternoster*:
the Lord's Prayer [C.5.87, C.5.107, B.5.341 (A.5.189, C.6.399),
B.5.394 (C.7.10), B.10.468, B.13.396 (C.6.283), B.14.49 (C.15.247),
C.16.323; other citations from the Paternoster occur at C.5.88,
B.13.396 (C.6.283), B.14.50 (C.15.249), B.15.179 (C.16.321),

C.16.374a, B.19.394a (C.21.394a)]; *placebo* and *dirige* [B.3.311 (C.3.464), B.15.125].

—**C.5.55** For by þe lawe of *leuyticy* þat oure lord ordeynede. The "lawe of leuyticy" referred to here—that tonsured clerks should not be forced to do manual labor, "knaues werkes"—is recorded in Numbers 18:20–24, which sets aside a living for priests or *Levitici* (see B.15.556) from the tithes of Israel. (Also notable is the wording of God's promise to the Levites in verse 20, "Ego pars et haereditas tua," wording repeated in Ps. 15:5, which the poem quotes just five lines further at C.5.60a.) Leviticus 21, proposed by Pearsall (100) as L's referent, is less to the point. [B.15.556 (C.17. 219)]

—**C.5.58a** *Non reddas malum pro malo.* Prov. 20:22, "Ne dicas: Reddam malum"; L's reading appears in Dionysius the Carthusian's comment on Levit. 19:18: "Et Salomon ait: Ne reddas malum pro malo" (*Opera Omnia* [Montreuil, 1897], 266); cf. Rom. 12:17, "Nulli malum pro malo reddentes"; 1 Thess. 5:15, "Videte ne quis malum pro malo alicui reddat"; and 1 Pet. 3:9, "Non reddentes malum pro malo."

—**C.5.60a** *Dominus pars hereditatis mee &c.* [B.12.189 (C.14.128)]

—**C.5.60b** *Clemencia non constringit.* Unidentified; however, as Pearsall says, the quotation relates "to the privileges of tonsured clerks" (100). It may echo (and be illuminated by) C.5.54, "Me[n] sholde constrayne no Clerk to no knaues werkes." Cf. "The quality of mercy is not strained" (Shakespeare, *Merchant of Venice*, 4.1.179).

—**C.5.86–87** *Non de solo ... viuit homo, / Nec in pane nec in pabulo.* Matt. 4:4, "Non in solo pane vivit homo, sed in omni verbo, quod procedit de ore Dei," quoting Deut. 8:3. [B.14.46a (C.15.244a)]

—**C.5.87** The paternoster wittenesseth. [C.5.46, C.5.107, B.5.341 (A.5.189, C.6.399), B.5.394 (C.7.10), B.10.468, B.13.396 (C.6.283), B.14.49 (C.15.247), C.16.323]

—**C.5.88** *Fiat voluntas dei* fynt vs alle thynges. [B.14.50 (C.15.249), B.15.179 (C.16.321); cf. C.5.46, B.10.468, B.13.396 (C.6.283), C.16.323, C.16.374a, B.19.394a (C.21.394a)]

—**C.5.98a** *Simile est regnum celorum thesauro abscondito in agro.* Matt. 13:44.

—**C.5.98a** *Mulier que inuenit dragmam.* Reference to Lk. 15:8–10, "Aut quae mulier habens drachmas decem, si perdiderit drachmam unam, nonne accendit lucernam, et everrit domum, et quaerit diligenter, donec inveniat? Et cum invenerit convocat amicas et vicinas, dicens: Congratulamini mihi, quia inveni drachmam quam perdideram. ..."

—**C.5.107** Seggyng my paternoster. [C.5.46, C.5.87, B.5.341 (A.5.189, C.6.399), B.5.394 (C.7.10), B.10.468, B.13.396 (C.6.283), B.14.49 (C.15.247), C.16.323]

Passus 5

B.5.39a (C.5.139a) *Qui parcit virge odit filium [suum].* Prov. 13:24; L's reading (i.e., without *suum*) appears also in *FM* (90). Numerous analogues cited in Walther 24441, 39847h1c.

—**C.5.171 (see B.10.325)**

—**C.5.172a (see B.10.327a)**

—**C.5.177a (see B.10.333a)**

B.5.55 *Amen dico vobis nescio vos.* Matt. 25:12. [B.9.67a, B.17.253a (C.19.219a)]

B.5.58 (Z.5.72, A.5.42, C.5.199) Sekeþ Seynt Truþe ... / *Qui cum patre & filio*; þat faire hem bifalle. Cf. the conventional close of a prayer, blessing, sermon; e.g., "To þe wiche blisse brynge vs he þat died on Rode Tre, *qui cum Patre et Spiritu viuit et regnat*" (*ME Sermons* 83). L's rearrangement of the formula suggests an identification of Truth with the Holy Spirit. See also the Nicene Creed (*Brev.* 2:484): "Et in Spiritum Sanctum ... Qui cum Patre et Filio simul adoratur et conglorificatur."

—**C.6.60a (see B.13.312a)**

—**C.6.64 (B.5.76 *var.*)** And cryede "*mea culpa*," corsynge alle his enemyes. Part of the formula of confession: "Peccavi nimis cogitatione, locutione, et opere, mea culpa" (*Brev.* 2:482, *Missale* 580).

—**C.6.76a (see B.13.330a)**

—**C.6.76b (see B.13.330b)**

B.5.168 They hadde þanne ben *Infamis*, þei kan so yuele hele counseil. In canon law, infamy constitutes an irregularity that prevents one from being ordained or from exercising such orders as may already have been received; discussion and additional examples in Alford 1984, 1988b, and Gray 59.

B.5.171 (C.6.153) Boþe Priour and Suppriour and oure *Pater Abbas.* "Father the Abbot"; the appellation is explained in the Benedictine *Rule* (2.7) and is based on Rom. 8:15, "Accepistis spiritum adoptionis filiorum, in quo clamamus: Abba, Pater."

B.5.186 (C.6.168) "*Esto sobrius!*" he seide and assoiled me after. 1 Pet. 5:8, "Sobrii estote, et vigilate: quia adversarius vester diabolus tanquam leo rugiens circuit, quaerens quem devoret." [B.5.442 (Z.5.111, A.5.214, C.7.56)]

B.5.243 I haue mo Manoirs þoruȝ Rerages þan þoruȝ *Miseretur &*
commodat. Ps. 111:5, "Iucundus homo qui miseretur et commodat,
disponet sermones suos in iudicio."

—**C.6.257** To assoyle the of thy synne *sine restitucione.* [see B.5.273a]

—**C.6.257a** *Numquam dimittitur peccatum &c.* [B.5.273a, B.17.310a
(C.19.290a)]

—**C.6.285a (see B.13.398a)**

—**C.6.290a** *Melius est mori quam male viuere.* [C.1.143a, C.17.40a]

B.5.269a-b (C.6.293a-b)

> *Seruus es alterius cum fercula pinguia queris;*
> *Pane tuo pocius vescere: liber eris.*

Unidentified; Walther 28183, cited by Pearsall (122) as a possible
analogue, has only a slight resemblance.

B.5.273a *Non dimittitur peccatum donec restituatur ablatum.* Maxim of
canon law, derived from Augustine; Gratian, causa 14, quest. 6,
cap. 1, "Quod vero penitencia agi non possit, nisi res aliena
reddatur, testatur Augustinus in epist. [LIV.] ad Macedonium. . . .
Si autem veraciter agitur, non remittetur peccatum, nisi restituatur
ablatum" (*CIC* 1:742); see also *Decretales* lib. 5, tit. 19, cap. 5 (*CIC*
2:812–13) and *Sext.*, "De regulis iuris," Reg. 4, "Peccatum non
dimittitur, nisi restituatur ablatum" (*CIC* 2:1122). For additional
citations, see Pennafort 173; Lyndwood 5.16.7 (149), and Bromyard 2:213/1. Examples from vernacular literature include *Spec.
Sacer.*, "For Seynt Austyn seiþ: 'Non dimittitur peccatum nisi
restituatur ablatum'" (71); *ME Sermons* 266; Brinton 1:27, 129,
199, 2:364, 373, 465, 407, 409, 437; *Impatient Poverty* (ed. J. S.
Farmer, *Lost Tudor Plays* [London: Early English Drama Society,
1907), 324, and *Nature*, translated as "And thereof to thy power
make due restitution; For erst shalt thou have of thy sin no remission" (Farmer 129). For additional examples, see Bennett, Alford
1975, 1988b, and Gray; and for a discussion of the place of the
quotation in the antimendicant tradition, see Scase 23–32. [C.6.
257a, B.17.310a (C.19.290a)]

B.5.277 In *Miserere mei deus [secundum magnam misericordiam tuam]*,
wher I mene truþe. Ps. 50:3, conventional prayer at confession; cf.
The Play of the Sacrament 677 (Manly 1:267), "O gracyows Lorde,
forgyfe me my mysdede! With lamentable hart: *miserere mei, Deus!*"
and *Mankind* 823 (Manly 1:347), "Aryse & aske mercy, Mankend
. . . for my lofe ope thy lyppys & sey *miserere mei, Deus!*" Recitation
of the Psalm was sometimes given as penance; see *Spec. Sacer.* 75,
88. [B.13.54]

B.5.277a (C.6.302) *Ecce enim veritatem dilexisti &c.* Ps. 50:8. As Pear-

sall explains: "The import of the gloss on this passage … is that
sin, though to be forgiven, cannot go unpunished, and the inward
truth that God desires must seek out and make restitution for
every dubious act, including the receipt of tithes properly paid but
ill-gotten" (122); cf. the gloss by Hugh of St. Cher: "Dilexisti
veritatem] in confitente accusante seipsum. quia si ipse accusat, tu
excusas, si ipse agnoscit, tu ignoscis."

B.5.278 *Cum sancto sanctus eris* [*et cum viro innocente innocens eris*]:
construwe me þis on englissh. Ps. 17:26. L's enjoining the reader
to "construe" the verse coincides with Hugh's introduction to it:
"Cum sancto sanctus eris. Quod sic construe; Tu Domine sanctus
in te, [eris cum sancto sanctus] effective, id est sanctifans." The
construction placed upon the verse in the *Fasciculus Morum*,
however, better fits the context here: "[W]e must abstain from
bad companionship. For the popular proverb says: 'He who
touches pitch gets dirty.' And the Psalmist declares: 'With the
holy, you will be holy,' and so forth" (641). [B.19.422 (C.21.422)]

B.5.281a *Misericordia* [*miserationes* Vulg.; *misericordiae* Ps. iuxta Heb.,
Weber] *eius super omnia opera eius &c.* Ps. 144:9. [B.11.139a (C.12.
74a), B.17.318a (C.19.298a)]

B.5.283a (C.6.338a) *Omnis iniquitas quantum ad* [*quantum ad = quoad*
C] *misericordiam dei est quasi sintilla in medio maris.* Bennett traces
the thought ultimately to St. Augustine's comment on Ps. 143:2,
"Unda misericordiae peccati ignis exstinguitur" (*Enarrationes in
Psalmos, PL* 37:1861). "But Augustine's text lacks the image of the
spark," notes Siegfried Wenzel, "whereas the quotation, in the
form in which it appears in Langland, is a commonplace in fourteenth-century preaching: it occurs, for instance, in Robert Hol-
cot's sermon 53 (Cambridge, Peterhouse MS 210, fol. 73ᵛ), in John
of Grimestone's collection of sermon commonplaces, under
'Misericordia' (Edinburgh, Advocates' Library MS 18.7.21, fol. 84),
and in *Fasciculus Morum* [e.g., pp. 126, 440, where the saying is
attributed to Bernard]" ("Medieval Sermons," in Alford 1988a,
156). However, as Pearsall notes (124), the text is attributed to
Augustine in the *Speculum Christiani,* "sicut scintilla ignis in medio
maris, sic omnis impietas uiri ad misericordiam dei" (EETS 182
[1933]), 73, 115, and in the *Prick of Conscience* 6314–17, "And
þar-for says Saynt Austyn þus, A gude worde þat may comfort us:
*Sicut scintilla ignis in medio maris, ita omnis impietas viri ad miseriam
dei.*" Gray (59) adds an example from the penitential tradition,
Serlo's *Summa de Penitentia,* 3, "Omnis malicia hominis ad dei
misericordiam tanquam scintilla in medio maris." See also the

Castle of Perseverance 3597a, "Pater sedens in judicio. Sicut sintilla in medio maris. / My mercy, Mankynd, ʒeue I þe" (EETS 262 [1969]), 109.

B.5.341 (A.5.189, C.6.399) He pissed a potel in a paternoster while. [C.5.46, C.5.87, C.5.107, B.5.394 (C.7.10), B.10.468, B.13.396 (C.6.283), B.14.49 (C.15.247), C.16.323]

B.5.390 (C.7.6) He bigan *Benedicite* with a bolk and his brest knokked. The opening of the formula for confession, "Bless me, father, for I have sinned."

B.5.394 (C.7.10) I kan noʒt parfitly my Paternoster. [C.5.46, C.5.87, C.5.107, B.5.341 (A.5.189, C.6.399), B.10.468, B.13.396 (C.6.283), B.14.49 (C.15.247), C.16.323]

B.5.412 Come I to *Ite missa est* I holde me yserued. The concluding words of the service of the mass (*Missale* 635–38). Cf. *FM* (on slothful persons): "If they should finally get there [to church] ... they really ought to remain until ... the priest says, 'Ite, missa est'" (403).

B.5.418 Bettre þan in *Beatus vir....* Ps. 1:1, "Beatus vir qui non abiit in consilio impiorum," or Ps. 111:1, "Beatus vir qui timet Dominum"; see also Ps. 31:2, "Beatus vir cui non imputavit Dominus peccatum," cited below (B.13.53). [B.10.326]

B.5.418 ... or in *Beati omnes*. Ps. 127:1, "Beati omnes qui timent Dominum, qui ambulant in viis eius." [B.6.250 (A.7.234)]

B.5.440a (C.7.54a) *Heu michi quia* [*quod* C] *sterilem vitam duxi* [transposed C] *Iuuenilem.* [B.1.141a (C.1.140a)]

B.5.442 (Z.5.111, A.5.214, C.7.56) Til *vigilate* þe veille [*vigilate &* *orate* var.] fette water at hise eiʒen. Matt. 26:41, "Vigilate et orate" (Bennett 180); cf. Mk. 13:33–37, Mk. 14:37–38, 1 Cor. 16:13, 1 Pet. 5:8. Jesus's words are interpreted traditionally as a command to repent, directed in particular against the sin of sloth. See the discussion above (13–14) and *ME Sermons* 46: "For þer ben many of vs ... þat slepeþ when þei preye.... By þis slepe is vndirstond dedely synne." L's usage may owe something as well to the *capitulum* for matins, feria 3 (*Vigilate*) and to the famous hymn by Prudentius, *Ales diei nuntius*, that follows (*Brev.* 2:111). [B.5.186 (C.6.168), C.9.259]

B.5.461 (Z.5.131, A.5.233, C.6.315) Roberd þe Robbere on *Reddite* loked. Cf. Rom. 13:7, "Reddite ergo omnibus debita...." [B.5.467 (Z.5.137, A.5.241, C.6.321), cf. B.19.187 (C.21.187), B.19.193 (C.21.193), B.19.259 (C.21.259), B.19.390 (C.21.390), B.20.308 (C.22.308)]

B.5.466 (Z.5.136, A.5.238, C.6.320) And haddest mercy on þat man for *Memento* sake. Lk. 23:42, "Domine, memento mei cum veneris in regnum tuum"; antiphon for Holy Week, *Brev.* 1:dccxciii. [cf. C.11.49]

B.5.467 (Z.5.137, A.5.241, C.6.321) So rewe on þis Robbere þat *Reddere* ne haue. Cf. Lk. 7:42, Rom. 13:7. [see B.5.461]

—Z.5.142 For *fodere non valeo*, so feble ar my bones. Lk. 16:3, "Fodere non valeo, mendicare erubesco."

—Z.5.143 Caucyon ant Y couthe, *caute* wolde Y make. Cf. Lk. 16:6, "Accipe cautionem tuam." Rigg and Brewer render the line: "If I could, I would prudently make a down payment" (with a pun on *caute / cautionem*).

B.5.474 (Z.5.148, A.5.248, C.6.328) That *penitencia* his pik he sholde polshe newe. Specific source, if any, unidentified. As Schmidt notes, "The penitential staff points to the idea [line 510] of pilgrimage as satisfaction for sin" (318); cf. C.10.95.

B.5.476 (Z.5.150, A.5.250, C.6.330) For he hadde leyen by *Latro*, luciferis Aunte. In legal usage, *latro* denotes a robber or thief; here it is used also to support a pun: *latro* "robber" / *lateo* "lie hid" / *latus* "side, flank." Cf. the account of the *latrones* crucified with Christ, Lk. 23:33–43. The identification of *Latro* as "luciferis Aunte" has not been explained.

—C.7.83a (see B.13.423a)

—C.7.86a (see B.13.426a)

—C.7.92a (see B.13.432a)

—C.7.100a (see B.13.440a)

—C.7.116 (see B.13.456)

—C.7.118a *Dare histrionibus &c.* (Skeat C.8.119a, *Qui histrionibus dat, demonibus sacrificat*). Cf. Augustine, *Supra Iohannem,* "Donare res suas istrionibus vitium est inmane, non virtus" (quoted by Gratian, *CIC* 1:299); Jerome, "Paria sunt histrionibus dare, et daemonibus immolare" (quoted by Peter the Cantor, *Verbum Abbreviatum, PL* 205:155). Cf. B.9.94a, B.15.343a.

B.5.483a (C.7.125a) *O felix culpa, o necessarium peccatum Ade &c.* From the canticle "Exultet," sung on Holy Saturday: "O certe necessarium Adæ peccatum et nostrum quod Christi morte deletum est. O felix culpa quæ talem ac tantum meruit habere redemptorem" (*Missale* 340). For a discussion of the doctrine, see Bennett 182.

B.5.486a *Faciamus hominem ad ymaginem et similitudinem nostram.* Gen. 1:26. The seminal discussion of the verse is Augustine's *De Trinitate* (e.g., 1.7, 12.6); for an interpretation of the verse in this context, see Bennett 183 and Daniel M. Murtaugh, *Piers Plowman and* *the Image of God* (Gainesville: Univ. Presses of Florida, 1978), 16–20. [B.9.36, B.9.43 (A.10.41a); cf. C.18.7]

B.5.486b *Qui manet in caritate in deo manet & deus in eo.* 1 Jn. 4:16, "Deus charitas est: et qui manet in charitate, in Deo manet, et Deus in eo," said in the daily grace (*Graces* 382). [C.3.403a, B.9.65a]

—**C.7.128a** *Ego in patre & pater in me est et qui me videt videt & patrem meum &c.* Jn. 14:9–10. [B.10.252a (C.11.153a)]

B.5.490a (C.7.130a) *Captiuam duxit captiuitatem.* Eph. 4:8, quoting Ps. 67:7, 19 ("Ascendisti in altum, cepisti captivitatem . . ."), associated with the Ascension (*Missale* 413; *Brev.* 1:dcccclix, dcccclxiv, dcccclxv, 2:235) and with the Harrowing of Hell (cf. Nico. 21:1).

B.5.493a (C.7.133a) *Populus qui ambulabat in tenebris vidit lucem magnam.* Isa. 9:2, quoted in Matt. 4:16 and Nico. 18:1, lesson for Monday, fourth week of Advent, and for Nativity vespers (*Missale* 51). The association with the descent into limbo is traditional (Bennett 185). [B.18.323 (C.20.366)]

B.5.498a (C.7.138a) *Non veni vocare iustos set peccatores ad penitenciam* [*ad pen.* om. C]. Lk. 5:32, cf. Matt. 9:13.

B.5.500a (C.7.140a) *Verbum caro factum est & habitauit in nobis* [*& . . . nobis* om. C]. Jn. 1:14. [C.3.356]

—**C.7.147a** *Quandocumque ingemuerit peccator omnes iniquitates eius non recordabor amplius.* Cf. Jer. 31:34b, "Quia propitiabor iniquitati eorum, et peccati eorum non memorabor amplius." The reading *non recordabor* occurs also in Jerome's quotation of the verse (in his comment on Isa. 54:12–13).

B.5.506 (C.7.151) Thanne hente hope an horn of *Deus tu conuersus viuificabis nos.* Ps. 84:7, quoted as a prayer following the *Confiteor* and *Misereatur* of the Mass (Wickham Legg 217; *Brev.* 2:53, 239, passim). The "horn of *Deus tu conuersus*" was suggested, quite likely, by the "horn of salvation" of Ps. 17:3 (Schmidt 319) and Lk. 1:69 (the song of Zacharias).

B.5.507 (C.7.152) And blew it wiþ *Beati quorum remisse sunt iniquitates* [*& quorum tecta sunt peccata* C]. Ps. 31:1, second of the penitential psalms. [B.12.177a (C.14.117a), B.13.53, B.13.54a, B.14.94]

B.5.509 (C.7.154) *Homines & iumenta saluabis* [*Domine,*] *quemadmodum multiplicasti misericordiam tuam, deus.* Ps. 35:7–8. [B.10.416a (C.11.248a)]

B.5.567a (C.7.216a) *Honora patrem* [*tuum*] *& matrem* [*tuum*] *&c.* Ex. 20:12, Deut. 5:16, Matt. 15:4, 19:19, Mk. 7:10, 10:19, Lk. 18:20, Eph. 6:2. The omission of *tuum* is common, e.g., Matt. 15:4, Mk. 10:19, and see the variants listed in the *Vetus Latina*, Hugh's comment on the verse, the citation in *Catonis Disticha* (*Auctores*

Octo sig. C[ii-b]), Brinton 1:23, and *FM* 86, 182, 370. For an explanation of L's somewhat puzzling use of the quotation in C.17.59a, see Wenzel (in Alford 1988a, 164). [C.17.59a]

B.5.603a (C.7.250a) *Per Euam cunctis clausa est et per Mariam virginem iterum patefacta est.* From an antiphon sung at lauds between Easter and Ascension day (*Brev.* 1:dccclxx).

—**C.7.260a** *Quodcumque pecieritis in nomine meo dabitur enim vobis.* Conflation of Jn. 14:13, "Et quodcumque petieritis Patrem in nomine meo, hoc faciam," and Matt. 7:7, "dabitur vobis." The word *Patrem,* missing in older texts of Jn. 14:13, is a scholastic addition (see Glunz 244, 291). [B.14.46a (C.15.244a)]

—**C.7.292** 3e! *villam emi,* quod oen, and now y moste thedre. Lk. 14:18.

—**C.7.304a (see B.14.3a)** *Vxorem duxi & ideo non possum venire.*

Passus 6

B.6.47a (C.8.44a) *Amice, ascende superius.* Lk. 14:10, antiphon for the seventeenth Sunday after the feast of Holy Trinity (*Brev.* 1:mccccxxxiii).

B.6.75 (A.7.67, C.8.77) *Deleantur de libro viuencium;* I sholde no3t dele wiþ hem. Ps. 68:29, continued below.

B.6.76a (A.7.68a, C.8.78a) *Quia* [*Et* A and Vulg.] *cum iustis non scribantur.* Ps. 68:29, continued from above.

—**C.8.86a** *Super Cathedram moysi sederunt &c.* [B.10.404a (C.11.235a), A.11.223]

—**C.8.90a** *Omnia que dicunt facite & seruate.* Matt. 23:3, "Omnia ergo quaecumque dixerint vobis, servate, et facite: secundum opera vero eorum nolite facere: dicunt enim, et non faciunt"; closer to L's wording is the quotation of the text in *Summa Virtutum,* "Que autem dicunt, facite" (231), and Gratian, *CIC* 1:385, "Que dicunt facite, que autem faciunt facere nolite."

B.6.86 (Z.7.72, A.7.78, C.8.95) *In dei nomine, amen.* "I make it myselue. / He shal haue my soule þat best haþ deserued." Usual formula at the beginning of a will (Alford 1988b, 72); e.g., *Foedera* 7:227; Madox, *Formulare Anglicanum* 427, 430, 434 (the last example in English: "In the name of God amen.... First y bequethe my Soule to Almi3ti God my Creatur"); cf. *Pilgrimage of the Life of Man,* "I be-quethe enterly / My soule vn-to my Fader dere" (EETS es 77 [1899], 126).

—**C.8.169** "Y preye the," quod Perus tho, "*pur charite,* sire hunger /

Awreke me of this wastors." [B.6.253 (Z.7.180, A.7.237, C.8.265), etc.]

—A.7.182 (Z.7.180) And preiȝede *pur charite* wiþ peris for to dwelle. [B.6.253 (A.7.237, C.8.265), etc.]

B.6.221a (C.8.230a) *Alter alterius onera portate* [*et sic adimplebitis legem Christi*]. Gal. 6:2, *capitulum* in the Psalter for Sunday at none, *Brev.* 2:68. L's use of the verse follows the standard interpretation; e.g., "Glossa: Alter alterius onera portantes sunt consilium et auxilium sibi invicem inpendentes" (*Summa Virtutum* 145). [B.11.211a, C.13.78a, B.17.74]

B.6.226a *Michi vindictam & ego retribuam*. Rom. 12:19, "Mihi vindicta: ego retribuam, dicit Dominus" (quoting Deut. 32:35, "Mea est ultio, et ego retribuam in tempore"), Heb. 10:30, Nico. 12:1. L's *vindictam* is the earlier reading; see *Vetus Latina*, Weber, Wordsworth, Hugh of St. Cher's gloss; see also *ME Sermons* 305 and *FM* 688. *Vindictam* is consistently the reading in Middle English grammars (Thomson 310). Skeat cites additional examples of *vindictam* from vernacular sources (2:115). [B.10.209a, B.10.374 (A.11.255), C.17.235a, B.19.446a (C.21.446a)]

B.6.228a (A.7.212a, C.8.234a) *Facite vobis amicos de mammona iniquitatis*. Lk. 16:9. [C.19.250a]

B.6.233 (Z.7.216, A.7.217, C.8.241a) *In sudore* and swynk þow shalt þi mete tilie [*In labore & sudore vultus tui vesceris pane tuo* C]. Gen. 3:19, "In sudore vultus tui vesceris pane ..."; response for Septuagesima Sunday, *Brev.* 1:ccccxciv. C's addition of *labore* may represent a conflation of the verse with Gen. 3:16, as given in the Breviary for Septuagesima, feria 6, lectio 3 (1:div), "In labore paries filios ..." (Pearsall 156).

B.6.236 (Z.7.219, A.7.220, C.8.245a) *Piger propter frigus* no feeld wolde tilie [*Piger propter frigus noluit arrare; mendicabit in yeme & non dabitur ei* C]. Prov. 20:4, "Propter frigus piger arare noluit, mendicabit ergo aestate, et non dabitur illi" (*ei* Hugh). Skeat suggests that L changes *aestate* to *yeme* in C "to suit our own climate" (2:115); Pearsall suggests that "the reading *hieme* arises by sympathetic association of winter and deprivation" (156). At any rate L's paraphrase of the verse two lines earlier shows that he knew the Vulgate reading: "The slowe caytif for colde a wolde no corn tylye; / In *somer* for his sleuthe he shal haue defaute."

B.6.239 (Z.7.222, A.7.223) *Seruus nequam* hadde a Mnam and for he nolde it vse. Reference to Lk. 19:11–28 (esp. 19:22), the parable of the talents; cf. the vespers antiphon *Serve nequam* for the twenty-second Sunday after the feast of Holy Trinity, *Brev.* 1:mccccxliii.

B.6.250 (Z.7.236, A.7.234) The Sauter seiþ, in þe psalme of *Beati omnes*. Ps. 127:1. [B.5.418]

B.6.252a (Z.7.237, A.7.234a, C.8.260a) *Labores manuum tuarum [quia manducabis* added A, B var., C][*beatus es, et bene tibi erit* added A var.]. Ps. 127:2.

B.6.253 (Z.7.239, A.7.237, C.8.265) Yet I preie þee ... *pur charite*. "For charity," a polite phrase used in requests and petitions (e.g., *CT* VII 891; Wright 257); also a concluding formula in prayers (*ME Sermons* 110, 150). In some instances, *pur charite* and "pure charite" (B.10.83, 10.320, 15.79) may be intended to recall each other. [C.8.169, A.7.182 (Z.7.180), B.8.11 (A.9.11, C.10.11), B.13.30 (C.15.32)]

−Z.7.267 *Honora medicum*, he seyt, for *necessitatem*. Ecclus. 38:1, "Honora medicum propter necessitatem."

−Z.7.271 *A regibus et principibus erit merces eorum*. [B.7.44a (Z.8.47, A.8.46a)]

B.6.311 (Z.7.315, A.7.295, C.8.333) And þat *chaud* and *plus chaud* for chillynge of hir mawe. "Hot" and "very hot" (no specific source).

B.6.315 (C.8.336a) *Paupertatis onus pacienter ferre memento*. Cato 1.21, "Infantem nudum cum te natura crearit, / paupertatis onus patienter ferre memento"; the second line is often quoted alone (e.g., *PL* 205:66). [cf.C.4.17]

Passus 7

B.7.3 (Z.8.3, A.8.3, C.9.3) And purchaced hym a pardoun *a pena & a culpa*. The phrase—meaning the remission of both the temporal punishment and the guilt of sin—has been interpreted in various ways; see Skeat 2:118, Bennett 216, Pearsall 161, and Alford 1988b. [B.7.19 (Z.8.21, A.8.21, C.9.23), C.9.187]

B.7.19 (Z.8.21, A.8.21, C.9.23) Ac noon *A pena & a culpa* þe pope wolde hem graunte. [B.7.3 (Z.8.3, A.8.3, C.9.3), C.9.187]

−C.9.45 But they *pre manibus* were payed for pledynge at þe barre. [C.3.300]

B.7.42a (Z.8.47, A.8.46a) *Super innocentem munera non accipies*. Ps. 14:5. [C.2.42, B.3.241a (A.3.221a)]

B.7.44a (Z.8.47, A.8.46a) *A Regibus & principibus erit merces eorum*. Probably from a comment on Ecclus. 38:2, "A Deo est enim omnis medela, et a rege accipiet donationem"; e.g., Denis the Carthusian: "*Et a rege accipiet donationem*, id est, reges et principes munera pretiosa et praemia copiosa peritis medicis largiuntur"

(*Opera Omnia* [Montreuil, 1897], 8:229); Hugh of St. Cher (on the following verse): "coram Principibus, & Regibus" (3:243^v). (For the application of the verse to lawyers specifically, see Alford 1984, 278–79.) Further evidence of the association with Ecclus. 38:2 appears in Z.7.267–71, where the phrase follows almost immediately a quotation from Ecclus. 38:1.

B.7.46 Than *pro dei pietate* pleden at þe barre. "For the love of God," a concluding formula in petitions of equity (Alford 1988b).

B.7.52a *Domine, quis habitabit in tabernaculo tuo.* Ps. 14:1. [B.2.39 (C.2.40), B.3.234a, B.13.127 (C.15.134)]

–Z.8.61 That *mercedem* for ys motyng of mene men resseyueth. The Latin of the Z manuscript may be intended to recall the earlier admonition that the *merces* of "motyng" should come not from poor clients but *a regibus et principibus* (Z.7.271); the reading in all other manuscripts is *mede* (A.8.60, B.7.59, C.9.54).

B.7.60a *Quodcumque vultis vt faciant vobis homines facite eis.* Matt. 7:12, "Omnia ergo quaecumque vultis ut faciant vobis homines, et vos facite illis" (cf. Luke 6:31); the "golden rule," the foundation of natural law (see Gratian, Dist. 1 [*CIC* 1:1]). L's reading "facite eis" is attested by several authorities (e.g., *VL* var. reading; St. Jerome, Peter Lombard [Glunz 256]). Other variations are common; e.g., *FM*, "Quia vulgariter dicitur: 'Hoc facies alii quod tibi vis fieri'" (536). [C.16.309]

B.7.73 (C.9.69) *Cui des videto* is Catons techyng. Cato, Prologue to *Disticha*, sententia 17. Scase notes (198n112) that this and the following quotation are linked also in Peter the Cantor, *Verbum Abbreviatum* (*PL* 205:150); see pp. 72–73 for her discussion of late medieval uses of the two quotations. For explicit references elsewhere to Cato, see C.4.17, B.6.314–15 (C.8.336a).

B.7.75 *Sit elemosina tua in manu tua donec studes cui des.* Variant of a common proverb, "Desudet eleemonsyna in manu tua, donec invenias iustum, cui des." Gray cites several examples from penitential texts (59), and Scase notes others in Bonaventure, Richard Maidstone, Peter the Cantor, and various canonists (198n112). Although L attributes the saying to the "clerk of the stories" (Peter Comester), it has not been found in the *Historica Scholastica*. The connection with Tob. 4:7 (Skeat 2:121) is very tenuous.

B.7.77a–b

> *Non eligas cui miserearis ne forte pretereas illum qui meretur accipere,*
> *Quia incertum est pro quo deo magis placeas.*

Attributed by Richard Maidstone (*Determinatio*, Bod. Lib. MS e

Mus. 94, fol. 6ʳ) to Isidore of Seville (Scase 198n114); Bennett (220n76) traces it to Jerome's comment on Eccles. 11:6: "Ne eligas cui bene facias ... Incertum est enim quod opus magis placeat Deo" (*PL* 23:1103). Scase demonstrates that this quotation, along with the two preceding, belongs to a pattern of authorities cited in the antimendicant controversy (72–73).

B.7.83a *Quare non dedisti pecuniam meam ad mensam vt ego veniens cum vsuris [utique] exegissem illam?* Lk. 19:23; several variant readings without *utique* are cited in Sabatier's notes to *Vetus Latina*. The verse is used to support the notion of "spiritual usury," on which see Pennafort 227 ff.; Hugh glosses the verse, "Bona usura est salus hominum."

B.7.86a *Satis diues est qui non indiget pane.* Jerome, Epistle 125 (*PL* 23:1085); cf. 1 Tim. 6:8.

—**C.9.120a** *Quando misi vos sine pane & pera &c.* Adaptation of Lk. 22:35 ("Quando misi vos sine sacculo, et pera, et calceamentis, numquid aliquid defuit vobis?"), alluding to Lk. 9:3 ("... neque peram, neque panem ..."); cf. Lk. 10:4, "Nolite portare sacculum, neque peram ... et neminem per viam salutaveritis" (cont. below).

—**C.9.123a** *Nemini salutaueritis per viam.* Lk. 10:4 (see above).

—**C.9.125a** *Et egenos vagosque induc in domum tuam.* Isa. 58:7, suggested possibly by Lk. 10:5 (continued from above), "In quamcumque *domum* intraveritis...." The verse is part of a grace said in Lent, "Frange esurienti panem tuum, & egenos vagosque induc in domum tuam: cum videris nudum operi eum. et carnem tuam ne despexeris: ait dominus omnipotens" (*Graces* 383). [B.10.85a (C.11.65a)]

—**C.9.127a** *Si quis videtur sapiens, fiet stultus vt sit sapiens.* 1 Cor. 3:18, "Nemo se seducat: si quis videtur inter vos sapiens esse in hoc saeculo, stultus fiat ut sit sapiens." L's abbreviated reading of the verse is broken up less when compared to the *Vetus Latina*: "Si quis videtur sapiens esse inter vos in hoc saeculo, stultus fiat ut sit sapiens."

B.7.89 (C.9.163) *Iunior fui etenim senui, & non vidi iustum derelictum nec semen eius querens panem [& non vidi ... panem om. C].* Ps. 36:25.

—**C.9.163** *Infirmata est vertus mea paupertate.* Ps. 30:11, "Infirmata est in paupertate virtus mea."

—**C.9.187** And pardon with the plouhman *A pena et a culpa.* [B.7.3 (A.8.3, C.9.3), B.7.19 (A.8.21, C.9.23)]

—**C.9.213a** *Non licet uobis legem voluntati, set voluntatem coniungere legi.* Similar statements appear in Pseudo-Chrysostom's comment on

Matt. 23, in Innocent III's *De contemptu mundi* 2.4, and elsewhere (Alford 1975, 1988b). Scase (214n59) connects the quotation to the admonition against false hermits in Benedict's *Rule*: "Qui bini aut terni aut certe singuli sine pastore, non dominicis sed suis inclusi ovilibus, pro lege eis desideriorum voluntas, cum quidquid putaverint vel elegerint, hoc dicunt sanctum, et quod noluerint, hoc putant non licere." Cf. the legal maxim "Intentio in servire debet legibus, non leges intentioni" (*Black's Law Dictionary*, 5th ed., 727).

—**C.9.258** Certes, hoso durste sygge hit, Simon *quasi dormit*. Cf. Mk. 14:37–38, "Et ait Petro, Simon, dormis? non potuisti una hora vigilare? Vigilate et orate," etc., continued below. Cf. the antiphon *Symon dormis, Brev.* 1:dcclxxi.

—**C.9.259** *Vigilare* were fayrere for thow haste a greet charge. Mk. 14:38, continued from above. [B.5.442 (Z.5.111, A.5.214, C.7.56)]

—**C.9.262** *Dispergentur oues*, þe dogge dar nat berke. Mk. 14:27, Matt. 26:31, quoting Zach. 13:7.

—**C.9.264** Here salue is of supersedeas in sumnoures boxes. [C.2.190, C.4.190]

—**C.9.265a**

> *Sub molli pastore &c.* [*lupus lanam cacat, et grex*
> *In-custoditus dilaceratur eo* added in some MSS.]

Liber Parabolarum, "Sub molli pastore capit lanam lupus et grex / Incustoditus dilaceratur eo" (*Auctores Octo*, sig. O^{7-b}). Skeat cites a translation in Chaucer's *Physician's Tale*: "Under a shepherde softe and necligent / The wolf hath many a sheep and lamb torent" (VI 101–2). Pearsall comments that L's substitution of *cacat* [befouls] for *capit* [seizes] "is appropriate enough for the allegorical reading ... but it has no literal sense" (172); nevertheless, the proverb appears exactly as L has it in the edition of *Liber Parabolarum* printed in *PL* 210:581 and in the collection of epigrams in MS Arundel 507, printed in Horstman 1:424.

—**C.9.273** *Redde racionem villicacionis* or in arrerage fall! Lk. 16:2, antiphon for the ninth Sunday after the feast of Holy Trinity (*Brev.* 1:mcccxvi) and the text of a famous sermon preached by Thomas Wimbledon about 1388; see Ione Kemp Knight, ed., *Wimbledon's Sermon: Redde Rationem Villicationis Tue* (Pittsburgh: Duquesne Univ. Press, 1967).

B.7.113–14 (Z.8.96, A.8.95–96, C.9.287–88)

> *Et qui bona egerunt ibunt in vitam eternam;*
> *Qui vero mala in ignem eternum.*

Verse 41 of the Athanasian creed, *Brev.* 2:48, recited at prime in the Sarum Rite; see Bennett 222. The article (an echo of Matt. 25:46) is associated chiefly with the Last Judgment: "In what wyze þat is wrathe may be suffred at þe Day of Iugemente. The gret clerke Athanasius answereþ in ys credo, 'Qui bona egerunt,' *et cetera*" (*ME Sermons* 29). Rosemary Woolf puts the association more strongly: "It is beyond any shadow of doubt that Verse 41 of the Athanasian Creed refers solely and emphatically to the Last Judgment" ("The Tearing of the Pardon," *Piers Plowman: Critical Approaches*, ed. S. S. Hussey [London: Methuen, 1969], 65). [C.12. 119a]

B.7.120–21 (Z.8.104, A.8.102–3) And seide, *"Si ambulauero in medio vmbre mortis / Non timebo mala quoniam tu mecum es."* Ps. 22:4, a gradual in the Mass for the Dead (*Brev.* 2:524, *Missale* 863*). [A.10.87, B.12.13a, B.12.293a]

B.7.128a (Z.8.111, A.8.110a) *Fuerunt michi lacrime mee panes die ac nocte.* Ps. 41:4, said as a versicle in the Mass for the Dead (*Brev.* 2:526, *Missale* 864*).

B.7.131 (Z.8.115, A.8.113) *Ne soliciti sitis* he seiþ in þe gospel. Matt. 6:25 (". . . ne solliciti sitis animae vestrae quid manducetis . . ."); cf. Lk. 12:22 ("Nolite solliciti esse . . ."). Piers's decision to leave off sowing and concentrate on "preieres and penaunce" may have been suggested by Philipp. 4:6 (*Brev.* 1:cxlvii), "Nihil sollicti sitis: sed in omni oratione, et obsecratione, cum gratiarum actione petitiones vestrae innotescant apud Deum." The *Summa Virtutum*'s comment on the verse distinguishes two kinds of solicitude, good and bad (245). On medieval interpretations of this important verse, see R. W. Frank, Jr., *Piers Plowman and the Scheme of Salvation* (New Haven: Yale Univ. Press, 1957), 31–33; and Scase 61–64 and passim. [B.14.33a]

B.7.141 As diuinour in diuinite, wiþ *Dixit insipiens* to þi teme. Ps. 13:1 and 52:1, "Dixit insipiens in corde suo: Non est Deus."

—A.8.123 (Z.8.125) *Quoniam literaturam non cognoui,* þat miȝte be þi teme. Ps. 70:15, "Quoniam non cognovi litteraturam."

B.7.143a (Z.8.127, A.8.125a) *Ejice derisores* [*derisorem* B var.] *& iurgia cum eis ne crescant &c.* [*& . . . &c. = & exibit cum eo iurgium cessabitque cause & contumelie* B var.]. Prov. 22:10, "Eiice derisorem, et exibit cum eo iurgium, Cessabuntque causae et contumeliae." For *Ejice* Rigg and Brewer read *Ecce*: "Langland probably wrote *Ecce,* which was 'corrected' by a few scribes" (*Piers Plowman: The Z Version* 111n).

B.7.156 (Z.8.138, A.8.134a) To sette sadnesse in Songewarie for *sompnia ne cures.* Cato 2.31, "Somnia ne cures, nam mens humana quod optat, / dum vigilat, sperat, per somnum cernit id ipsum."

B.7.168 (Z.8.149, A.8.145, C.9.312) Thanne Iacob iugged Iosephes sweuene: / "*Beau fit3*," quod his fader. "Fair son," a polite form in general use (see *MED* "beau" 2[d]).

B.7.181a (Z.8.164, A.8.159a, C.9.327a) *Quodcumque ligaueris super terram erit ligatum & in celis &c.* Matt. 16:19, "Et quodcumque ligaveris super terram, erit ligatum et in caelis" (cf. Matt. 18:18); antiphon associated with St. Peter, e.g., *Missale* 714; *Brev.* 3:180, 376, 575. See also Gratian, *CIC* 1:65 ff.; *Prick of Conscience* 3846 ff.

Passus 8

B.8.11 (A.9.11, C.10.11) And preide hem, *pur charite*. [B.6.253 (Z.7. 239, A.7.237, C.8.265), etc.]

B.8.20 (A.9.16, C.10.20) "*Contra!*" quod I as a clerc and comsed to disputen. University students, usually in the third and fourth years of the arts curriculum, were expected to take part in public disputations, first as an opponent raising objections to a stated thesis (as here), later as a respondent answering objections; see William J. Courtenay *Schools and Scholars in Fourteenth-Century England* (Princeton: Princeton Univ. Press, 1987), 33. For lists of *quaestiones* at Oxford, see A. G. Little and F. Pelster, *Oxford Theology and Theologians* (Oxford: Clarendon, 1934), 104–45, 287–362; for the use of *contra* to introduce an objection, see 351. Cf. *quodlibet* at B.15.382 and *ergo* at B.8.24 (A.9.20, C.10.28), etc. [B.10.349 (A.11. 232), B.12.280 (C.14.202)]

B.8.20a (A.9.16a, C.10.21) *Sepcies in die cadit Iustus.* Variant of Prov. 24:16, "Septies enim cadet iustus." L's wording appears in commentaries on the verse (e.g., Hugh 7:347b), in penitential texts (see the examples recorded by Gray, and also *Summa Virtutum* 84), and elsewhere (e.g., *Prick of Conscience* 3432; MS Digby 102 [EETS 124], 37; *The Book of Vices and Virtues* [EETS 217], 72; *ME Sermons* 67, *Gesta Romanorum* [EETS es 33], 74; *Handlyng Synne* [EETS 123], 355; *FM* 518; Brinton 1:26, 136). Apparently the phrase *in die* was inserted to improve the parallelism with Ps. 118:164 ("Septies in die laudem dixi tibi"), often quoted as a companion verse.

B.8.24 (A.9.20, C.10.28) *Ergo* he nys no3t alwey at hoom amonges yow freres. For other instances of disputational language, see the entries under *Contra* and *Quodlibet* in Index 3. [B.14.62 (C.15.261), B.14.287 (C.16.122a), B.14.292 (C.16.127), B.18.340 (C.20.388), B.19.19 (C.21.19)]

B.8.93 (A.9.83a, C.10.90) *Libenter* [*enim*] *suffertis insipientes cum sitis ipsi sapientes* [*cum . . . sap.* om. C]. 2 Cor. 11:19.

—**C.10.95** And with the pyk pulte adoun *preuaricatores legis.* Possibly an allusion to Rom. 2:23–27, "per praevaricationem legis Deum in honoras . . .; si autem praevaricator legis sis . . .; praevaricator legis es?" or 2 Macc. 13:7, "Et tali lege praevaricatorem legis contigit mori," or Ps. 118:119, "Praevaricantes reputavi omnes peccatores terrae," which Hugh glosses as "prevaricatio contra legem" (Alford 1975). On the use of the "pyk" to put down *preuaricatores legis,* see *The Pilgrimage of the Life of Man,* in which Reason explains to the vicar, "Thyn hornys & pyk also / Be yove to the . . . / ffor Punysshyng & for chastysyng / Off folkys Rebel in werchyng" (EETS es 77 [1899], 43; cf. 45–46). Cf. C.17.285a-b (the bishop's *baculus*) and B.5.474 (Z.5.148, A.5.248, C.6.328) (the "pik" of *penitencia*).

—**C.10.99a** *Nolite timere eos qui possunt occidere corpus &c.* Matt. 10:28, "Et nolite timere eos qui occidunt corpus, animam autem non possunt occidere." L's reading agrees exactly with Jerome's, in his commentary on Ephesians, liber 3, cap. 6 (*PL* 26:575); the construction *possunt occidere* is common in some manuscripts of the *Vetus Latina* and in other church fathers' quotations of the verse as well (see *VL* critical apparatus).

Passus 9

B.9.7 (A.10.7, C.10.134) *Anima* she hatte. [B.9.16 (C.10.142), B.9.23 (C.10.149), B.9.55 (A.10.44, C.10.172), B.9.59 (A.10.47, C.10.174), B.15.23 (C.16.183)]

B.9.8 (A.10.8, C.10.135) A proud prikere of Fraunce, *Princeps huius mundi.* Jn. 12:31, 14:30, 16:11. [A.10.62, B.18.315a (C.20.349a)]

B.9.16 (C.10.142) By his leryng is lad þat lady *Anima.* [B.9.7 etc.]

B.9.23 (C.10.149) Thise sixe ben set to saue þis lady *anima.* [B.9.7 etc.]

B.9.33a (A.10.34a) *Dixit & facta sunt* [*ipse mandauit &c.; et vniversa mandauit et creata* added A vars.]. Ps. 148:5 (also 32:9), "Quia ipse dixit, et facta sunt; ipse mandavit, et creata sunt." [C.14.165a, B.14.61a (C.15.260a)]

B.9.36 For he was synguler hymself and seide *faciamus.* Gen. 1:26, cf. Gen. 2:18. On *faciamus* see Schmidt 327–28. [B.5.486a, B.9.43 (A.10.41a)]

B.9.43 (A.10.41a) *Faciamus hominem ad imaginem nostram* [*nostram =*

et similitudinem nostram A var.]. Gen. 1:26, "Faciamus hominem ad imaginem et similitudinem nostram." [B.5.486a, B.9.36]

B.9.50 (A.10.38) That is þe Castel þat kynde made; *caro* it hatte. For possible scriptural associations, see Mary Clemente Davlin, *A Game of Heuene: Word Play and the Meaning of Piers Plowman* (Cambridge: Brewer, 1989), 54–55. The image of the body as castle is conventional (e.g., *Sawles Warde*, Grosseteste's *Castle of Love*). [B.17.110]

B.9.55 (A.10.44, C.10.172) For loue of þe lady *anima* þat lif is ynempned. [B.9.7 etc.]

B.9.59 (A.10.47, C.10.174) Ac Inwit . . . lokeþ / What *anima* is leef or looþ. [B.9.7 etc.]

—A.10.50 For þoruȝ his connyng is kept *caro & anima*. Source, if any, unidentified.

B.9.62a *Quorum deus venter est.* Philipp. 3:19, "Multi enim ambulant, quos saepe dicebam vobis (nunc autem et flens dico) inimicos crucis Christi: quorum finis interitus: quorum Deus venter est: et gloria in confusione ipsorum, qui terrena sapiunt."

B.9.65a *Qui manet in caritate in deo manet [et Deus in eo].* 1 Jn. 4:16, a daily grace (*Graces* 382). [C.3.403a, B.5.486b]

B.9.67a *Amen dico vobis, nescio vos.* Matt. 25:12. [B.5.55]

B.9.67a (C.10.165a) *Et dimisi eos secundum desideria [cordis] eorum.* Ps. 80:13.

—A.10.62 Thanne haþ þe pouk power, sire *princeps huius mundi*. [B.9.8 (A.10.8, C.10.135), B.18.315a (C.20.349a)]

B.9.94a *Proditor est prelatus cum Iuda qui patrimonium christi minus distribuit; Et alibi, Perniciosus dispensator est qui res pauperum christi inutiliter consumit.* Skeat (2:141) cites similar words in Peter the Cantor's *Verbum Abbreviatum* (*PL* 205): "Sic dantibus objici potest, quod similes sunt Judae ... quanto magis furtum et sacrilegium committit, qui patrimonium crucifixi, pauperibus erogandum, non dico ad horam, dat carni et sanguini, sed officium dispensandi res pauperum, dum vixerit, nepoti" (col. 135), and "Malum est indignis de patrimonio Christi dare, periculosum est, de illis dispensatores rerum pauperum constituere" (col. 150). Cf. C.7.118a, B.15.343a.

B.9.96a (A.10.81a) *Inicium sapiencie timor domini.* Ps. 110:10, Ecclus. 1:16.

—A.10.87 *Virga tua & baculus tuus ipsa me consolata sunt.* Ps. 22:4. [B.7.120–21 (Z.8.104, A.8.102–3), B.12.13a, B.12.293a]

B.9.100a *Qui offendit in vno in omnibus est reus.* Jas. 2:10, "Quicumque autem totam legem servaverit, offendat autem in uno, factus est omnium reus." Cf. Gelasius, *Epistola* 8: "Qui enim in uno offenderit, omnium reus est" (cited in *VL*). [B.11.309 (C.13.122a)]

—**A.10.90** For *intencio i*[*u*]*dicat hominem* [*quemquam* A var.] *&c.* Canon law maxim. Kane's interpretation of the minims to read *indicat* is clearly incorrect; cf. Hostiensis, "Quicquid agant homines, intentio iudicat omnes" (*Summa Aurea*, "De simonia" [Venice, 1574], col. 1492); similarly, Panormitanus, *Commentaria in Decretalium Libros*, lib. 3, tit. 1, cap. 10 (Venice, 1588); and the sixteenth-century play *St. John the Evangelist*, ed. J. S. Farmer, *Lost Tudor Plays* (London: Early English Drama Society, 1907), 357. Other citations are given in Alford 1984, 1988b.

B.9.109a (C.10.202a) *Inquirentes autem dominum non minuentur omni bono.* Ps. 33:11. [B.11.282a]

—**A.10.94a** *Qui agit contra conscientiam* [*edificat ad iehennam*]. Gratian, *Decretum*, secunda pars, causa 28, questio 1, caput 14 (*CIC* 1:1088); quoted by Pennafort, "Qui facit contra conscientiam ... edificat ad gehennam" (207); Gregory IX (*CIC* 2:287); Bromyard, on *conscientia*, "Idem patet Rom. 14. Ubi habetur, quod omne quod non est ex fide, peccatum est, Glo. Omne quod fit contra conscientiam edificat ad gehennam" (1:130/1); Lucas de Penna, "Non debet aliquid contra conscientiam agere, ut aedificet ad gehennam" (Walter Ullmann, *The Medieval Idea of Law* [1946; repr. New York: Barnes and Noble, 1969], 128n.); and Menot 155.

—**A.10.98** *Cum recte viuas ne cures verba malorum.* Cato 3.2, "Cum recte vivas, ne cures verba malorum, / arbitri non est nostri, quid quisque loquatur." Quoted in "Song on the Scottish Wars" (Wright 162).

—**A.10.108a** *Qui circuit omne genus in nullo genere est.* The original context might have been grammatical, though the closest analogue is Ranulph Higden, *Polychronicon*, lib. 1: "Immo nonnulli omne genus circueuntes in nullo genere sunt, omnem ordinem attemptantes nullius ordinis sunt" (Alford 1984).

—**A.10.112** *In eadem vocacione qua vocati estis state* [*permaneatis* A var.]. 1 Cor. 7:20, "Unusquisque in qua vocatione vocatus est, in ea permaneat." Cf. Brinton 1:68, "Unusquisque *stet* in ea vocacione qua vocatus est." [C.5.43a]

—**A.10.120a** [*Qui se exaltabit humiliabitur et* added A var.] *Qui se humiliat exaltabitur &c.* Lk. 14:11, 18:14, "Quia omnia, qui se exaltat, humiliabitur: et qui se humiliat, exaltabitur"; Matt. 23:12, "Qui autem se exaltaverit, humiliabitur: et qui se humiliaverit, exaltabitur." [cf. B.15.552a (C.17.215a)]

B.9.125a (A.10.150, C.10.212a) *Concepit dolorem* [*in dolore* A var., C] *& peperit iniquitatem.* Ps. 7:15, "Ecce parturiit iniustitiam; Concepit dolorem, et peperit iniquitatem"; Job 15:35, "Concepit dolorem et peperit iniquitatem." On the reading in C, Pearsall comments: "L substitutes *in dolore* for Vg. *dolorem* under the influence of Gen. 3:16: *in dolore paries filios,* 'in pain you shall bring forth children' " (189). One A-text manuscript substitutes *Quare via impiorum prosperatur bene est omnibus qui peruerse & inique agunt,* Jer. 12:1, quoted below, B.10.25a (A.11.23a).

B.9.133a (A.10.162, C.10.222) *Penitet me fecisse hominem* [*Penitet me fecisse eos .i. homines* A var.]. Conflation of Gen. 6:6, "Poenituit eum quod hominem fecisset in terra," and Gen. 6:7, "Poenitet enim me fecisse eos"; second lesson on Sexagesima Sunday, *Brev.* 1:dxiv.

B.9.149 (C.10.236a) *Filius non portabit iniquitatem patris et pater non portabit iniquitatem filij* [*et ... filij* om. C]. Ezek. 18:20, a Lenten verse; see *Missale* 161 and *capitulum* for vespers, feria 2, first week in Lent, *Brev.* 1:dxcii; cf. Jn. 9:1–3. [B.10.114]

B.9.155a (C.10.244a) *Numquam colligunt de spinis vuas nec* [*aut* Vulg.] *de tribulis ficus* [*nec ... ficus* om. C]. Matt. 7:16, "Numquid colligunt de spinis uvas, aut de tribulis ficus?" Cf. Lk. 6:44.

—C.10.244b *Bona Arbor bonum fructum facit.* Var. of Matt. 7:17, "Sic omnis arbor bona fructus bonos facit." [B.2.27b (C.2.29a)]

B.9.164 (C.10.255) "I am *via & veritas*," seiþ crist, "I may auaunce alle." Jn. 14:6, "Ego sum via, et veritas, et vita. Nemo venit ad Patrem, nisi per me."

B.9.186a-b (C.10.287a-b)
> *Dum sis vir fortis ne des tua robora scortis;*
> *Scribitur in portis, meretrix est ianua mortis.*

Several versions of this proverb circulated in the Middle Ages. E.g., "Cum sis vir fortis, ne des tua munera [*robora var.*] scortis, / Scribitur in portis: Meretrix est ianua mortis" (Walther 4447); John of Bridlington, "Dedita gens scortis morietur fulmine sortis, / Scribitur in portis, meretrix est ianua mortis" (cited by Skeat). The proverb appears with a ME verse translation in Windsor Castle, St. George's Chapel MS E.1.1:
> Si sis vir fortis, non des tua robora scortis;
> Scribitur in portis: Meritrix est ianua mortis.

(Sarah M. Horrall, "Latin and Middle English Proverbs in a Manuscript at St. George's Chapel, Windsor Castle," *Mediaeval Studies* 45 [1983]: 375). The first half of the proverb appears also in a school notebook from the fifteenth century: "Si sis vri [*sic*] fortis non des tua robora scortis" (see Nicholas Orme, "A School Note-Book from Barlinch Priory," *Education and Society in Medieval and*

Renaissance England [London: Hambledon, 1989], 118). Part of the second line, "meretrix est ianua mortis," circulated as a separate proverb (Walther 38242c1). The ultimate source of the proverb, as Skeat implies, is probably Prov. 7:26–27, "Multos enim vulneratos deiecit, Et fortissimi quique interfecti sunt ab ea. Viae inferi domus eius, Penetrantes in interiora mortis"; cf. Prov. 29:3.

B.9.194a (C.10.293a) *Bonum est vt vnusquisque vxorem suam habeat propter fornicacionem.* 1 Cor. 7:1–2, "Bonum est homini mulierem non tangere: propter fornicationem autem unusquisque suam uxorem habeat, et unaquaeque suum virum habeat." Pennafort cites the text in arguing that marriage has two principal causes: the education of children and *vitatio fornicationis* (514).

Passus 10

B.10.9 (A.11.9, C.11.7) And seide, *"nolite mittere,* man, margery perles."* Matt. 7:6, "Nolite dare sanctum canibus: neque mittatis margaritas vestras ante porcos." The wording *mittere* coincides with that of Ambrose on Ps. 118: "Nolite mittere margaritas vestras porcis"; cf. Jerome's version, quoted in Gratian, *CIC* 1:650, "Nolite mittere sanctum canibus, neque margaritas vestras ante porcos." See also the discussion above (15).

—C.11.18a-b
Qui sapiunt nugas & crimina lege vocantur;
Qui recte sapiunt lex iubet ire foras.
Unidentified.

—C.11.22a *Ducunt in bonis dies suos & in fine descendunt ad infernum.* Job 21:13, "Ducunt in bonis dies suos, Et in puncto ad inferna descendunt." [cf. B.18.111 (C.20.114)]

—C.11.23a *Ibunt* [*Introibit usque* Vulg.] *in progenie patrum suorum & usque in eternum non videbunt* [*videbit* Vulg.] *lumen.* Ps. 48:20; Ps. iuxta Heb. reads ". . . non videbunt lucem."

B.10.25a (A.11.23a) *Quare impij viuunt? bene est omnibus qui preuaricantur & inique agunt? A* reads, *Quare via impiorum prosperatur, bene est omnibus qui praue agunt & inique?* Conflation of Job. 21:7, "Quare ergo impii vivunt?" (*VL:* "Quare impii vivunt"?) and Jer. 12:1, "Quare via impiorum prosperatur? Bene est omnibus qui praevaricantur, et inique agunt?" (second lesson for Tuesday in Holy Week, *Brev.* 1:dcclxiv).

B.10.26a (C.11.23b) *Ecce ipsi peccatores! [et] habundantes in seculo obtinuerunt diuicias [habundantes . . . diuicias* om. C]. Ps. 72:12.

B.10.29a (C.11.25a) *Que perfecisti destruxerunt; iustus autem &c.* [*iustus autem &c.* om. C]. Ps. 10:4, "Quoniam quae perfecisti destruxerunt; Iustus autem quid fecit?"

B.10.45 Than Munde þe Millere of *Multa fecit deus.* Ps. 39:6, "Multa fecisti tu, Domine Deus meus, mirabilia tua."

—A.11.55 (C.11.49) And so seiþ þe sauter, seke it in *Memento.* First word of Ps. 131, "Memento, Domine, David, et omnis mansuetudinis eius," quoted immediately following. [B.15.490; cf. B.5.466 (Z.5.136, A.5.238, C.6.320)]

B.10.69a (A.11.55a, C.11.49a) *Ecce audiuimus eam* [*i.e. caritatem* added in C var.] *in effrata; inuenimus eam in campis silue.* Ps. 131:6; see the comment by Schmidt 330. [B.15.490a]

B.10.85a (C.11.65a) *Frange esurienti panem tuum &c.* Isa. 58:7, said in the grace for Lent (*Graces* 383) and as the *capitulum* at none, feria 2, first week in Lent, *Brev.* 1:dxcii. [C.9.125a]

B.10.89a (C.11.69a) *Si tibi sit copia habundanter tribue; si autem exiguum illud impertiri stude libenter* [*libenter stude* B var., C]. Tob. 4:9, "Si multum tibi fuerit, abundanter tribue: si exiguum tibi fuerit, etiam exiguum libenter impertiri stude." Early biblical variants include "Si tibi copiosa fuerit . . ." (cited in notes to *VL*).

B.10.114 *Filius non portabit iniquitatem patris &c.* Ezek. 18:20, associated liturgically with Isa. 58:7 above (B.10.85a), *Brev.* 1:dxcii. [B.9.149 (C.10.236a)]

B.10.116a *Vnusquisque portabit onus suum* [*honus suum portabit* B var.] *&c.* Gal. 6:5, "Unusquisque enim onus suum portabit." *Enim* is omitted also in Brinton 2:410.

B.10.121 (A.11.74) *Non plus sapere quam oportet* [*sapere*]. Rom. 12:3; *sapere* is omitted also in *FM* 304. For use of the verse directed at the clergy, as here, see Gratian, *CIC* 1:154. [B.15.69 (C.16.229–30)]

B.10.195–96 (A.11.147–48)

> Qui simulat verbis nec corde est fidus amicus,
> Tu quoque fac simile; sic ars deluditur arte.

Cato 1.26, "Qui simulat verbis nec corde est fidus amicus, / tu qui fac simile: sic ars deluditur acte." L's version appears verbatim in the Loeb edition.

B.10.204a *Dum tempus est* [*habemus* 11 MSS] *operemur bonum ad omnes, maxime autem ad domesticos fidei.* Gal. 6:10, "Ergo dum tempus habemus, operemur bonum ad omnes, maxime autem ad domesticos fidei." [A.11.245a]

B.10.209a *Michi vindictam & ego retribuam.* [B.6.226a, B.10.374 (A.11.255), C.17.235a, B.19.446a (C.21.446a)]

—A.11.154a *Necesse est vt veniant scandala.* Matt. 18:7, "Necesse est enim ut veniant scandala: verumtamen vae homini illi, per quem scandalum venit." [B.16.157a (C.18.174a)]

—A.11.192a *Ecce quam bonum & quam iocundum habitare Fratres in vnum.* Ps. 132:1. [B.18.423a (C.20.466a)]

—A.11.193a *Gaudere cum gaudentibus Et* [*Et* om. Vulg., A var.] *flere cum flentibus.* Rom. 12:15; L's reading coincides with that of Ambrose in *Liber de Lapsu Virginis* (var. cited in *VL*), and of Robert of Flamborough, *Liber Poenitentialis* (Toronto: Pontifical Institute of Mediaeval Studies, 1971), 113.

—A.11.196a *Qui facit* [*fecerit* A var.] *& docuerit magnus* [*hic magnus* A var.] *vocabitur in regno celorum.* [see B.13.118a (C.15.126a)]

B.10.246a *Deus pater, deus filius, deus spiritus sanctus.* Athanasian creed, *Brev.* 2:47. [cf. C.2.31, C.3.406a, C.18.51, B.16.223a, B.18.68a (C.20.70a)]

B.10.252a (C.11.153a) *Ego in patre et pater in me est, et qui videt me videt et patrem meum* [C reads *Ego in patre & pater in me est; Et qui me videt, patrem meum videt qui in celis est,* the last clause added from the Lord's Prayer]. Jn. 14:9–10, "Philippe, qui videt me, videt et Patrem [*VL:* Patrem meum]. . . . Non creditis quia ego in Patre, et Pater in me est?" [C.7.128a]

B.10.256a (C.11.157a) *Fides non habet meritum vbi humana racio prebet experimentum.* Gregory's Homily 26 on the Gospels (*PL* 76:1197), quoted in the first lesson at matins on the Sunday after Easter (*Brev.* 1:dcclx).

B.10.261a *Appare quod es vel esto quod appares.* Pseudo-Chrysostom, *Homilia 45 in Matthaeum:* "Ergo aut esto quod appares, aut appare quod es" (*PG* 56:885). The saying is attributed to Chrysostom by Hugh and other commentators on Matt. 23:29 (see Alford 1975), and by *Fasciculus Morum,* which gives it as "Ergo aut appare quod es aut esto quod appares" (514). The idea itself is commonplace; e.g., "Be suche within, as ye outward seme," *Twenty-Six Political and Other Poems,* ed. J. Kail (EETS 124 [1904]), 83.

B.10.266a–b

> Si culpare velis culpabilis esse cauebis;
> Dogma tuum sordet cum te tua culpa remordet.

Proverbial. Basel, MS University A.11.67 (early fifteenth century), folio 213ᵛ, "Si culpare velis, culpabilis esse cavebis: / Dogma tuum sordet, tua quod doctrina remordet," in Jacob Werner, *Lateinische Sprichwörter und Sinnspruche des Mittelalters,* 2d ed. (Heidelberg: Winter, 1966), 111 (no. 77). The first line of L's quotation appears also in John Rylands Library, MS Latin 394 (Walther 28372), cited above at B.1.141a. The second line circulated separately; cf. Walther 6232, "Dogma tuum sordet, cum te tua culpa remordet."

B.10.268a *Quid consideras festucam in oculo fratris tui, trabem* [*autem* B var.] *in oculo tuo &c?* Lk. 6:41, "Quid autem vides festucam in oculo fratris tui, trabem autem, quae in oculo tuo est, non consideras?" continued below (cf. Matt. 7:3).

B.10.270a *Ejice primo* [*primum* Vulg., B var.] *trabem de oculo tuo &c.* Lk. 6:42; cf. Matt. 7:5. The reading *primo* appears also in *FM*, "Ipocrita, eice primo trabem de oculo" (530).

B.10.281a *Dum cecus ducit cecum ambo in foueam cadunt.* Variant of Matt. 15:14 ("... caecus autem si caeco ducatum praestet, ambo in foveam cadunt"; cf. Lk. 6:39), as quoted in penitential texts, e.g., Robert of Flamborough, *Liber Poenitentialis* (Toronto: Pontifical Institute of Mediaeval Studies, 1971), "Quia si caecus caecum ducit ambo in foveam cadunt" (56–57). (Additional examples in Gray.) Cf. Brinton, Sermon 54, "Quod si cecus ducat cecum ..." (2:245). [B.12.185 (C.14.124a)]

B.10.288 *Archa dei* myshapped and Ely brak his nekke. 1 Reg. 4:18, "Cumque ille nominasset arcam Dei, cecidit de sella retrorsum iuxta ostium, et fractis cervicibus mortuus est." [Cf. C.Prol.108, 112, B.12.113, 119 (C.14.58)]

B.10.291 *Existimasti inique quod ero tui similis; arguam te & statuam contra faciem tuam.* Ps. 49:21. [B.11.95 (C.12.29a)]

B.10.293a *Canes* [*muti* inserted in B var.] *non valentes latrare.* Isa. 56:10, "Canes muti non valentes latrare...." The verse is commonly cited in reproof of negligent priests; e.g., Gratian, "De discretione predicationis, et silenti," *CIC* 1:153–55; *Spec. Sacer.* 68; Brinton 2:362–63. Further examples in A. L. Kellogg, "Langland and the 'canes muti,' " *Essays in Literary History, Presented to J. Milton French* (New Brunswick: Rutgers Univ. Press, 1960), 25–35; and Morton Bloomfield, *Piers Plowman as a Fourteenth-Century Apocalypse* (New Brunswick: Rutgers Univ. Press, 1962), 215n64.

B.10.325 (C.5.171) And puten hem to hir penaunce, *Ad pristinum statum ire.* Formula in canon law discussions of the effectiveness of penitence in reviving merit. The primary source is Gratian, who writes in *Decretum* Dist. 50, cap. 28, "Illos enim ad pristinos grados redire canones precipiunt ..." (*CIC* 1:189), and inquires in *De poenitentia*, "Quare sit institutum post septem annos in pristinum statum penitentem redire" (*CIC* 1:1155). In both cases his authority is Isidore of Seville, who is talking specifically about religious (see *PL* 83:899–902). In what sense a penitent cleric is restored *ad pristinum statum* is a question that further occupies Isidore and later commentators on the *Decretum,* such as Guido de Baysio (Archidiaconus) and Bartolomeo da Brescia (see Alford 1984). In discussions of the doctrine of the reviviscence of merit, the phrase applies more generally to both clerics and laymen (see *The New Catholic Encyclopedia,* 12:449-50, 13:79). Undoubtedly it lies behind Grace-Dieu's assurance to the pilgrim in Lydgate's *Pilgrimage of the Life of Man:* only repent and with the help of grace thou shalt be "restoryd to thy ffyrste place" (ed. F. J. Furnivall, EETS es 83 [1901], line 12612). But in the present context, L seems less concerned with the reviviscence of merit as such than with the restoration of a penitent clergy's "right" to perform its vocational duties. Cf. Brinton 1:138. For contrasting interpretations, see Scase 88 ff., 202n14; and Anna P. Baldwin, "The Historical Context" (Alford 1988a), 75.

B.10.326 And Barons wiþ Erles beten hem þoruȝ *Beatus vir*res techyng. Ps. 1:1 or Ps. 111:1. [B.5.418, B.13.53]

B.10.327a (C.5.172a) *Hij in curribus & hij in equis ipsi obligati sunt* [*et ceciderunt* C] *&c.* Ps. 19:8-9, "Hi in curribus, et hi in equis; Nos autem in nomine Domini Dei nostri invocabimus. Ipsi obligati sunt, et ceciderunt, Nos autem surreximus, et erecti sumus"; antiphon sung in celebration of the Name of Jesus, *Brev.* 3:620.

B.10.333a (C.5.177a) *Quomodo cessauit exactor, quieuit tributum?* [*Quomodo . . . tributum?* om. C] *contriuit dominus baculum impiorum, et* [*et* om. C] *virgam dominancium cedencium* [*cedencium* om. C] *plaga insanabili.* Isa. 14:4-6, "Quomodo cessavit exactor, Quievit tributum? Contrivit Dominus baculum impiorum, Virgam dominantium, Caedentem populos in indignatione Plaga insanabili, Subiicientem in furore gentes, Persequentem crudeliter."

B.10.336 Thanne is dowel and dobet . . . *dominus* and knyȝthode? As a title, *dominus* is applied to virtually anyone having lordship over others, from God to the merest litigant in control of a legal action. In the previous quotation (B.10.333a), *dominus* refers to the Lord; here it refers to a king (cf. 10.38 "kynghod") or only "lord(ship)" in general. The deflation of the title in this passage mirrors its historical fortune—on which, see Georges Duby, *The Chivalrous Society,* trans. Cynthia Postan (Berkeley: Univ. of California Press, 1980), 18, 34, 42, 77-78, 103, 108, 134, 174, 178-81.

—A.11.223 *Super cathedram moisi sederunt principes.* Matt. 23:2, "Super cathedram Moysi sederunt scribae et pharisaei." [C.8.86a, B.10.404a (C.11.235a)]

—C.11.163 And saide, "*multi multa sciunt & seipsos nessiunt.*" [see B.11.3]

—**C.11.172, 176, 189 (B.11.13, etc.)** *Concupiscencia carnis.* [C.11.307, 310]

—**C.11.201a** *Ita possibile est diuiti intrare in regnum celorum sicut camelus &c.* [B.14.212a]

B.10.342a *Nichil [est] iniquius quam amare pecuniam.* Ecclus. 10:10.

B.10.343a *Dilige denarium set parce dilige formam.* Cato 4.4, "Dilige denarium, sed parce dilige formam / quam nemo sanctus nec honestus captat habere."

B.10.349 (A.11.232) *"Contra!"* quod I, "by crist! þat kan I wiþseye." [B.8.20 (A.9.16, C.10.20), B.12.280 (C.14.202)]

—**A.11.234** *Qui crediderit et baptizatus fuerit saluus erit [Qui vero non crediderit condempnabitur* added A var.]. Mk. 16:16. [B.11.124a (C.12.59a), C.13.87a]

B.10.352 (A.11.235) "That is *in extremis,*" quod Scripture, "as Sarȝens & Iewes." "The words *in extremis* probably refer to the case of people lying at the point of death" (Skeat 2:159). On baptism *in extremis,* see Lyndwood's *Provincial* lib. 1, tit. 7; lib. 3, tit. 24; and, also in Lyndwood, the *Constitutions* of Othobon, lib. 1, tit. 1 (Lyndwood, *Provinciale* [Oxford, 1679], 41 ff., 241 ff., 80 f.).

—**A.11.242** *Dilige deum &c., Et proximum tuum sicut teipsum.* The Two Commandments of the New Law (though derived, as L notes at B.15.584, from the Old Testament), e.g., Matt. 22:37–39, Mk. 12:30–31, Lk. 10:27, Jas. 2:8; cf. Deut. 6:5 and Lev. 19:18. [B.13.127 (C.15.-134), C.15.140, B.15.584, B.17.13 (C.19.14), cf. C.17.140a]

B.10.359a *Si cum christo surrexistis &c.* Col. 3:1, "Igitur, si consurrexistis cum Christo: quae sursum sunt quaerite, ubi Christus est in dextera Dei sedens"; also part of the grace for Easter eve, "Si consurrexistis cum christo . . ." (*Graces* 384). L's reading *surrexistis* is attested by both Ambrose and Augustine (see *VL*).

—**A.11.245a** *Dum tempus est [habemus* A var.] *operemur bonum ad omnes, maxime autem ad domesticos fidei.* [B.10.204a]

B.10.372 (A.11.254) But if I sende þee som tokene, and seiþ *Non mecaberis.* Ex. 20:14, Deut. 5:18, Lk. 18:20. Skeat explains L's mistranslation ("slee noȝt") as a confusion of *mecari* (to commit adultery) and *necare* (to kill); a number of manuscripts, in fact, show *necaberis* as a scribal correction. However, the wording may owe something to James 2:9–11 and its commentaries; see E. Talbot Donaldson, "Langland and Some Scriptural Quotations," in *The Wisdom of Poetry,* ed. Larry D. Benson and Siegfried Wenzel (Kalamazoo: Medieval Institute, 1982), 70; and Margaret Goldsmith, "Will's Pilgrimage in *Piers Plowman* B," in *Medieval Literature and Antiquities,* ed. Myra Stokes and T. L. Burton (Cambridge:

Brewer, 1987), 119-31. Cf. *FM* 681, "Adultery ... is like man-slaughter because husband and wife are one flesh: he who takes someone's wife from him, does the same thing as taking her husband away."

B.10.374 (A.11.255) For *michi vindictam et ego retribuam.* [B.6.226a, B.10.209a, C.17.235a, B.19.446a (C.21.446a)]

B.10.382a (A.11.263a, C.11.207a) *Nemo ascendit ad celum* [*in celum* A, B var.] *nisi qui de celo descendit* [*descendit de celo* A, B var.]. Jn. 3:13, "Et nemo ascendit in caelum, nisi qui descendit de caelo." L's order (*de celo descendit*) is the older form; see Glunz 110, Hugh of St. Cher's text, and the variant readings cited by *VL* from Athanasius and Augustine.

—**C.11.213a** *Nec michi nec tibi* [*sit*], *set diuidatur.* 3 Reg. 3:26.

—**C.11.232a** *Eadem mensura &c.* [B.1.178a (C.1.174a), B.11.228]

B.10.404a (C.11.235a) *Super cathedram Moysi &c.* Matt. 23:2, a standard text against clerical hypocrisy (Gratian, *CIC* 1:528; Bromyard 2:462/3; *FM* 418). Also the incipit of a famous bull that governed relations between regular and secular clergy, issued by Boniface VIII in 1300; see Szittya 75, 125, 134. [C.8.86a, A.11.223]

—**C.11.244** For *Archa Noe, nymeth hede, ys no more to mene* / Bote *holy churche.* The interpretation of Noah's ark as a type of the church is an exegetical commonplace, following Origen and Augustine (e.g., *De Civ. Dom.* 15.26). The phrase *Archa Noe,* which appears nowhere in the Bible, may reflect Hugh of St. Victor's elaborate allegorization, *De Archa Noe Morali* (*PL* 176).

B.10.415 (C.11.246) The *culorum* of þis clause curatours is to mene. [B.3.280 (A.3.258, C.3.433)]

B.10.416a (C.11.248a) *Homines & iumenta saluabis, domine &c.* [*domine* om. C]. Ps. 35:7. [B.5.509 (C.7.154)]

B.10.436a (C.11.271a) *Sunt iusti atque sapientes, & opera eorum in manu dei sunt* [*sunt* om. Vulg.] *&c.* Eccles. 9:1.

B.10.445 For *quant oportet vient en place il nyad que pati.* Proverbial (Alford 1984). Cf. *Roman des deduis,* "Quant Oportet vient en place, il convient que l'on le face" (vv. 3095-96), cited by James Woodrow Hassell, Jr. (*Middle French Proverbs, Sentences and Proverbial Phrases* [Toronto: Pontifical Institute of Mediaeval Studies, 1982], 183). Hassell gives references to several other examples as well. Not cited by Hassell but closely related to the imagery of judgment in the present context is Michel Menot's comment on 2 Cor. 5:10 ("Omnes enim nos manifestari oportet ante tribunal Christi"): "*Oportet.* Cum oportet in medium adducitur, nihil est quin oporteat."

Quant *oportet* vient en place,
Il n'est chose qui ne se face.

Ratio: Quia citamur peremptorie, nec possumus iudicem repellere vel recusare tanquam suspectum, vel ut non nostrum, quia omnium Iudex est. Ideo oportet" (Menot 310). The editor cites additional examples of the proverb on page lv. It is worth noting that the English version—"And, when *oportet* cums in plas, / Thou knawys *miserere* has no gras" (Skeat 2:163)—makes even clearer the connection with the theme of judgment.

B.10.450a (A.11.296, C.11.275a) *Dum steteritis ante Reges [vel presides &c. C] & presides nolite cogitare [& . . . cogitare om. C].* Part of a response at matins on the Nativity of an Apostle, *Brev.* 2:366, adapted from Mk. 13:9-11 (cf. Matt. 10:17-19).

B.10.461 (A.11.305, C.11.287) *Ecce ipsi ydiote [indocti A var.] rapiunt celum vbi nos sapientes [cum doctrinis nostris A var.] in inferno mergimur.* Augustine, *Confessions,* viii.8: "Surgunt indocti et caelum rapiunt, et nos cum doctrinis nostris ecce ubi volutamur in carne et sanguine!" (Loeb ed., 442). Schmidt (333) tries to rationalize L's wording, and Goldsmith (see above B.10.372) explains it as a deliberate "misquotation," but many versions were current in the Middle Ages; for example, Hugh on Ps. 70:15, "Unde dicit Aug. Heu indocti celum rapiunt, & nos cum doctrinis nostris ad inferna demergimur," and on Ps. 134:6, "Augustinus. Simplices, & idiotae rapiunt sibi celum, nos autem cum litteris nostris ad inferna demergimur"; *Legenda Aurea,* "surgunt indocti et coelum rapiunt et nos cum doctrinis nostris in infernam demergimur" (551); and *The Lantern of Light,* "Quid patimur? quid audimus? surgunt indocti & celum rapiunt. & nos cum doctrinis nostris in infernum dimergimur" (EETS 151 [1917], 6). The phrase "rapiunt celum" is an allusion to Matt. 11:12, "Regnum caelorum vim patitur, et violenti rapiunt illud." L's use of the quotation is discussed by C. David Benson, "An Augustinian Irony in *Piers Plowman,*" *N&Q* 23 (1976): 51-54.

B.10.468 Percen wiþ a Paternoster þe paleys of heuene. [C.5.46, C.5.87, C.5.107, B.5.341 (A.5.189, C.6.399), B.5.394 (C.7.10), B.13.396 (C.6.283), B.14.49 (C.15.247), C.16.323; other quotations from the Paternoster at C.5.88, B.14.50 (C.15.249), B.15.179 (C.16.321), C.16.374a, B.19.394a (C.21.394a)]

—C.11.295a (also A.11.303a in Skeat's edition) *Breuis oratio penetrat celum.* Common proverb based on Ecclus. 35:21, "Oratio humiliantis se nubes penetrabit"; see the Vernon lyrics (EETS 117 [1901]), 552, and *The Book of the Knight of the Tower* (EETS supp.

ser. 2 [1971]), 17: "And therfore saith the hooly scripture that the short prayer perceth heuen." See also Walther 35313 and Whiting P357. The development of the proverb, along with numerous other examples, is traced briefly in Alford 1975, to which may be added *FM* 510 and *Gesta Romanorum* (EETS es 33 [1879], 47).

B.10.473 That euere þei kouþe konne on book moore þan *Credo in deum patrem*. Opening of Apostles' creed, *Brev.* 2:2. [C.16.322, B.15.608 (C.17.316); cf. C.3.357, C.3.481]

B.10.481a *Ite* [*et*] *vos in vineam meam*. Matt. 20:4. [B.15.500]

—A.12.19a *Vidi preuaricantes & tabescebam*. Ps. 118:158. L's translation, "I saw synful ... þerfore I seyde no þing," is faulted by Skeat: "It is clear that William translates *tabescebam* as if it were *tacebam*" (2:164); however, *tabesco* early acquired the secondary meaning "to grow quiet or mild" (see R. E. Latham, *Revised Medieval Latin Word-List* [London: British Academy, 1965]). L may simply be exploiting a possible meaning of the word to fit the context.

—A.12.22a *Audiui archana uerba que non licet homini loqui*. [B.18.395a (C.20.438a)]

—A.12.28 *"Quid est ueritas?"* quod he; "verilyche tel vs." Jn. 18:38, Nico. 3:2.

—A.12.50–52, 56–57 *Omnia probate ... quod bonum est tenete*. [B.3.339–43 (C.3.491–95), C.20.234a)]

Passus 11

B.11.3 And seide *"Multi multa sciunt et seipsos nesciunt."* Opening words of the *Meditationes Piisimae de Cognitione Humanae Conditionis* (*PL* 184:485), attrib. to Bernard of Clairvaux; Middle English translation, beginning "Many knoweth many thynges & knoweth not hem selfe," in MS Rawlinson C 894 (ff. 74ʳ-86ᵛ) and Royal 17.C.xviii (ff. 89ᵛ–104ᵛ); see also *ME Sermons* 98, "Where-fore Seynt Bernarde [seyþ] ... in his Meditacions, que sic incipit, 'Multi multa sciunt'...." For a discussion of the saying see Joseph Wittig, *"Piers Plowman* B, Passus IX–XII: Elements in the Design of the Inward Journey," *Traditio* 28 (1972): 211–80. [C.11.163]

B.11.13, 17, 30, 40, 43 (C.11.172, etc.) *Concupiscencia carnis* men called þe elder mayde. 1 Jn. 2:16. [C.11.307, 310]

B.11.37–38 (C.11.303–4) *Homo proponit ... And Deus disponit*. Proverbial (Walther 11102, 37258a; Whiting M162; Rossell Hope Robbins, *Historical Poems of the XIIIth and XIVth Centuries* (New York: Columbia Univ. Press, 1959), 227; Whiting, *Proverbs in the Earlier English Drama* [New York: Octagon, 1969], 380 [no. 102], "L'homme propose et Dieu dispose"). Cf. Prov. 16:9, "Cor hominis disponit viam suam, Sed Domini est dirigere gressus eius," on which Hugh of St. Cher comments, "Hoc est, quod vulgariter dicitur: Homo proponit, sed Deus disponit." [B.20.33a (C.22.33a)]

—**C.11.307, 310** *Concupiscencia carnis.* [B.11.13, 17, etc. (C.11.172 etc.)]

B.11.58 (C.12.10) And preien for þee pol by pol if þow be *pecuniosus.* The context is unidentified.

B.11.58a (C.12.10a) *Pena pecuniaria non sufficit pro spiritualibus delictis* [*pro . . . delictis* om. C]. Maxim of canon law; cf. Lyndwood, *Provinciale: Constitutio Domini Othoboni,* tit. 10, "Et quia non sufficit pecuniaria poena, ubi est Spirituale delictum" (99).

B.11.81a *Sola contricio delet peccatum.* A common saying in the long controversy concerning the importance of oral confession in the sacrament of penance (Alford 1975, 1988b; Gray; Scase 39); Brinton 1:81, "Econtra vero sola contritio delet omnem maculam . . . ." (cf. B.14.92).

B.11.82a *Nisi quis renatus fuerit* [*ex aqua & spiritu sancto &c* added B var.]. Jn. 3:5, "Amen, amen dico tibi, nisi quis renatus fuerit ex aqua, et Spiritu sancto, non potest introire in regnum Dei."

B.11.88 *Non oderis fratres secrete in corde tuo set publice argue illos.* Levit. 19:17, "Non oderis fratrem tuum in corde tuo, sed publice argue eum, ne habeas super illo peccatum"; cf. 1 Tim. 5:20. *Frater* is made plural in L's version to apply to the friars. The verse is a commonplace in antimendicant writings (Scase 162). [B.11.93 (C.12.34)]

B.11.90 (C.12.31) *Nolite iudicare quemquam.* Matt. 7:1, "Nolite iudicare, ut non iudicemini"; Lk. 6:37, "Nolite iudicare, et non iudicabimini"; Jn. 7:24, "Nolite iudicare secundum faciem, sed iustum iudicium iudicate" (used as the text of Richard Fitzralph's *Defensio Curatorum* [Scase 161]). [B.12.89a, B.14.293 (C.16.128)]

B.11.93 (C.12.34) *Non oderis fratrem* [*secrete in corde &c.* C]. [B.11.88]

B.11.95 (C.12.29a) *Existimasti inique quod ero tui similis:* [*Arguam te & statuam contra faciem tuam* C]. [B.10.291]

B.11.96 It is *licitum* for lewed men to legge þe soþe . . . ; ech a lawe it graunteþ. The term (meaning "licit, permitted") appears regularly in both canon and civil law ("ech a lawe"), especially in cases open to question.

B.11.106a (C.12.40a) *Parum lauda; vitupera parcius.* Seneca (attrib.),

De Quattuor Virtutibus, "Lauda parce, vitupera partius, similiter enim reprehensibilis est nimia laudatio ut immoderata vituperatio." The expression is also quoted and attributed to Seneca by Hugh of St. Cher (6:167^r); Alan of Lille, *Ars Praedicandi,* cap. 23 (*PL* 210:158); Vincent of Beauvais, *Speculum Doctrinale* 5.69; and the commentary on Cato in *Auctores Octo* (sig. C^{vi}). Vernacular sources include *Dives and Pauper* (EETS 280), "Therfor Seneca seith: Lauda parce, vitupera parcius" (9).

B.11.112 (C.12.47) *Multi* to a mangerie and to þe mete were sompned. Matt. 22:14, "Multi enim sunt vocati, pauci vero electi"; antiphon said during Septuagesima, *Brev.* 1:ccccxcix. Cf. "Song on the Scottish Wars": "Electi pauci sunt, multi vero vocati" (Wright 173). [continued below]

B.11.114 (C.12.49) And plukked in *Pauci* pryueliche and leet þe remenaunt go rome. [see above]

B.11.120a (C.12.55a) *O vos omnes sicientes [scientes* B var.] *venite [ad aquas* added B var., C] *&c.* Isa. 55:1, "Omnes sitientes, venite ad aquas; et qui non habetis argentum, properate, emite, et comedite: venite, emite absque argento et absque ulla commutatione vinum et lac," echoed in Apoc. 21:6, 22:17; introit, Sabbato post Laetere (*Missale* 232). Bromyard adopts the reading *scientes* in his article on *Scientia* (2:347/2). On the possibility of word play between *sitientes* (thirsting) and *scientes* (knowing), see Robertson and Huppé 135.

B.11.124a (C.12.59a) *Qui crediderit & baptiʒatus fuerit &c.* Mk. 16:16, response, Ascension day, *Brev.* 1:dcccclxx. [A.11.234, C.13.87a]

B.11.139a (C.12.74a) *Misericordia eius super omnia opera eius.* [B.5.281a, B.17.318a (C.19.298a)]

B.11.161 The *legenda sanctorum* yow lereþ. The reference is to the *Legenda Sanctorum* of Jacobus a Vorgine (ca. 1230–1298), a book so popular that it became known as the "Golden Legend" or *Legenda Aurea.* [B.11.220, B.15.269, C.17.157]

B.11.176a (C.12.99a) *Qui non diligit manet in morte.* 1 Jn. 3:14, "Qui non diligit, manet in morte: omnis qui odit fratrem suum, homicida est."

B.11.191a (C.12.103a) *Cum facitis conuiuia nolite inuitare [vocare* C] *amicos.* Lk. 14:12–13, "Cum facis prandium, aut coenam, noli vocare amicos tuos, neque fratres tuos, neque cognatos, neque vicinos divites . . . ; sed cum facis convivium, voca pauperes, debiles, claudos, et caecos."

B.11.203 (C.12.111) As *quasi modo geniti* gentil men echone. 1 Pet. 2:2, as quoted in the Introit for Low Sunday, the first after Easter,

Missale 385: "Quasi modo geniti infantes, alleluya: rationabiles sine dolo lac concupiscite, alleluya, alleluya, alleluya" (see Pearsall 216 for discussion of figurative meaning); the use of the phrase as a formula in contemporary law may also have relevance to the passage (Alford 1988b).

B.11.204a (C.12.112a) *Qui facit peccatum seruus est peccati.* Jn. 8:34. [Cf. B.Prol.39 (A.Prol.39, C.Prol.40)]

B.11.207 (C.12.115) And after his resurexcion *Redemptor* was his name. Job 19:25, "Scio enim quod Redemptor meus vivit, Et in novissimo die de terra surrecturus sum," quoted as a response in the Office of the Dead; see also Easter matins, lectio 2, "Illa Redemptoris nostri resurrectio" (*Brev.* 1:dcccxi) and lectio 3, "de Redemptore nostro dicitur" (*Brev.* 1:dcccxiii). The word occurs only once in the New Testament, Acts 7:35.

B.11.211a *Alter alterius onera portate* [*et sic adimplebitis legem Christi*]. [B.6.221a (C.8.230a), C.13.78a, B.17.74]

—C.12.119a *Et qui bona egerunt, ibunt &c.* [B.7.113–14 (Z.8.96, A.8.95, C.9.287–88)]

B.11.218 That *Fides sua* sholde sauen hire and saluen hire of synnes. Lk. 7:50, "Dixit [i.e. Christus] autem ad mulierem: Fides tua te salvam fecit: vade in pace."

B.11.220 Of logyk ne of lawe in *legenda sanctorum* / Is litel alowaunce maad. [B.11.161, B.15.269, C.17.157]

B.11.228 *Eadem mensura qua mensi fueritis remecietur vobis.* [B.1.178a (C.1.174a), C.11.232a]

B.11.231 *Melius est scrutari scelera nostra quam naturas rerum.* Analogue noted by Robertson and Huppé (141n): "Melius est enim scire infirmitatem nostram, quam naturas rerum. Laudabilior enim est animus cui nota est infirmitas sua, quam qui ea non respecta, siderum viam scrutator, et terrarum fundamenta et coelorum fastigia" (attributed to Augustine by Peter Lombard, *Collectanea*, in *PL* 191:1601).

B.11.252 (C.12.138) *Domine, non est tibi cure quod soror mea reliquit me solam ministrare?* Lk. 10:40.

B.11.255a (C.12.141a) *Maria optimam partem elegit que non auferetur ab ea.* Lk. 10:42.

B.11.269a (C.12.154a) *Pauper ego ludo dum tu diues meditaris.* Proverbial (Walther 20907), possibly from Alexander of Villa Dei, *Doctrinale,* verse 1091 (ed. Dietrich Reichling, Monumenta Germaniae Paedogogica, no. 12 [Berlin 1893]).

B.11.271 *Diuicias nec paupertates &c.* L's attribution of the quotation ("Salomon seide") suggests Prov. 30:8, "Vanitatem et verba mendacia longe fac a me. Mendicitatem et divitias ne dederis mihi; tribue tantam victui meo necessaria." L's version (the substitution of *paupertas* for *mendicitatem*) was current in polemical writings against the friars (Scase 57–58); it appears also in *FM* 572 as "Divicias et paupertates ne dederis michi, set tantum, etc."

—C.12.160a *Quicumque reliquerit patrem & matrem &c.* Matt. 19:29, "Et omnis qui reliquerit domum, vel fratres, aut sorores, aut patrem, aut matrem, aut uxorem, aut filios, aut agros propter nomen meum, centuplum accipiet, et vitam aeternam possidebit." The wording of this verse is considerably varied in early biblical manuscripts and citations by the Fathers; closest to L's quotation is Ambrose's comment on Ps. 118: "Quicunque reliquerit patrem, aut matrem, domum, aut fratres . . ." (cited in apparatus to *VL*).

B.11.274a (C.12.167a) *Si vis perfectus esse vade & vende [quae habes, et da pauperibus, et habebis thesaurum in caelo: et veni, sequere me].* Matt. 19:21. A classic authority for mendicancy, e.g., the opening text of the Rule of St. Francis (1221), the first authority cited by Bonaventure in "De Paupertate quoad Abrenuntiationem" (Scase 57–59).

B.11.281a *Nichil inpossibile volenti.* Proverbial (Walther 44445a1b: "Volenti nil impossibile"), based on Matt. 17:19, "si habueritis fidem, sicut granum sinapis . . . nihil impossibile erit vobis." Cf. John Heywood, "Nothing is impossible to a willyng hart" (*Proverbs*, pt. 1, chap. 4); Stephen Hawes, "To a wyllynge herte is nought impossyble" (*Pastime of Pleasure* [EETS 173], 10); other vernacular examples in Whiting N157.

B.11.282a *[Divites eguerunt, et esurierunt;] Inquirentes autem dominum non minuentur omni bono.* Ps. 33:11. [see B.9.109a (C.10.202a)]

—C.12.171a *Nisi renunciaueritis omnia que possidetis &c.* Lk. 14:33, "Sic ergo omnis ex vobis, qui non renuntiat omnibus quae possidet, non potest meus esse discipulus."

—C.12.179a *Nisi granum frumenti cadens in terram mortuum fuerit &c.* Jn. 12:24, antiphon sung on the nativity of a martyr, *Brev.* 2:384.

—C.12.207a *Tristicia vestra vertetur in gaudium.* Jn. 16:20.

—C.12.215a *O stulte, ista nocte anima tua egredietur.* Lk. 12:20, "Stulte, hac nocte animam tuam repetunt a te: quae autem parasti, cuius erunt?"

—C.12.215a *Tezaurisat, & ignorat &c.* Ps. 38:7, "Thesaurizat, et ignorat cui congregabit ea," suggested by Lk. 12:21, "Sic est qui sibi thesaurizat . . ." (continued from above).

—C.13.4a *Tanquam nichil habentes &c.* 2 Cor. 6:10, "Quasi tristes, semper autem gaudentes: sicut egentes, multos autem locuple-

tantes: tanquam nihil habentes et omnia possidentes."
—C.13.17–18
> And for a song in his sorwe, *"si bona accepimus a domino &c,*
> Derworthe and dere god, do we so *mala."*

Job. 2:10, "[S]i bona suscepimus de manu Dei, mala quare non suscipiamus?" Both Ambrose and Gregory read *accepimus:* "Si bona accipimus de manu Domini, quae mala sunt cur non sustineamus?" (*De interpellatione Job et David* 3.2 [*PL* 14:878]); "Si bona accepimus de manu Domini, mala quare non sustineamus" (*Moralia, PL* 75:619).

—C.13.44a (cf. B.20.10, C.22.10) *Necessitas non habet legem.* Maxim of natural law; see *CIC* 1:374, Pennafort 33, 114, 192, 224, and, for a commentary pertinent to L's use of the maxim, *Dives and Pauper* (EETS 280 [1980]), 141, "For ȝif ony man or woman for myschef of hungyr or of þrest or of cold ... take so onyþing in peryl of deth or in gret myschef, nede excusith hym from þefte and fro synne ... for in gret nede alle þing is comoun.... And also for nede hat no lawe. Example ha we in þe gospel, wher we fyndyn þat þe discyplis of Crist for hyngyr tokyn herys in þe feld & gnoddyn is & etyn is for hyngyr [Matt. 12:1–8].... For it is a general reule in þe lawe þat nede hat no lawe." Aquinas expresses the rule as "necessitas non subditur legi" (*Summa Theologica* 1.2 q. 96 art. 6). See also Walther 16295c, 38635; for numerous examples in English, Whiting N51; and for its special association with friars, Szittya 270, 277, passim, and Scase 66. The theory itself is discussed by Ullmann, 153–54.

—C.13.78a *Alter alterius onera portate* [*et sic adimplebitis legem Christi*]. [B.6.221a (C.8.230a), B.11.211a, B.17.74]

—C.13.87a *Qui crediderit & baptizatus fuerit &c.* [B.11.124a (C.12.59a), A.11.234]

—C.13.98a *Amen dico vobis quia hec vidua paupercula &c.* Lk. 21:3, "Vere dico vobis, quia vidua haec pauper, plus quam omnes misit"; L's reading reflects the *Vetus Latina,* "Vere dico vobis, quia vidua haec paupercula...."

B.11.286a *Iudica me deus & discerne causam meam* [*de gente non sancta, ab homine iniquo et doloso erue me*]. Ps. 42:1, specifically associated (like the quotation immediately following) with the priesthood; see the Ordinary of the Mass, *Missale* 579 (*Brev.* 2:481 passim), and the collection of treatises known as *Judica Me Deus,* addressed primarily to parish priests (Hope Emily Allen, *Writings Ascribed to Richard Rolle* [New York: Modern Language Association, 1927], 93–113).

B.11.287 (C.13.101) *Spera in deo* spekeþ of preestes þat haue no spendyng siluer. Ps. 42:5. The words are particularly appropriate to the priesthood, according to Peter Lombard (Robertson and Huppé 142); they are said by the priest as he approaches the altar: "Introibo ad altare Dei.... Spera in Deo" (*Brev.* 2:481); cf. Ps. 36:3, 41:6. [B.15.180]

B.11.309 (C.13.122a) *Qui offendit in vno in omnibus est reus.* [B.9.100a]

B.11.311 (C.13.123a) *Psallite deo nostro; psallite quoniam rex terre deus Israel* [*Israel* om. B var., C]; *psallite sapienter.* Ps. 46:7–8, "Psallite Deo nostro, psallite; Psallite regi nostro, psallite; Quoniam rex omnis terrae Deus, Psallite sapienter."

B.11.313 (C.13.125) That crouneþ swiche goddes kny3tes, þat konneþ no3t *sapienter*. Quoted from above.

B.11.316–317 (C.13.128) ... *Ignorancia / Non excusat episcopos nec* [*episcopos nec* om. C] ydiotes preestes. A maxim of canon law (Alford 1988b). See Pennafort 195, "Ignorantia iuris ... non excusat"; Peckham's *Constitutions*, "Ne quis per ignorantiam se excuset ...," where the essential points of knowledge belonging to priests are set forth (Lyndwood, *Provinciale* 1); and Bromyard 1.35/4, "Ignorantia non excusat sacerdotem in his, quae ad officium suum pertinent." Cf. *Sext.*, "De regulis iuris," Regula 13, "Ignorantia facti, non iuris, excusat" (*CIC* 2:1122). In lay matters the thinking was different; for example, Lucas de Penna would excuse ignorance of the law where no evil intention was involved: "Nam tunc quaelibet ignorantia, etiam juris, excusat" (Ullmann 156).

B.11.383a *Propter deum subiecti estote omni creature.* 1 Pet. 2:13, "Subiecti igitur [*igitur* om. in *VL* and Weber] estote omni humanae creaturae propter Deum."

B.11.385–86 (C.13.203–4)

> *Bele vertue est suffrance; mal dire est petite vengeance.*
> *Bien dire et bien suffrir fait lui suffrable a bien venir.*

MS Bodl. 14525 (ca. 1400) contains an English translation: "A fayre vertew is gwode suffrance: A fowle vyce is petite venjawnce" (Whiting S861). Cf. Chaucer's *Franklin's Tale* (V 773–80), "Pacience is an heigh vertu ... / For every word men may nat chide or pleyne. / Lerneth to suffre, or elles, so moot I goon, / Ye shul it lerne, wher so ye wole or noon; / For in this world, certein, ther no wight is / That he ne dooth or seith somtyme amys" (*CT* 179). As Pearsall notes (231), the same passage also translates the tag quoted by L at B.11.404, *Nemo sine crimine viuit.*

B.11.395 (C.13.196a) *De re que te non molestat noli certare.* Ecclus. 11:9, "De ea re quae te non molestat ne certeris; Et in iudicio peccantium ne consistas."

B.11.398a *Et vidit* [*Viditque* Vulg., *Et vidit* VL] *deus cuncta que fecerat & erant valde bona.* Gen. 1:31, versicle, Septuagesima Sunday, *Brev.* 1:cccclxxxvi.

B.11.404 (C.13.212) Caton acordeþ þerwiþ: *Nemo sine crimine viuit.* Cato 1.5, "Si vitam inspicias hominum, si denique mores, / cum culpant alios nemo sine crimine vivit"; the quotation appears also in sermons (Brinton 2:348) and penitential texts, e.g., Pennafort, *Summa de Poenitentia* (259, 459); Peter the Cantor, *Summa*; and Hostiensis, *Summa Aurea* (Gray 58); cf. Chaucer's translation of the tag in the *Franklin's Tale*, quoted above (B.11.385).

B.11.416a (C.13.224a) *Philosophus esses si tacuisses.* Proverbial. See Bromyard 1:450/2, "Si tacuisses, philosophus fuisses, sed loquendo philosophum se non esse ostendit"; Thomas Wright, ed., *Political Poems and Songs*, Rolls Series 14 (London: Longman, 1859), 1:262: "With an O and an I, Si tunc tacuisses, / Tu nunc stulto similis philosophus fuisses." As noted by Skeat (2:178) the proverb is adapted from Boethius, *Consolation of Philosophy*, lib. 2, prosa 7: " 'Iam tandem,' inquit, 'intellegis me esse philosophum?' Tum ille nimium mordaciter: 'Intellexeram,' inquit, 'si tacuisses' " (ed. E. K. Rand and S. J. Tester, Loeb Classical Library [Cambridge, Mass.: Harvard, 1918], 220). Vernacular examples cited in Whiting F441, P156.

—**C.13.224b** *Locutum me aliquando penituit, tacuisse nunquam.* Cf. Cato 1.12, "Rumores fuge, ne incipias novus auctor haberi, / nam nulli tacuisse nocet, nocet esse locutum" (Walther 30954b).

Passus 12

B.12.9a *Si non in prima vigilia nec in secunda &c.* Cf. Lk. 12:38, "Et si venerit in secunda vigilia, et si in tertia vigilia venerit, et ita invenerit, beati sunt servi illi."

B.12.12a *Quem diligo castigo.* Heb. 12:6, "Quem enim diligit Dominus, castigat"; cf. Apoc. 3:19, Prov. 3:12.

B.12.13a *Virga tua & baculus tuus, ipsa me consolata sunt.* Ps. 22:4, associated with bishops (whose sign is the *baculus*) in the Office of the Dead, *Missale* 863*, *Brev.* 2:524. [B.7.120–21 (Z.8.104, A.8.102–3), A.10.87, B.12.293a]

B.12.22a *Interpone tuis interdum gaudia curis.* Cato 3.6, "Interpone tuis interdum guadia curis, / ut possis animo quemvis sufferre laborem"; also quoted by Bromyard 2:216/2, and Voragine 112.

B.12.29a *Fides, spes, caritas et maior horum &c.* 1 Cor. 13:13, "Nunc autem manent, fides, spes, caritas, tria haec; et maior horum est charitas." [B.17.1 (C.19.1), etc.; B.2.35, etc.]

B.12.50a *Sunt homines nequam, bene de virtute loquentes.* Gottfried of Winchester, epigram 169, "Imitandum esse quem magis aspectu provaveris quam auditu":

Illum proponas tibi, Caelestine, sequendum,

Quem magis aspectu quam aure probatum habeas.

Sunt homines nequam, bene de virtute loquentes,

Non hos sed verbum pectore fige tuo.

From Thomas Wright, *The Anglo-Latin Satirical Poets and Epigrammatists of the Twelfth Century*, Rolls Series 59 (London: Longman's, 1872), 2:130. Cf. Walther 30735.

B.12.54a *Date & dabitur vobis.* [B.1.201 (Z.1.124, A.1.175, C.1.196)]

—C.14.14 Ac to louye and to lene ... / Is ycalde *Caritas*, kynde loue an engelysche. See B.12.29a. [B.2.35, C.18.14, C.18.32, C.18.39]

—C.14.16a *Beacius est dare quam petere.* Acts 20:35, "Beatius est magis dare, quam accipere."

B.12.56a (C.14.18a) *Scientes et non facientes varijs flagellis vapulabunt* [*vapulabit* B var.]. Adapted from Lk. 12:47, "Ille autem servus qui cognovit voluntatem domini sui, et non praeparavit, et non fecit secundum voluntatem eius, vapulabit multis"; cf. Jn. 13:17.

B.12.57a *Sapiencia inflat, [charitas vero aedificat].* 1 Cor. 8:1.

B.12.63a (C.14.27a) *Spiritus vbi vult spirat.* Jn. 3:8.

—C.14.32a *Vultus huius seculi sunt subiecti vultibus celestibus.* Unidentified.

B.12.65a (66, 67) *Quod scimus loquimur, [et] quod vidimus testamur.* Jn. 3:11.

B.12.69a *Nescit aliquis vnde venit aut quo vadit* [*vadat* Hm] *&c.* Jn. 3:8, "sed nescis unde veniat, aut quo vadat," continued from B.12.63a.

—C.14.42a *Quis vestrum sine peccato est, [primus in illam lapidem mittat].* Jn. 8:7.

B.12.89a *Nolite iudicare & non iudicabimini.* Lk. 6:37; cf. Matt. 7:1. [B.11.90 (C.12.31), B.14.293 (C.16.128)]

B.12.113 (119) (C.14.58) *Archa dei,* in þe olde lawe, leuytes it kepten. Cf. 1 Para. 15:1-2, Num. 1:50-51, 3:31; 1 Reg. 13:7-14, 15:9-22; 2 Reg. 6:1-8. [Cf. C.Prol.108, 112, B.10.288]

B.12.125a (C.14.69a) *Nolite tangere christos meos &c.* Ps. 104:15, one of the standard texts used to support the notion of clerical privilege; see the discussion in Hugh's comment on the verse. Ambrose quotes 1 Reg. 24:7 as "Nolite tangere Christum Domini" (*Apologia Prophetae David, PL* 14:902).

B.12.138a (C.14.83a) *Sapiencia [enim] huius mundi stulticia est apud* *deum.* 1 Cor. 3:19. *Enim* also omitted in *Prick of Conscience* 1356 (38) and *ME Sermons* 105.

B.12.142 (C.14.86a) *Pastores loquebantur ad inuicem.* Lk. 2:15, opening of lesson 8, the third nocturn on Nativity day, *Brev.* 1:clxxxiii.

B.12.144a (C.14.88a) *Ibant magi ab oriente.* Matt. 2:1, "ecce Magi ab oriente venerunt Ierosolymam, dicentes." [B.19.85 (C.21.85)]

B.12.147a *Set non erat ei locus in diuersorio, et pauper non habet diuersorium.* Lk. 2:7, "quia non erat eis locus in diversorio"; *VL* reads "quia non erat ei locus." A source for the second part of the quotation has not been found; it may have been added by Langland (see Schmidt's explanation, 338).

B.12.150 (C.14.94) And songe a song of solas, *Gloria in excelsis deo.* [B.3.328, B.19.74a (C.21.74a)]

B.12.177a (C.14.117a) *Beati quorum remisse sunt iniquitates & quorum tecta sunt [peccata] &c.* [& ... &c. om. C]. [B.5.507 (C.7.152), B.13.53, B.13.54a, B.14.94]

B.12.185 (C.14.124a) *Dum cecus ducit cecum &c.* [B.10.281a]

B.12.189 (C.14.128) *Dominus pars hereditatis mee [mee om. C]* is a murye verset. Ps. 15:5, quoted in ceremony of tonsuring new clerks (Alford 1988b). See the Roman Pontifical, "De clerico faciendo," and St. Jerome on a clergyman's duties (*Select Letters* [Loeb edition], 200). Cf. Hugh on Matt. 12:35. [C.5.60a]

—**C.14.134a** *Nolo mortem peccatoris &c.* Ezek. 33:11, "... nolo mortem impii"; cf. Ezek. 18:23, 32. L's reading (*peccatoris*) occurs also in the *Vetus Latina* and is common in other texts; e.g., Ambrose, *Liber de Lapsu Virginis* (*PL* 16:399); Gratian, *CIC* 1:513, 1220; Bromyard 2:459/4, 460/2; *ME Sermons* 155, 165, 216; *Spec. Sacer.* 137; *FM* 108, 124, 642; Brinton 1:72, 155, 165, 2:346.

B.12.207a (C.14.146a) *De peccato propiciato* [Vulg. transposes] *noli esse sine metu.* Ecclus. 5:5.

B.12.213a (C.14.152a) *Quia [Qui B var., Et C] reddit vnicuique iuxta opera sua.* Rom. 2:6, "... qui reddet unicuique secundum opera eius." Variations of the verse are extremely common: 2 Par. 6:30, Ps. 61:13, Prov. 24:12, 29, Wisd. 10:17, Jer. 25:14, 50:29, Matt. 16:27, 2 Tim. 4:14, Apoc. 22:12. L's wording (*iuxta ... sua*) coincides with that of Hugh on Job 21:4; *Spec. Sacer.* 69; *ME Sermons* 270; *FM* 82; and Brinton 2:350. [C.5.32a]

B.12.216a (C.14.155a) *Quare placuit? quia voluit [deus voluit B var.].* Adapted possibly from texts like Job 23:13, Ps. 113b:3, 134:6; see Pearsall 242.

—**C.14.165a** *Dixit & facta sunt.* Ps. 148:5. [B.9.33a (A.10.34a), B.14.61a (C.15.260a)]

B.12.280 (C.14.202) *"Contra!"* quod Ymaginatif þoo and comsed to loure. [B.8.20 (A.9.16, C.10.20), B.10.349 (A.11.232)]

B.12.281 (C.14.203) And seide, *"Saluabitur vix* [transposed B var., C] *Iustus in die Iudicij."* 1 Pet. 4:18, "Et si iustus vix salvabitur, impius et peccator ubi parebunt?" quoted in the *Dies Irae* ("Cum vix justus sit securus") and in the *Officium pro defunctis* for Hereford, in *Manuale et Processionale ad Usum Insignis Ecclesiae Eboracensis*, Surtees Society 63 (Durham, 1875), 124*. Also quoted in school grammars of the period, apparently to point a lesson regarding the word *vix* (see Thomson 107). Skeat remarks on L's stress upon *vix*, "since the just man shall *scarcely* be saved, it follows that he *shall* be saved" (2:188); this is in fact the same interpretation found in *The Prick of Conscience* 5396–5403, "If þe rightwys man . . . sal *unnethes* þan saved be . . . Ryghtwysmen . . . *Sal* be saf þan and nan elles." [B.13.19 (C.15.22); cf. C.15.118]

B.12.282 (C.14.204) *"Ergo saluabitur,"* quod he and seide na moore latyn. [*Ergo* is used also at B.8.24 (A.9.20, C.10.28), B.14.62 (C.15. 261), B.14.287 (C.16.122a), B.14.292 (C.16.127), B.18.340 (C.20. 388), B.19.19 (C.21.19).]

B.12.286a (C.14.208a) *Aduenit ignis diuinus non comburens set illuminans &c.* From an antiphon sung at Pentecost, *Brev.* 1:mvi, mxvi, based on Acts 2:3.

—**C.14.214a** *Quia super pauca fuisti fidelis [super multa te constituam].* Matt. 25:23.

B.12.293 For *Deus dicitur quasi dans eternam vitam suis, hoc est fidelibus.* An anagram, perhaps inspired by 1 Jn. 5:11 ("Et hoc est testimonium, quoniam vitam aeternam dedit nobis Deus"), Jn. 10:28 ("Et ego vitam aeternam do eis"), or Jn. 17:2 (". . . det eis vitam aeternam"). Schmidt (304) translates as follows: "God is called *Deus* because his name spells salvation to his people—i.e. 'dans eternam vitam suis' gives 'devs.' " As Schmidt notes (crediting J. A. Burrow for the reference), this etymological *interpretatio* of the word *Deus* appears in a gloss to Evrard of Béthune's *Laborintus*, a standard grammatical text (see E. Faral, *Les arts poétiques du XIIe et du XIIIe siècle* [Paris, 1924], 65).

B.12.293a *Si ambulauero in medio vmbre mortis [non timebo mala quoniam tu mecum es domine* B var.]. [B.7.120–121 (Z.8.104, A.8.102– 103), A.10.87, B.12.13a]

Passus 13

B.13.19 (C.15.22) And siþen how ymaginatif seide *"vix saluabitur iustus."* [B.12.281 (C.14.203)]

B.13.30 (C.15.32) And preyde *"pur charite,* for a pouere heremyte." [B.6.253 (Z.7.180, A.7.237, C.8.265), etc.]

B.13.39a (C.15.44a) *Edentes & bibentes que apud eos [illos* Vulg., B var.] *sunt.* Lk. 10:7. A verse commonly cited in the mendicant controversy; e.g., *Friar Daw's Reply,* "And so to his prechours Crist also þus seide: *In quamcumque domum intraueritis, manete in eadem edentes et bibentes etc."* (*Upland* 92). [B.2.123 (A.2.86a)]

B.13.44 (C.15.49) In a morter, *Post mortem,* of many bitter peyne. "After death," that is, in purgatory. The image of the mortar and the admonition in the following line that the Doctor and his man should "synge for tho soules" (of benefactors) suggests also a prayer for the dead in purgatory, "Deus, cui soli competit medicinam praestare post mortem, tribue, quaesumus, ut anima famuli tui ab omnibus exuta peccatis, electorum tuorum societatibus aggregetur" (*Missale* 873*). Scase sees an allusion to the Doctor's "sinful receipt and abuse of bequests ('*Post mortem*')" (105). Inquests following the death of a property-holder (to determine, among other things, what was due to the Crown), were known as *Inquisitiones post mortem*; see, for example, *Calendarium Inquisitionum Post Mortem sive Escaetarum,* vol. 15 [1–7 Richard II] (London: Her Majesty's Stationery Office, 1970).

B.13.45a (C.15.50a) *Vos qui peccata hominum comeditis, nisi pro eis lacrimas & oraciones effuderitis, ea que in delicijs comeditis in tormentis euometis.* Source not identified, but probably derived from Osee 4:8, "Peccata populi mei comedent"; cf. Gratian, *CIC* 1:391, "Sacerdotes ... peccata populi comedunt," also *CIC* 1:409.

B.13.49 (C.15.55) He sette a sour loof toforn vs and seide *"Agite penitenciam."* Job 21:2, Ezek. 18:30, repeated (transposed) in Matt. 3:2, "Poenitenciam agite: appropinquavit enim regnum caelorum"; also Acts 2:38 and, in the singular ("Age") Apoc. 2:5, 2:16, 3:3, 3:19. *FM* 484 quotes Matt. 3:2 as "Agite penitenciam."

B.13.50 (C.15.56) And siþe he drouȝ vs drynke, *Diu [Dia* B var.] *perseuerans.* Source unknown, but cf. Matt. 10:22, "Qui autem perseveraverit usque in finem, hic salvus erit." The relevance of Matt. 10:22 to the present context is indicated by the comment in *FM*: "For the prize is not promised to those who begin a life of penance, but rather to those who firmly persevere in it, for it is written: 'Qui autem perseveraverit ... ' " (431). Schmidt prints the phrase as *Dia perseverans*, thus preserving a possible pun on Middle English *dia*, "potion, medicament" (cf. B.20.174: "Lyf leeued þat lechcraft ... sholde ... dryuen awey deeþ wiþ Dyas and drogges"). See also his discussion of the quotation in *The Clerkly Maker: Langland's Poetic Art* (Cambridge: Brewer, 1987), 92.

B.13.53 And he brouȝte vs of *Beati quorum* of *Beatus vir*res makyng. Ps. 31:1 and Ps. 31:2; also Ps. 1:1, Ps. 111:1. The quotations from Ps. 31 are especially appropriate in this context: it is one of the seven "Penitential Psalms" (*Brev.* 2:242–49), each associated with a deadly sin (Ps. 6, Ire; Ps. 31, Pride; Ps. 37, Gluttony; Ps. 50, Lechery; Ps. 101, Avarice; Ps. 129, Envy; Ps. 142, Sloth [see the next five quotations]). Their recitation during Lent was ordered by Innocent III (1198–1216). [B.5.418, B.5.507 (C.7.152), B.10.326, B.12.177a (C.14.117a), B.13.54a]

B.13.54 And þanne a mees of ooþer mete of *Miserere mei deus*. Ps. 50:3, one of the seven "Penitential Psalms" (see above). [B.5.277]

B.13.54a *Et quorum tecta sunt peccata* [*& beatus vir cui non imputauit* added B var.]. Ps. 31:1–2, "Beati quorum remissae sunt iniquitates, et quorum tecta sunt peccata. Beatus vir cui non imputavit Dominus peccatum" (see B.13.53). [B.5.507 (C.7.152), B.12.177a (C.14.117a)]

B.13.55 In a dissh of derne shrifte, *Dixi & confitebor tibi*. Ps. 31:5, "Dixi: confitebor adversum me iniustitiam meam Domino" (see B.13.53).

B.13.57 (C.15.60) And þanne hadde Pacience a pitaunce, *Pro hac orabit ad te omnis sanctus in tempore oportuno*. Ps. 31:6 (see B.13.53).

B.13.58a (C.15.62) *Cor contritum & humiliatum deus non despicies*. Ps. 50:19 (see B.13.53). [B.15.194 (C.16.336a)]

B.13.61a (C.15.65a) *Ve vobis* [*vobis* om. Vulg.] *qui potentes estis ad bibendum vinum*. Isa. 5:22. As Schmidt observes (339), the preceding verse (Isa. 5:21) "accounts for the one quoted: 'Woe to you that are wise in your own eyes and prudent in your own conceits' (appropriate for the Doctor)."

B.13.67 (C.15.73a) *In fame & frigore* and flappes of scourges. 2 Cor. 11:27, "in fame et siti ... in frigore et nuditate."

B.13.67a *Ter cesus sum & a iudeis quinquies quadragenas &c.* 2 Cor. 11:24–25, "A Iudaeis quinquies quadragenas, una minus, accepi. Ter virgis caesus sum...."

B.13.70 (C.15.75a) *Periculum est in falsis fratribus*. (See below.)

B.13.73a *Vnusquisque a fratre se custodiat quia vt dicitur periculum est in falsis fratribus*. The source of this allusion to 2 Cor. 11:26 ("... periculis in falsis fratribus") is unknown; similar quotations based on 2 Cor. 11:26 are commonplace in antimendicant literature (*Upland* 111; Szittya 110; Scase 219n12). Brinton (2:436) also uses the singular *periculum*.

—**C.15.116a** *Et visitauit & fecit redempcionem &c.* Lk. 1:68, "Benedictus Dominus Deus Israel, Quia visitavit, et fecit redemptionem plebis suae."

—**C.15.118** But dowel endite ʒow *in die iudicij*. The phrase is too common in Scripture to trace to a specific source. However, the context (the hypocritical friar) suggests Matt. 12:34, 36, "[H]ow can you speak good things, whereas you are evil? But I say unto you, that every idle word that men shall speak, they shall render an account for it in the day of judgment [*in die iudicii*]." L has used the phrase earlier (B.12.281 [C.14.203]) as a gloss on "saluabitur vix iustus." It appears in a number of litanies as part of the prayer, "In die judicii, libera nos Domine" (e.g., *Brev.* 2:252).

B.13.118a (C.15.126a) *Qui facit [autem fecerit* Vulg., B var.] *& docuerit [hic* Vulg., B var.] *magnus vocabitur in regno celorum [in . . . celorum* om. C]. Matt. 5:19. [A.11.196a]

B.13.127 (C.15.134) *Dilige deum [& proximum* C]. Matt. 22:37, Mk. 12:30, Lk. 10:27, quoting Deut. 6:5. [A.11.242, C.15.140, B.15.584, B.17.13 (C.19.14); cf. C.17.140a]

B.13.127 (C.15.134) *Domine quis habitabit [in tabernaculo tuo]*. Ps. 14:1. [B.2.39 (C.2.40), B.3.234a, B.7.52a]

—**C.15.135a** *Nemo bonus [nisi unus Deus]*. Mk. 10:18, "Iesus autem dixit ei: Quid me dicis bonum? Nemo bonus, nisi unus Deus"; cf. Lk. 18:19, "Nemo bonus nisi solus Deus" (the phrase "solus Deus" occurs also in C.18.190).

B.13.135a (C.15.137) *Pacientes vincunt &c.* Proverbial, in the singular form, e.g., "Patientia vincit omnia" (Walther 20833f, 39248c, 39415b1), and "Patience conquers all" (Whiting P61), but L offers the only example in the plural; cf. Matt. 10:22, Jas. 1:12, 5:7–11. [B.13.171a (C.15.156a), B.14.33c, B.14.54 (C.15.253), B.15.268, B.15.598a]

B.13.137 (cf. C.15.140) *"Disce,"* quod he, *"doce, dilige inimicos."* The triad *disce, doce, dilige* has the character of a school maxim, to which L may have added the objects *inimicos* (after Matt. 5:44 or Lk. 6:27, "diligite inimicos vestros") and *deum* (below). Cf. Walther 5888a, "Disce timere Deum, dilige semper eum!"

—**C.15.140** That *disce, doce, dilige Deum* and thyn enemy. See above; *dilige deum*. [A.11.242, B.13.127 (C.15.134), B.15.584, B.17.13 (C.19.14); cf. C.17.140a]

B.13.151 Wiþ half a laumpe lyne in latyn, *Ex vi transicionis*. Grammatical terminology; see R. E. Kaske, " 'Ex vi transicionis' and its

Passage in *Piers Plowman,*" *JEGP* 62 (1963): 32–60. For a full discussion of "ex vi" terminology, see Cynthia Bland, "Langland's Use of the Term *Ex vi transicionis*," *YLS* 2 (1988): 125–35.

B.13.163a (cf. C.15.164a) *Caritas nichil timet.* 1 Jn. 4:18, "Timor non est in charitate: sed perfecta charitas foras mittit timorem."

—C.15.164a *Caritas expellit omnem timorem.* Variant or gloss on 1 Jn. 4:18 (above); cf. Ambrose, "Perfecta enim charitas timorem expellit foras" (*PL* 16:1461), and Hugh of St. Cher, "Charitas expellit servilem timorem."

B.13.171a (C.15.156a) *Pacientes vincunt.* [B.13.135a (C.15.137), B.14.33c, B.14.54 (C.15.253), B.15.268, B.15.598a]

B.13.195 Than 3acheus for he seide "*dimidium bonorum meorum do pauperibus.*" Lk. 19:8, "Ecce dimidium bonorum meorum, Domine, do pauperibus" (*VL* omits "Domine").

B.13.197 Than alle þo þat offrede into *Ga3ophilacium?* Lk. 21:1–4. [cf. C.13.98a]

B.13.224 (C.15.193) I am a Mynstrall ... my name is *Actiua vita.* On the concept of the active life, especially as it relates to *Piers,* see T. P. Dunning, "Action and Contemplation in *Piers Plowman,*" *Piers Plowman: Critical Approaches,* ed. S. S. Hussey (London: Methuen, 1969), 213–25. [B.14.28, C.15.272, C.16.117, C.18.80, C.18.82a]

B.13.249a (C.15.221a) *In nomine meo demonia ejicient &* [*In ... &* om. C] *super egros manus imponent & bene habebunt.* Mk. 16:17–18, "Signa autem eos qui crediderint, haec sequenter: In nomine meo daemonia eiicient: linguis loquenter novis: serpentes tollent: et si mortiferum quid biberint, non eis nocebit: super aegros manus, imponent, et bene habebunt."

B.13.254a (C.15.224a) *Argentum & aurum non est michi; quod autem habeo tibi do; in nomine domini* [*in nomine Iesu Christi Nazareni* Vulg.] *surge et ambula* [*in ... ambula* om. C]. Acts 3:6. L's reading "in nomine domini" is attested by ancient biblical manuscripts (see critical notes to *VL*).

—C.15.229a *Habundancia panis & vini turpissimum peccatum aduenit.* Pearsall (257) cites a similar sentence in Peter the Cantor, "Et abundantia panis causa fuit peccati Sodomorum" (*PL* 205:331), also prompted by the same verse from Ezekiel that follows here — "Ecce haec fuit iniquitas Sodomae, sororis tuae: superbia, saturitas panis et abundantia, et otium ipsius, et filiarum eius" (16:49), which L renders as, "Plente of payn the peple of Sodoume / And reste and ryche metes rebaudes hem made." The passage is quoted in *FM* as "Hec fuit iniquitas Sodome, saturitas panis et ocium" (420). [B.14.77a]

B.13.312a (C.6.60a) *Si [adhuc] hominibus placerem christi seruus non essem.* Gal. 1:10; *adhuc* is omitted in some Old Latin versions (viz. notes to *VL*).

B.13.312a (C.6.60a) *Nemo potest duobus dominis seruire.* Matt. 6:24.

B.13.330a (C.6.76a) *Cuius malediccione os plenum est & amaritudine [et dolo* Vulg., B var.]; *sub lingua eius labor et dolor.* Ps. 9b:7.

B.13.330b (C.6.76b) *Filij hominum dentes eorum arma & sagitte et lingua eorum gladius acutus.* Ps. 56:5.

B.13.396 (C.6.283) Ne neuere penaunce parfournede ne Paternoster seide. [C.5.46, C.5.87, C.5.107, B.5.341 (A.5.189, C.6.399), B.5.394 (C.7.10), B.10.468, B.14.49 (C.15.247), C.16.323; other quotations from the Paternoster at C.5.88, B.14.50 (C.15.249), B.15.179 (C.16.321), C.16.374a, B.19.394a (C.21.394a)]

B.13.398a *Vbi [Vbi est* B var.] *thesaurus tuus ibi & cor tuum [tuum est* B var.]. Matt. 6:21, "Ubi enim est thesaurus tuus, ibi est et cor tuum." L's wording coincides exactly with Ambrose's, "Ubi thesaurus tuus, ibi et cor tuum" (*PL* 14:785). [C.6.285a]

B.13.423a (C.7.83a) *Ve vobis qui ridetis &c.* Lk. 6:25, "Vae vobis, qui saturati estis: quia esurietis. Vae vobis, qui ridetis nunc: quia lugebitis et flebitis."

B.13.426a (C.7.86a) *Consencientes & agentes pari pena punientur.* Canon law maxim (Alford 1975, 1988b, and Gray); see also Gratian, *CIC* 1:816; Innocent V, *In IV. Librum Sententiarum Commentaria* 4.15.3 (Toulouse, 1651; repr. Ridgewood, NJ: Gregg, 1964), 165; Bromyard 1:21/3, 1:107/4, 1:192/3, 2:462/1; Brunne's *Handlyng Synne* (EETS 119 [1901]), 242; *Dives et Pauper* (EETS 275 [1976]), 238; Menot 480. The maxim is versified by Gower in *Vox Clamantis*, "Iura volunt quod homo facinus qui mittit, et alter / Qui consentit ei, sint in agone pares" (1.1123–24), and Englished by Chaucer in *The Parson's Tale*, "Wherfore they that eggen or consenten to the synne been parteners of the synne, and of the dampnacioun of the synnere" (965–70). The notion is frequently embedded in the wording of English laws and ordinances (e.g., *Liber Albus* [Rolls Series 12.3], 145). For a discussion of the theory in Lucas de Penna ("Facientes et consentientes par poena constringit"), see Ullmann 157.

B.13.432a (C.7.92a) *Non habitabit in medio domus mee qui facit superbiam & [& om.* C] *qui loquitur iniqua [non direxit in conspectu oculorum meorum].* Ps. 100:7.

B.13.440a (C.7.100a) *Qui vos spernit me spernit.* Lk. 10:16; cf. Jn. 5:23, 12:48, 13:20.

B.13.456 (C.7.116) Wiþ *turpiloquio*, a lay of sorwe, and luciferis fiþele. [B.Prol.39 (A.Prol.39, C.Prol.40)]

Passus 14

B.14.3a (C.7.304a) *Vxorem duxi & ideo non possum venire.* Lk. 14:20. For the allegorical application of this verse to the present context (*uxor* = concupiscence), see Alford, "Haukyn's Coat," *MAE* 43 (1974): 133–38.

B.14.17a–21a *Cordis contricio . . . Oris confessio . . . Satisfaccio.* Formulaic expression of the steps in the sacrament of penance; e.g., Thomas of Cobham, *Summa Confessorum,* 1.1: "Tria autem, sicut dictum est, sunt in penitentia, ut contritio cordis, oris confessio, satisfactio operis" (Gray 59). See also Bromyard 2:212/1; *Spec. Sacer.* 63; *FM* 124 (quoting Bernard); Brinton 1:78; and the discussion by Skeat 2:204–5. [C.16.29–31a]

B.14.28 Than Haukyn wil þe wafrer, which is *Actiua vita.* [B.13.224 (C.15.193), C.15.272, C.16.117, C.18.80, C.18.82a]

B.14.33a *Ne soliciti sitis* [*animae vestrae quid manducetis, neque corpori vestro quid induamini*]. Matt. 6:25, continued below; cf. Lk. 12:22. [B.7.131 (Z.8.115, A.8.113)]

B.14.33b *Volucres celi deus pascit* [*eos* B var.] *&c.* Matt. 6:26, continued from above, "Respicite volatilia caeli . . . et Pater vester caelestis pascit illa"; cf. Lk. 12:24.

B.14.33c *Pacientes vincunt &c.* [B.13.135a (C.15.137), B.13.171a (C.15.156a), B.14.54 (C.15.253), B.15.268, B.15.598a]

B.14.46a (C.15.244a) *Quodcumque pecieritis a patre* [*Patrem* Vulg.] *in nomine meo* [*dabitur vobis* added B var., C, from Matt 7:7]. Jn. 14:13. Neither *Patrem* nor *a patre* appears in the Sixto-Clementine version (Glunz 244, 291); the *Vetus Latina* reads, "Et quodcunque ab illo petieritis." [C.7.260a]

B.14.46a (C.15.244b) *Non in solo pane viuit homo set in omni verbo quod procedit de ore dei* [*set . . . dei* om. C]. Matt. 4:4, quoting Deut. 8:3. [C.5.86–87]

B.14.49 (C.15.247) A pece of þe Paternoster. [C.5.46, C.5.87, C.5.107, B.5.341 (A.5.189, C.6.399), B.5.394 (C.7.10), B.10.468, B.13.396 (C.6.283), C.16.323]

B.14.50 (C.15.249) And þanne was it *fiat voluntas tua* sholde fynde vs alle. Matt. 6:10, "Fiat voluntas tua" (part of the Lord's Prayer); also a response and versicle in Holy Week: *Brev.* 1:dcclxxv. [C.5.88, B.15.179 (C.16.321); other citations from the Lord's Prayer at C.5.46, B.10.468, B.13.396 (C.6.283), C.16.323, C.16.374a, B.19.394a (C.21.394a)]

B.14.54 (C.15.253) Prison ne peyne, for *pacientes vincunt.* [B.13.135a (C.15.137), B.13.171a (C.15.156a), B.14.33c, B.15.268, B.15.598a]

B.14.60a (C.15.259a) *Si quis amat christum mundum non diligit istum* [*sed quasi fetorem spernes illius amorem* added in C var.]. *Cartula*, "Si quis amat christum mundum non diligit istum / Sed quasi feto-rem spernens illius amorem" (*Auctores Octo*, sig. G^v-b); printed as *Carmen Paraeneticum ad Rainaldum* in *PL* 184:1307, "Quisque amat Christum, mundum non diligit istum: / Sed quasi fetores sper-nens illius amores." The basis of the verse is 1 Jn. 2:15, "Si quis diligit mundum, non est charitas Patris in eo." Other examples cited in Walther 28959.

B.14.61a (C.15.260a) *Dixit & facta sunt* [*fuerunt* C] *&c.* [B.9.33a (A.10.34a), C.14.165a)]

B.14.62 (C.15.261) *Ergo* þoruȝ his breeþ boþe men and beestes lyuen. [B.8.24 (A.9.20, C.10.28), B.14.287 (C.16.122a), B.14.292 (C.16.127), B.18.340 (C.20.388), B.19.19 (C.21.19)]

B.14.63a (C.15.262a) *Aperis tu manum tuam & imples omne animal benediccione* [*& ... benediccione* om. C]. Ps. 144:16, part of a daily grace (*Graces* 382; cf. C.3.339a). [C.16.320]

—C.15.271a *Dabo tibi secundum peticionem tuam.* Ps. 36:4, "Delectare in Domino, et dabit tibi petitiones cordis tui."

—C.15.272 "What is properly parfit pacience?" quod *Actiua vita.* [B.13.224 (C.15.193), B.14.28, C.16.117, C.18.80, C.18.82a]

B.14.73 Ac vnkyndenesse *caristiam* makeþ amonges cristen peple. The word does not occur in the Vulgate Bible; its use may be intended to invoke a legal context (Alford 1988b).

B.14.77a *Ociositas & habundancia panis peccatum turpissimum nutriuit.* Cf. Brinton, Sermon 48 (216), "Immo ocium et habundancia panis fuerunt causa subuersionis Sodome et Gomorre"—a rough para-phrase of Ezek. 16:49, "Ecce haec fuit iniquitas Sodomae, sororis tuae: superbia, saturitas panis et abundantia, et otium ipsius, et filiarum eius." Cf. *Pilgrimage of the Life of Man*, "ffor the Prophete Ezechel / Writeth ... Idelnesse, plente of bred, / caused ... / of Sodom the distruccioun" (EETS es 77 [1899], 633). The same quotation appears in slightly different form above at C.15.229a.

B.14.92 *Per confessionem* to a preest *peccata occiduntur.* Penitential maxim; cf. Pennafort 286, "Licet enim peccatum sit deletum per paenitentiam"; Brinton 2:437, "Peccata per confessionem delen-tur" (cf. B.11.81a).

B.14.94 As Dauid seiþ in þe Sauter: *et quorum tecta sunt peccata.* [B.5.507 (C.7.152), B.12.177a (C.14.117a), B.13.53, B.13.54a]

B.14.104 (C.15.279) "Ye? *quis est ille?*" quod Pacience; "quik, *lauda-bimus* [*laudamus* C] *eum!*" Ecclus. 31:9, "Quis est hic? et lauda-bimus eum." [cf. B.15.234a (C.16.359a)]

B.14.123 (C.15.299) And diues in deyntees lyuede and in *douce vie.*
Allusion to the parable of Dives and Lazarus, Lk. 16:19–31. The
words are translated as "delicat lyf" in C.8.277. [C.19.240a]

B.14.131a (C.15.306) *Dormierunt* [*somnum suum,*] *& nichil inuenerunt*
[*omnes viri divitiarum in manibus suis*]. Ps. 75:6.

B.14.131b (C.15.306a) *Velud sompnium surgencium domine in Ciuitate
tua, et ad nichilum rediges &c.* [*domine . . . &c* om. C]. Ps. 72:20,
"Velut somnium surgentium, Domine, In civitate tua imaginem
ipsorum ad nihilum rediges."

B.14.144a *De delicijs ad delicias difficile est transire* [*ascendere* B var.]. St.
Jerome, *Epistola ad Julianum,* "Difficile, imo impossibile est . . . ut
de deliciis transeat ad delicias" (*PL* 22:965); quoted frequently,
e.g., Bromyard 1:6/3, "unde Hiero. Impossibile est transire de
delicijs ad delicias; hic implere ventrem et ibi mentem"; Voragine
162^v; Menot 346. The saying is based on Matt. 19:23.

B.14.169 Of þe good þat þow hem gyuest *ingrati* ben manye. Cf. Lk.
6:35, "et eritis filii Altissimi, quia ipse benignus est super ingratos
et malos"; for the word's legal implications, see Alford 1984,
1988b (additional citations from Roman law in Bromyard 1:280/2,
299/1, 340/4). Langland's wordplay (*gratus* / grace) is paralleled
in *Floretus,* "Non sis ingratus domino si vis fore gratus" (*Auctores
Octo,* sig. T$^{ii–b}$). [B.17.257 (C.19.223)]

—C.16.29–31a *Cordis contricio . . . oris confessio . . . Cordis contricio, Oris
confessio, Operis satisfaccio.* [B.14.17a-21a]

B.14.180a *Conuertimini ad me & salui eritis.* Isa. 45:22; the verse has
strong associations with Advent, *Brev.* 1:xxxv, lii, lviii, passim.

B.14.181 Thus *in genere* of gentries Iesu crist seide. Scholastic (Alford
1984) or grammatical terminology; cf. C.3.356, "He acordeth with
crist in kynde, *verbum caro factum est.*"

B.14.190a *Pateat &c.* [*Pateant vniuersi* B var.]. Formula in letters
patent (Alford 1988b).

B.14.190b *Per passionem domini* [*nostri iesu christi* B var.]. Continuation of the legal form suggested by *pateat,* above; the phrase
indicates by whose warrant the "Acquitaunce" was issued, in
imitation of letters patent of the time. E.g., "Per Concilium," "Per
ipsum Regem," "Per ipsum Regem & Concilium" (*Foedera* 7:302,
305, 315). Cf. the litany for feria 2 in Quadragesima, "Per Passionem et Crucem tuam, Libera nos Domine," *Brev.* 2:252.

B.14.212a *Ita inpossibile* [*possibile* 11 MSS] *diuiti &c.* Cf. Matt. 19:23,
". . . quia dives difficile intrabit in regnum caelorum"; Mk. 10:25,
Lk. 18:25. [C.11.201a]

B.14.213a (C.16.54a) *Opera enim illorum sequuntur illos.* Apoc. 14:13, said in the Mass for the Dead, *Missale* 863*, *Brev.* 2:524.

B.14.215a *Beati pauperes* [*pauperes spiritu* Vulg., B var.] *quoniam ipsorum est regnum celorum.* Matt. 5:3; as here, *spiritu* is often omitted in patristic quotations of the passage, probably under the influence of Lk. 6:20, "Beati pauperes, quia vestrum est regnum Dei"; similarly, *spiritu* is sometimes added as a gloss to *pauperes* in Luke 6:20 (Glunz 188).

B.14.276 (C.16.116)
> "*Paupertas*," quod Pacience, "*est odibile bonum, Remocio curarum, possessio sine calumpnia, donum dei, sanitatis mater, absque sollicitudine semita, sapiencie temperatrix, negocium sine dampno, Incerta fortuna, absque sollicitudine felicitas.*"

Popular definition attributed to Secundus Philosophus, quoted by Vincent of Beauvais, John Bromyard, Hugh of St. Cher, Chaucer, and others; see A. V. C. Schmidt, "Two Notes," *N&Q*, ns 16 (1969): 168–69, and Alford 1975. [B.286a, 293a, 296a, 300a, 303a, 309, 312a, 315a, 320a (C.16.122a, 128a, 136a, 138a, 143a, 146a, 149a, 155a)]

—C.16.117 "Y can nat construe al this," quod *Actiua vita.* [B.13.224 (C.15.193), B.14.28, C.15.272, C.18.80, C.18.82a]

B.14.286a (C.16.123a) *Ergo paupertas est odibile bonum.* This excerpt from Patience's definition of poverty at B.14.276 is sometimes quoted alone: "Unde secundus philosophus, interrogatus quid esset paupertas? Respondit odibile bonum" (Voragine, Sermo 1, Dom. 2 post oct. Epiph., 49). [B.14.276 (C.16.116)]

B.14.286 And Contricion confort and *cura animarum.* "The cure of souls," technically defined as "the exercise of a clerical office involving the instruction, by sermons and admonitions, and the sanctification, through the sacraments, of the faithful in a determined district, by a person legitimately appointed for the purpose," *The Catholic Encyclopedia* (New York: The Encyclopedia Press, 1913), 4:572. [cf. B.20.233 (C.22.233)]

B.14.292 (C.16.127) *Ergo* pouerte and poore men parfournen þe comaundement. [B.8.24 (A.9.20, C.10.28), B.14.62 (C.15.261), B.14.287 (C.16.122a), B.18.340 (C.20.388), B.19.19 (C.21.19)]

B.14.292a (C.16.128) *Nolite iudicare quemquam.* [B.11.90 (C.12.31), B.12.89a]

B.14.293a (C.16.128a) *Remocio curarum.* [B.14.276 (C.16.116)]

B.14.296a (C.16.132a) *Possessio sine calumpnia.* [B.14.276 (C.16.116)]

B.14.300a (C.16.136a) *Donum dei.* [B.14.276 (C.16.116)]

B.14.303a (C.16.138a) *Sanitatis mater.* [B.14.276 (C.16.116)]

B.14.307a *Cantabit paupertas coram latrone viator.* Juvenal, "Cantabit

vacuus coram latrone viator" (*Satires* 10.22); quoted frequently,
e.g., Matthew of Vendome, *Ars Versificatoria*, ed. E. Faral, *Les Arts
poétiques du XII et du XIII siècle* (Paris: Champion, 1962), 138;
Bernard of Cluny, *De Contemptu Mundi* 2.349, ed. and trans.
Ronald E. Pepin (East Lansing, Mich.: Colleagues Press, 1991), 96;
numerous other examples in Walther 2306. The substitution of
paupertas for *vacuus* appears also in Bromyard 1:86/1; and Duran-
dus, *Speculum Iuris*, lib. 3, "De accusatione" (Basel, 1574; repr.
Aalen: Scientia, 1975), 2:15. The saying is translated by Chaucer in
the Wife of Bath's tale (*CT* III 1193-94), and in *Pilgrimage of the
Life of Man*: "I am 'Wylleffull Pouerte;' And, off myne owne
volunte, I despyse alle rychesse; Slepe in Ioye and sekyrnesse, Nor
theves may not robbe me" (EETS es 77 [1899], 605-6).

B.14.309a (C.16.143a) Forþi seiþ Seneca *Paupertas est absque sollicitudine semita*. No source in Seneca has been identified; the saying
has already been quoted above, B.14.276 (C.16.116).

B.14.312a (C.16.146a) *Sapiencie temperatrix*. [B.14.276 (C.16.116)]

B.14.315a (C.16.149a) *Negocium sine dampno*. [B.14.276 (C.16.116)]

B.14.320a (C.16.155a) *Absque sollicitudine felicitas*. [B.14.276 (C.16.116)]

—**C.16.158, 162, 165, 173, 182, etc.** *Liberum arbitrium*. [B.16.16 etc.]

Passus 15

B.15.23 (C.16.183) The whiles I quykne þe cors ... called am I
anima. [B.15.39a (C.16.201a); see also B.9.7 (A.10.7, C.10.134),
etc.]

B.15.24 (C.16.184) And whan I wilne and wolde *animus* ich hatte.
[B.15.39a (C.16.201a)]

B.15.25 (C.16.185) And for þat I kan and knowe called am I *mens*.
[B.15.39a (C.16.201a)]

B.15.26 (C.16.186) And whan I make mone to god *memoria* is my
name. [B.15.39a (C.16.201a), B.20.366 (C.22.366)]

B.15.28 (C.16.188) Thanne is *Racio* my riȝte name, reson on
englissh. [B.15.39a (C.16.201a)]

B.15.29 (C.16.189) And whan I feele þat folk telleþ my firste name is
sensus. [B.15.39a (C.16.201a)]

—**C.16.194** Thenne am y *liberum Arbitrium*. [B.16.16, etc.]

B.15.34 (C.16.196) Thanne is lele loue my name, and in latyn *Amor*.
[B.15.39a (C.16.201a)]

B.15.36 (C.16.198) *Spiritus* þanne ich hatte. [B.15.39a (C.16.201a)]
B.15.39a (C.16.201a)

> *Anima pro diuersis accionibus diuersa nomina sortitur: dum viuificat corpus anima est; dum vult animus est; dum scit mens est; dum recolit memoria est; dum iudicat racio est; dum sentit sensus est; dum amat Amor est;* [*dum declinat de malo ad bonum, liberum Arbitrium est* added C]; *dum negat vel consentit consciencia est; dum spirat spiritus est.*

Isidore of Seville, *Etymologiae* 11.1.13. Skeat criticizes L's rendering of *recolit* in lines 26 ("make mone to God") as a mistranslation (2:215); Pearsall calls it "odd" (268n185). However, the translation is perfectly explicable as a reference to confession. "As Boethius and Augustine so clearly emphasize," Russell Peck notes in another connection, "confession is remembering" (ed., *Confessio Amantis* [New York: Holt, 1968], xvi). Cf. the phrase "to recollect oneself to God" (cited above, B.4.120). [B.9.7 (A.10.7, C.10.134), B.9.16 (C.10.142), B.9.23 (C.10.149), B.9.55 (A.10.44, C.10.172), B.9.59 (A.10.47, C.10.174), B.15.23 (C.16.183)]
B.15.41–43 (C.16.203–5)

> For bisshopes yblessed bereþ manye names,
> *Presul* and *Pontifex* and *Metropolitanus*,
> And oþere names an heep, *Episcopus* and *Pastor*.

The point is a common one, based primarily on the discussion in Gratian, *CIC* 1:67 ff. [B.15.516 (C.17.267)]
B.15.51a (C.16.213a) *Ponam pedem meum in aquilone & similis ero altissimo* [*& . . . altissimo* om. C]. [B.1.119 (C.1.111a)]
B.15.55 (C.16.217) And seiþ, *Sicut qui mel comedit multum* [*multum comedit* Vulg., *comedit multum* Hugh] *non est ei bonum, Sic qui scrutator est maiestatis opprimitur a gloria.* Prov. 25:27.
B.15.60–61 (C.16.222–23)

> "*Beatus est,*" seiþ Seint Bernard, "*qui scripturas legit
> Et verba vertit in opera* fulliche to his power."

Bernard, *Tractatus de Ordine Vitae* (*PL* 184:566): "Beatus qui divinas Scripturas legens, verba vertit in opera." This is closer to L's quotation than the version in Bernard's epistle 201, cited by Skeat, though neither is necessarily the source. The idea, common throughout Bernard's writings, is probably based on Matt. 7:24 ("Everyone therefore that heareth these my words, and doth them, shall be likened to a wise man that built his house upon a rock"), concerning which Pseudo-Chrysostom comments, "Verba enim, quae non convertuntur ad opus, arena sunt spargibilis" (*PG* 56:746).
B.15.63a (C.16.225a) *Sciencie appetitus hominem inmortalitatis gloriam*

spoliauit. Bernard, *Sermo IV in Ascensione Domini* (*PL* 183:311), quoted by Hugh on Eph. 4:9; see Alford 1975.

B.15.69 (C.16.229–30) That is *Non plus sapere quam oportet sapere.* [B.10.121 (A.11.74)]

B.15.81a *Confundantur omnes qui adorant sculptilia.* Ps. 96:7.

B.15.81b *Vt quid diligitis vanitatem & queritis mendacium?* Ps. 4:3.

B.15.88 (C.16.241a) That seide to hise disciples, *"Ne sitis personarum acceptores"* [transposed B var., C]. Probably a legal maxim; echoes a number of biblical texts, e.g., Lev. 19:15, Deut. 1:17, Prov. 24:23, Acts 10:34, and esp. James 2:1 (cf. Hugh's very full comment); see Alford 1988b.

B.15.115 Ye aren enblaunched wiþ *bele paroles* and wiþ *bele* cloþes. Allusion to Matt. 23:27, perhaps triggered by Jas. 2:2 ("vir ... in veste candida"), continued from Jas. 2:1 above. See A. V. C. Schmidt, *"Lele Wordes* and *Bele Paroles*: Some Aspects of Langland's Word-Play," *RES* ns 34 (1983): 137–50.

B.15.118 (C.16.273)

> *Sicut de templo omne bonum progreditur, sic de templo omne malum procedit. Si sacerdocium integrum fuerit tota floret ecclesia; Si autem corruptum fuerit omnium fides marcida est. Si sacerdocium fuerit in peccatis totus populus conuertitur ad peccandum. Sicut cum videris arborem pallidam & marcidam intelligis quod vicium habet in radice, Ita cum videris populum indisciplinatum & irreligiosum, sine dubio sacerdocium eius non est sanum.*

Gloss on Matt. 21:12 ff., attributed to John Chrysostom (Homily 38, *PG* 56:839).

B.15.125 Ac a Porthors þat sholde be his Plow, *Placebo* to sigge. [B.3.311 (C.3.464), C.5.46]

B.15.149a (C.16.298a) *Nisi [conuersi fueritis et] efficiamini sicut paruuli non intrabitis in regnum celorum [non ... celorum* om. C]. Matt. 18:3. L is not alone in omitting the words *conuersi fueritis et;* cf. *Prick of Conscience* 398–99 (12): "Nisi efficiamini sicut parvulus, non intrabitis in regnum celorum."

B.15.157 (C.16.291a) *Non inflatur, non est ambiciosa, non querit que sua sunt [non ... sunt* om. C]. 1 Cor. 13:4–5.

B.15.162a (C.16.296a) *Hic in enigmate, tunc facie ad faciem.* 1 Cor. 13:12, "Videmus nunc per speculum in aenigmate: tunc autem facie ad faciem."

—C.16.309 *Quodcumque vultis vt faciant vobis homines, facite eis.* [B.7.60a]

—C.16.320 Oen *aperis-tu-manum* alle thynges hym fyndeth. [B.14.63a, C.15.262a]

B.15.179 (C.16.321) *Fiat voluntas tua* fynt hym eueremoore. Matt. 6:10. [C.5.88, B.14.50 (C.15.249); cf. C.5.46, B.10.468, B.13.396 (C.6.283), C.16.323, C.16.374a, B.19.394a (C.21.394a)]

—**C.16.322** And also a can clergie, *credo in deum patrem*. [B.10.473, B.15.608 (C.17.316); cf. C.3.357, C.3.481]

B.15.180 And if he soupeþ eteþ but a sop of *Spera in deo*. [B.11.287 (C.13.101)]

—**C.16.323** And purtraye wel þe paternoster and peynten hit with Auees. The Lord's Prayer [C.5.46, C.5.87, C.5.107, B.5.341 (A.5.189, C.6.399), B.5.394 (C.7.10), B.10.468, B.13.396 (C.6.283), B.14.49 (C.15.247)] and the Ave Maria (*Brev.* 2:2).

B.15.191 (C.16.333) And leggen on longe wiþ *Laboraui in gemitu meo*. Ps. 6:7, one of the "Penitential Psalms" (see B.13.53).

—**C.16.335a** [*Asperges me hyssopo, et mundabor;*] *Lauabis me & super niuem dealbabor*. Ps. 50:9, one of the seven "Penitential Psalms" (see B.13.53). L's association of the verse with the tears of contrition (line 335) is conventional; see Gratian, *CIC* 1:186; Brinton 1:84. Cf. *The Play of the Sacrament*, line 680 (Manly 1:268), "Lord, by the water of contrycion lett me aryse: *Asparges me, Domine, ysopo, et mundabor*."

B.15.194 (C.16.336a) *Cor contritum & humiliatum deus non despicies*. Ps. 50:19 (see above). [B.13.58a (C.15.62)]

B.15.200a (C.16.340a) *Et vidit* [*i.e.* God] *deus cogitaciones eorum*. Lk. 11:17, "Ipse autem ut vidit [i.e. Jesus] cogitationes eorum"; cf. Matt. 9:4. Schmidt (344) suggests that L "heightens the effect" by substituting God for Jesus in the quotation.

—**C.16.342a** *Operibus credite* [*ut cognoscatis, et credatis quia Pater in me est, et ego in Patre*]. Jn. 10:38.

B.15.212 But Piers þe Plowman, *Petrus id est christus*. An association based on 1 Cor. 10:4, "Petra autem erat Christus," and reflected in numerous comments, e.g., Hugh on Deut. 32:13, Ps. 39:3, Ps. 77:15–16, 20, Ps. 136:9, Is. 48:21, Matt. 16:18. For interpretations of the phrase, see Alford 1988a, 55–56.

B.15.215 Fy on faitours and *in fautores suos*! Legal phrase common in both canon and common law; see Gray 60 and Alford 1988b.

B.15.219a (C.16.344a) [*Cum autem ieiunatis*] *Nolite fieri sicut ypocrite tristes &c*. Matt. 6:16, antiphon sung at lauds on Ash Wednesday, *Brev.* 1:dlvii.

B.15.234a (C.16.359a) *Beatus est* [*est om. B var.*] *diues* [*sine macula C*] *qui &c*. Ecclus. 31:8, "Beatus dives qui inventus est sine macula, et qui post aurum non abiit." [cf. B.14.104 (C.15.279)]

—**C.16.374a** *Panem nostrum cotidianum, &c*. Matt. 6:11, part of the

Lord's Prayer; other parts quoted at C.5.46, C.5.88, B.10.468, B.13.396 (C.6.283), B.14.50 (C.15.249), B.15.179 (C.16.321), C.16.323, B.19.394a (C.21.394a).

B.15.254a *In pace in idipsum dormiam [et requiescam].* Ps. 4:9; prayer in the ordinary of compline, *Brev.* 2:239; antiphon sung on Holy Saturday, *Brev.* 1:dccxcv. [B.18.186–87 (C.20.191–92)]

B.15.268 *Pacientes Vincunt verbi gracia,* and verred ensamples manye. [B.13.171a (C.15.156a), B.13.135a (C.15.137), B.14.33c, B.14.54 (C.15.253), B.15.598a]

B.15.269 Lo! in *legenda sanctorum,* þe lif of holy Seintes. [B.11.161, B.11.220, C.17.157]

—C.17.5a *Caritas omnia suffert.* 1 Cor. 13:7, "[Caritas] omnia suffert, omnia credit, omnia sperat, omnia sustinet" (cf. C.16.291a, 296a).

—C.17.23 Marie *Egipciaca* eet in thritty wynter. St. Mary of Egypt; her name appears in the *Legenda Aurea* (cited at B.11.161, B.11.220, B.15.269, and C.17.157) as *Maria Ægyptiaca* (Pearsall).

B.15.286 (C.17.13) Poul *primus heremita* hadde parroked hymselue. Paul of Thebes, first of the desert fathers. The title "primus heremita" is used by both Jerome and Peter the Cantor (Skeat 2:223–24); it appears also in *Pierce the Ploughmans Crede* (line 308), possibly borrowed from this passage: "We friers be þe first and founded vpon treuþe. / Paul *primus [heremita]* put vs him-selue / Awey into wildernes . . ." (EETS 30). Concerning the place of Paul *primus heremita* in the antimendicant tradition, see Scase 94–95.

—C.17.40a *Videte ne furtum sit.* Tobias 2:21, "Videte, ne forte furtivus sit, reddite eum dominis suis, quia non licet nobis aut edere ex furto aliquid, aut contingere"; cf. Bromyard 2:473/1, "Videte ne forte furtivum sit. Thob. 2"; Matthew of Vendome, *Tobias,* "Reddite, Tobias clamat, furtiva videte" (*PL* 205:941).

—C.17.40a *Melius est mori quam male viuere &c.* [C.1.143a, C.6.290a]

B.15.318 (C.17.53) *Numquid, dicit Iob [dicit Iob* om. Vulg.]*, rugiet onager cum herbam habuerit [habuerit herbam* Vulg., B var., C] *aut mugiet bos cum ante plenum presepe [praesepe plenum* Vulg.] *steterit? brutorum animalium natura te condempnat, quia cum eis pabulum commune sufficiat; ex adipe prodijt iniquitas tua.* Job 6:5; the second part of the quotation ("brutorum animalium . . .") probably comes from a commentary. Skeat (2:225) cites similar wording in Bruno's *Expositio in Librum Iob:* "Vel ipsa vos bruta animalia doceant, qui quandiu necessarii abundant, neque r[u]giunt, neque mugiunt" (Venice: Bertanos, 1651), 329.

—C.17.59a *Honora patrem & matrem &c.* [B.5.567a (C.7.216a)]

B.15.327 *Dispersit, dedit pauperibus? [Iusticia eius manet in saeculum* *saeculi* added B var.]. Ps. 111:9, 2 Cor. 9:9; versicle, feast of St. Lawrence, *Brev.* 3:655 (see also *Missale* 856). On the biblical and liturgical contexts of the verse, see M. T. Tavormina, "*Piers Plowman* and the Liturgy of St. Lawrence," *SP* 84 (1987): 245–71. The verse also served as an after-dinner grace, "Dispersit, dedit pauperibus: Iusticia eius manet in seculum seculi" (*Graces* 383), continued below in the C version.

—**C.17.66a** *Iusticia eius manet in eternum* [*in saeculum saeculi* Vulg., C var.; *in aeternam*, Ps. iuxta Heb.]. Ps. 111:9 (see Tavormina, ibid.), 111:3, Ps. 110:3, 2 Cor. 9:9. Ambrose consistently quotes the verse as "iustitia ejus manet *in aeternum*" (e.g., *PL* 14:777, 16:1456). A continuation of the grace begun in B.15.327.

B.15.343a

> *Quia sacrilegium est res pauperum non pauperibus dare. Item, peccatoribus dare est demonibus immolare. Item, monache, si indiges & accipis pocius das quam accipis; Si autem non eges & accipis rapis. Porro non indiget monachus si habeat quod nature sufficit.*

Skeat (2:226) identifies these lines as a pastiche of quotations from St. Jerome, also found together in Peter the Cantor, *Verbum Abbreviatum* (*PL* 205), "Sacrilegium est res pauperum dare non pauperibus" (col. 147, quoting Jerome, *Epist.* 66, sect. 8, "Pars sacrilegii est rem pauperum dare non pauperibus"); "vitio nunquam dederis, quia paria sunt, et dare peccatoribus, et immolare daemonibus" (col. 149); "Maximum periculum est, de patrimonio crucifixi pauperibus non dare" (col. 152); "O monache, si indiges et accipis, potius das quam accipis; si non indiges et accipis, rapis, quia distribuenda pauperibus tibi usurpas" (col. 152); "Paria sunt histrionibus dare, et daemonibus immolare" (col. 155). Other examples or variants of the first quotation are given in Scase 99–100 and 205n58. The last quotation ("Porro non indiget...") seems to be a reminiscence of 1 Tim. 6:8, "Habentes autem alimenta, et quibus tegamur, his contenti simus." See also C.7.118a, B.9.94a.

B.15.382 And answere to Argument3 and assoile a *Quodlibet.* "Any question in philosophy or theology proposed as an exercise in argument or disputation" (*Oxford English Dictionary*). In contrast to the ordinary academic disputations, usually centered on a theme, quodlibetal disputations could be on any topic whatever and took place twice a year, in Advent and Lent. More than 350 sets of quodlibetal questions have come down to us; see P. Glorieux, *La Littérature quodlibetique*, 2 vols. (Paris, 1925–35). Cf. *Contra* at B.8.20 (A.9.16, C.10.20).

B.15.388 (C.17.120) As clerkes in *Corpus Christi* feeste syngen and reden. "The feast of Corpus Christi was held on the Thursday after Trinity Sunday, in memory, as was supposed, of the miraculous confirmation of the doctrine of transubstantiation under Pope Urban IV; it was instituted between 1262 and 1264, and confirmed by the council of Vienne in 1311" (Skeat 2:227).

B.15.389 (C.17.121) That *sola fides sufficit* to saue wiþ lewed peple. From the hymn *Pange lingua gloriosi* (stanza four: *Ad firmandum cor sincerum Sola fides sufficit*), sung at Lauds on Corpus Christi day (*Brev.* 1:mlxiv).

—C.17.140a *Dilige deum propter deum, id est propter veritatem; & inimicum tuum propter mandatum, id est propter legem; & Amicum propter Amorem, id est propter caritatem.* Unidentified. [cf. A.11.242, B.13. 127 (C.15.134), C.15.140, B.15.584, B.17.13 (C.19.14)]

—C.17.157 By þe legende *sanctorum*. [B.11.161, B.11.220, B.15.269]

—C.17.163–64

> *Beaute sanȝ bounte* blessed was hit neuere
> Ne kynde *sanȝ cortesie* in no contreye is preysed.

The first line is part of a well-known proverb (Whiting B152); the phrase in the second line has not been identified.

B.15.428a *Petite & accipietis* [*querite & inuenietis pulsate (et aperietur vobis)* added from Matt. 7:7 in B var.; cf. B.15.503a]. Jn. 16:24, antiphon sung on fifth Sunday after Easter, *Brev.* 1:dccccxlix, *Missale* 409.

B.15.429a *Vos estis sal terre &c.* Matt. 5:13.

B.15.431a *Et* [*Quod* Vulg.] *si sal euanuerit in quo salietur?* Matt. 5:13, continued from above.

B.15.464a *Ecce altilia mea & omnia parata sunt.* Matt. 22:4, "Ecce prandium meum paravi, tauri mei et altilia occisa sunt, et omnia parata: venite ad nuptias."

B.15.490 Boþe Mathew and Marc and *Memento domine* dauid. Ps. 131:1. [A.11.55, C.11.49]

B.15.490a *Ecce audiuimus eam in effrata &c.* Ps. 131:6, continued from above. For the appropriateness of the quotation, see Schmidt 345–46. [B.10.69a (A.11.55a, C.11.49a)]

B.15.491a (C.17.191) *Ite in vniuersum mundum & predicate* [*euangelium* added B var.] *&c.* [*& . . . &c* om. C]. Mk. 16:15, "Et dixit eis: Euntes in mundum universum praedicate Evangelium omni creaturae" (quoted in Nico. 14:1); L's wording reflects the *Vetus Latina,* "Ite in universam orbem, & praedicate Evangelium omni creaturae"; cf. the response on Ascension day, *Brev.* 1:dccclxv: "Ite in orbem universum et . . ."; cf. Matt. 28:19.

B.15.497a (C.17.193a) *Bonus pastor animam suam ponit* [*pro ouibus suis* C] *&c.* Jn. 10:11, "Bonus pastor animam suam dat pro ovibus suis." *Ponit* is the Old Latin reading. Cf. Ambrose on Ps. 118: "Bonus pastor animam sua ponit pro ovibus suis"; also Gregory's *Moralia* (Glunz 17, 21); Voragine 152; Hilarius on Ps. 131, the first lesson at matins on the second Sunday after Easter (*Brev.* 1:dcccxciii); and Hugh of St. Cher on Jn. 10:11. [C.17.291a]

B.15.500 *Ite* [*et*] *vos in vineam meam &c.* Matt. 20:4. [B.10.481a]

B.15.503a *Querite & inuenietis &c.* Matt. 7:7, antiphon sung at lauds on Rogation Monday, *Brev.* 1:dcccclii. [Cf. B.14.46a var. (C.15. 244a), B.15.428a var.]

B.15.516 (C.17.267) And bicam man of a maide and *metropolitanus.* See B.15.41–43 (C.16.203–5).

B.15.530a *Nolite mittere falsem in messem alienam.* Canon law maxim, derived from Deut. 23:25 ("Si intraveris in segetem amici tui, franges spicas, et manu conteres: falce autem non metes"). Gray states that the process of modification begins in Gratian's *Decretum,* causa 6, q. 3, c. 1 ("Alterius parochianum alicui iudicare non licet: Scriptum est in lege: 'Per alienam messem transiens falcem mittere non debes, sed manu spicas conterere et manducare.' Falcem enim iudicii mittere non debes in ea segete, que alteri uidetur esse conmissa"), though in fact modification appears much earlier in Gregory's comment on the verse ("Falcem judicii mittere non potes in eam segetem, quae alteri videtur esse commissa"). As Gray notes, "The maxim is used, in *Piers Plowman* as in canon law and the penitential texts, as the *auctoritas* prohibiting confessors from hearing the confessions of those who come under another's jurisdiction." See also Scase 37–38. The maxim appears as well in the commentary on the school text *Facetus* (*Auctores Octo*). Further discussion in Alford 1988b. [C.17.280a]

B.15.537a (C.17.198a) *Absit nobis* [*mihi* B var.] *gloriari nisi in cruce domini nostri &c.* Gal. 6:14, "Mihi autem absit gloriari, nisi in cruce Domini nostri Iesu Christi." The plural appears also in Ambrose, *Liber de Tobia,* cap. 20, "Nobis autem absit gloriari, nisi in cruce Domini Jesu" (*PL* 14:825). Cf. Feria tertia post Dominicam in Ramis Palmarum: "Nos autem gloriari oportet in cruce Domini nostri Jesu Christi" (*Missale* 277; also 300, 742, 748*).

B.15.552 (C.17.215) Shal þei demen *dos ecclesie,* and depose yow for youre pride. "The endowment of the Church"; for commentary see Pearsall 288 and Scase 84. [B.15.560 (C.17.223)]

B.15.552a (C.17.215a) *Deposuit potentes de sede* [*et exaltavit humiles*]. Lk. 1:52; the Magnificat (*Brev.* 2:221). [cf. A.10.120a]

B.15.556 (C.17.219) And lyuen as *Leuitici* as oure lord yow techeþ. The Levites or priests of Israel (cf. B.12.113, "*Archa dei*, in þe olde lawe, leuytes it kepten"). As in C.5.55 concerning "þe lawe of *leuyticy*," the allusion is to Num. 18:20-24, where the Lord ordains that Levites "shall possess nothing" but shall live off the tithes of Israel. [C.5.55]

B.15.556a (C.17.219a) *Per primicias & decimas &c.* Unidentified. Although both Schmidt and Pearsall, following Skeat, cite Deut. 12:6 ("Et offeretis in loco illo holocausta et victimas vestras, decimas et primitias manuum vestrarum"), this verse has little to do with L's argument on priests' livings. That *Levitici* should be supported *per primicias & decimas* is based on Num. 18 (see above), and L's wording may derive from a comment on, or a tract inspired by, this *locus classicus*.

B.15.560 (C.17.223) *Dos ecclesie* þis day haþ ydronke venym. [B.15.552 (C.17.215)]

—**C.17.235a** *Mihi vindictam &c.* [B.6.226a, B.10.209a, B.10.374 (A.11.255), B.19.446a (C.21.446a)]

—**C.17.238** The pope with alle prestes *pax vobis* sholde make. Lk. 24:36, Jn. 20:19, 21, 26; said with the kiss of peace (in the singular, *pax tibi*) in the mass (*Missale* 624); cf. Nico. 27:2. [B.19.169 (C.21.169)]

B.15.576a *In domo mea non est panis neque vestimentum et ideo nolite constituere me Regem.* Isa. 3:7, "Et in domo mea non est panis neque vestimentum; nolite constituere me principem populi."

B.15.578 *Inferte omnes decimas in orreum meum vt cibus in domo mea.* Mal. 3:10, "Inferte omnem decimam in horreum, et sit cibus in domo mea." For L's readings *orreum meum* and *ut*, see Hugh, "Inferte omnem decimam in horreum meum, ut sit cibus in domo mea"; Gratian, *CIC* 1:800, "Inferte omnem decimationem in horreum meum, ut sit cibus in domo mea."

—**C.17.280a** *Nolite mittere falcem in messem alienam &c.* [B.15.530a]

—**C.17.285a–b**

> In baculi forma sit, presul, hec tibi norma;
>
> Fer, trahe, punge gregem, seruando per omnia legem.

"Leonine verses, closely resembling three lines copied in B.L. MS Lansdowne 397, f. 9ᵛ" (Pearsall 290, after Walther, *Initia Carminum ac Versum Medii Aevi Posterioris Latinorum* no. 8828); how "closely" is problematic, since Walther cites only the incipit "In baculi forma." On the symbolism of the bishop's *baculus* see C.10.95. Such verses on the *baculus pastoris* are commonplace. Five examples appear in Robert of Flamborough, *Liber Poenitentialis*

(Toronto: Pontifical Institute of Mediaeval Studies, 1971), 115.

—**C.17.291a** *Bonus pastor &c.* [B.15.497a (C.17.193a)]

B.15.584 *Dilige deum & proximum* is parfit Iewen lawe. Cf. Deut. 6:5, "Diliges Dominum Deum tuum," and Lev. 19:18, "Diliges amicum tuum," conflated in Matt. 22:37–40, Mk. 12:30, Lk. 10:27; cf. James 2:8. [A.11.242, B.13.127 (C.15.134), C.15.140, B.17.13 (C.19.14); cf. C.17.140a]

B.15.594a *Laȝare veni foras.* Jn. 11:43. [cf. below]

—**C.17.303** *Quadriduanus* coeld quyk dede hym walke. Jn. 11:39, "Domine, iam foetet, quatriduanus est enim." [B.16.114 (C.18.144)]

B.15.598a *Pacientes vincunt* [*Maliciam* added B var.]. [B.13.135a (C.15.137), B.13.171a (C.15.156a), B.14.33c, B.14.54 (C.15.253), B.15.268]

B.15.600 *Cum sanctus sanctorum veniat cessabit vnxio vestra.* The prophecy is derived from Dan. 9:24–27 (see Hugh's comment), though the wording is from the pseudo-Augustinian sermon *Contra Judaeos* (*PL* 42:1124), as used in a lesson for the fourth Sunday in Advent, "Dic, sancte Daniel, dic de Christo quod nosti. Cum venerit, inquit, Sanctus sanctorum, cessabit unctio vestra" (*Brev.* 1:cxxxvii). [B.18.109a (C.20.112a)]

B.15.601 (C.17.309) And ȝit wenen þo wrecches þat he were *pseudopropheta.* Matt. 24:11, "Et multi pseudoprophetae surgent ..."; a verse made familiar by antimendicant writings (see Szittya 56, 61, 87, 175, 177, 226).

B.15.608–13 (C.17.316–21)

> Konne þe firste clause of oure bileue, *Credo in deum patrem omnipotentem* [*omnipotentem* om. C]
> Prelates of cristene prouinces sholde preue if þei myȝte
> Lere hem litlum and litlum *et in Iesum Christum filium,*
> Til þei kouþe speke and spelle *et in Spiritum sanctum,*
> Recorden it and rendren it wiþ *remissionem peccatorum*
> *Carnis resurreccionem et vitam eternam amen.*

The Apostles' Creed, *Brev.* 2:2. [B.10.473, C.16.322; cf. C.3.357, C.3.481]

Passus 16

—**C.18.1, 3** *Liberum Arbitrium.* [B.16.16, etc.]

—**C.18.4** Til we cam into a contre, *cor hominis* hit heihte. A common expression in the Bible; most pertinent to the context is 1 Cor. 2:9, "Sed sicut scriptum est: Quod oculos non vidit, nec auris

audivit, nec in cor hominis ascendit, quae praeparavit Deus iis qui
diligunt illum."
—**C.18.7** That hihte *ymago dei*, graciousliche hit growede. Cf. Gen.
1:27, "Et creavit Deus hominem ad imaginem suam: ad imaginem
Dei creavit illum . . ."; Gen. 9:6, "ad imaginem quippe Dei factus
est homo"; 1 Cor. 11:7, 2 Cor. 4:4, Col. 1:15. L's use of the phrase
may owe something to the hymn *Nos ymago Trinitatis, Brev.* 2:321 (*In
festo Yconiae Domini Salvatoris*); the preceding antiphon, "Fructus
ligni perdidit genus hujus seculi," may have suggested the tree
imagery. Extended discussion of the concept of *imago Dei* appears
in Daniel M. Murtaugh, *Piers Plowman and the Image of God*
(Gainesville: University Presses of Florida, 1978). For a discussion
of the tree imagery, see Ben H. Smith, *Traditional Imagery of
Charity in Piers Plowman* (The Hague: Mouton, 1966), esp. 60. [Cf.
B.5.486a]
—**C.18.14** The whiche is *Caritas* ykald, Cristes oune fode. [B.2.35,
C.14.14, C.18.32, C.18.39]
B.16.16 And *liberum arbitrium* haþ þe lond to ferme. "Free will"; for
the history and definition of the phrase, see A. V. C. Schmidt,
"Langland and Scholastic Philosophy," *MAE* 38 (1969): 134–56.
[C.16.158, C.16.162, C.16.165, C.16.173, C.16.182, C.16.194,
C.18.1, C.18.3, C.18.104, B.16.46, B.16.50, C.18.137, C.18.179]
B.16.25a *Cum ceciderit iustus non collidetur quia dominus supponit
manum suam.* Ps. 36:24 (*iustus* appears in the *Vetus Latina* but is
dropped in the Vulgate). L's wording coincides with that of Hugh
of St. Cher and Richard Rolle (*The Psalter or Psalms of David and
Certain Canticles with a Translation and Exposition in English by
Richard Rolle of Hampole*, ed. H. R. Bramley [Oxford: Clarendon
Press, 1884]).
—**C.18.32** Couetyse cometh of þat wynde and *Caritas* hit abiteth.
[B.2.35, C.14.14, C.18.14, C.18.39]
B.16.30 (C.18.34) Thanne with þe firste pil I palle hym doun, *potencia dei patris.* For the seminal discussion of this aspect of the
Trinity, see Augustine, *De Trinitate*, beginning with book 6 ("How
the Apostle calls Christ 'the Power of God, and the Wisdom of
God' " [1 Cor. 1:24]).
—**C.18.39** And al forbit *Caritas* rihte to þe bare stalke. [B.2.35,
C.14.14, C.18.14, C.18.32]
B.16.36 (C.18.40) Thanne sette I to þe secounde pil, *sapiencia dei
patris.* Sapience or wisdom, that is, Christ, an identification based
primarily on 1 Cor. 1:24; see Augustine, *De Trinitate*, book 7, esp.
chap. 3, "Why the Son chiefly is intimated in the Scriptures by the

name of Wisdom"; cf. the morality play *Wisdom*, esp. the prologue (EETS 262 [1969], 114).

B.16.47a *Videatis qui peccat in spiritum sanctum numquam remittetur &c.* Matt. 12:32, "[Q]ui autem dixerit contra Spiritum sanctum, non remittetur ei"; cf. Mk. 3:29, Lk. 12:10. The substitution of *peccat* for *dixerit* represents a gloss on the verse (cf. Hugh on Matt. 12:32, "Quod aliquid fit peccatum in spiritum sanctum ..."), though it may also reflect earlier readings, e.g., "Qui autem in Spiritum Sanctum peccaverit," "Qui peccaverit in Spiritum Sanctum," "Quicunque in Spiritu Sancto peccaverit" (see critical notes to *VL*). Robertson and Huppé argue that Piers "quotes Matt. 12.32, but verses 30 and 31 are implied" (195). [B.17.200a-1 (C.19.166a-67)]

B.16.47b *Hoc est idem qui peccat per liberum arbitrium non repugnat.* Unidentified comment on the quotation above; the connection with Heb. 12:4, proposed by Skeat (2:236), is very tenuous. [cf. B.16.16 etc. (C.18.1 etc.)]

—C.18.51 The whiche is *spiritus sanctus* and sothfaste bileue. [C.3.406a, B.10.246a, B.16.90 (C.18.123)]

—C.18.80 That lyf *Actiua* lettred men in here langage calleth. [B.13.224 (C.15.193), B.14.28, C.15.272, C.16.117, C.18.82a]

—C.18.82a *Actiua vita & contemplatiua vita.* The division of Christian life into active and contemplative is commonplace. The biblical types are Martha and Mary (Lk. 10:38–42; see Hugh 6:195–96, and Brinton 2:352–53). [B.13.224 (C.15.193), B.14.28, C.15.272, C.16.117, C.18.80]

—C.18.104 Leue *liberum Arbitrium*, lat some lyf hit shake. [B.16.16 etc.]

B.16.84 (C.18.115) And made of holy men his hoord *In limbo Inferni.* "In the borderlands of hell"—according to Pearsall (298), "a common phrase," though he cites no other examples. The reference is evidently to the *limbus patrum*, since the inhabitants are called "holy men," but L's statement that the devil is "maister" of limbo—at variance with Church doctrine (see *The Catholic Encyclopedia* [New York: Encyclopedia Press, 1913], 9:257)—needs further study.

—C.18.117 Thenne moued hym moed *in magestate dei.* Source unidentified.

—C.18.118 That *libera voluntas dei* lauhte þe myddel Shoriare. Source unidentified (cf. C.20.20, *Liberum dei Arbitrium*).

B.16.88 (C.18.120) *Filius* by þe fader wille and frenesse of *spiritus sanctus.* [C.3.406a, B.10.246a, B.16.90 (C.18.123), B.16.186 (C.18.193), B.17.212, B.17.229 (C.19.195)]

B.16.90 (C.18.123) And þanne spak *spiritus sanctus* in Gabrielis
mouþe. Cf. Lk. 1:35, "Et respondens angelus [Gabriel] dixit ei:
Spiritus sanctus superveniet in te...." [C.3.406a, B.10.246a,
B.16.88 (C.18.120), B.16.90 (C.18.123), B.17.212]

B.16.93 (C.18.126) Til *plenitudo temporis* tyme comen were. Gal. 4:4,
"At ubi venit plenitudo temporis, misit Deus Filium suum factum
ex muliere, factum sub lege ..."; said during Advent, *Brev.* 1:c,
cxxxix, passim. Cf. *ME Sermons* 188 ("For þe holy apostell Poule
calleþ here [the Virgin] þe fulnesse of tyme"); also Bennett 184.
The verse is quoted in *FM* 236 as an example of attribution of the
Incarnation to the Father. [C.18.138]

B.16.99a (C.18.132a) *Ecce ancilla domini; fiat michi secundum verbum
tuum* [*fiat ... tuum* om. C]. Lk. 1:38; antiphon sung at compline in
the service of the Blessed Mary during Advent, *Brev.* 2:285, and on
Annunciation day, *Brev.* 3:245, passim.

—**C.18.137** Ac *liberum Arbitrium* lechecraeft hym tauhte. [B.16.16,
etc.]

—**C.18.138** Til *plenitudo temporis* hy tyme aprochede. [B.16.93
(C.18.126)]

B.16.110a *Non est sanis opus medicus set infirmis* [*male habentibus* B
var.]. Matt. 9:12, "Non est opus valentibus medicus, sed male
habentibus"; cf. Mk. 2:17, "Non necesse habent sani medico, sed
qui male habent," and Lk. 5:31, "Non egent qui sani sunt medico,
sed qui male habent." Conflation of these verses is common; e.g.,
Gratian, *CIC* 1:446, "Non est ... necessarius sanis medicus, sed
male habentibus." However, L's reading is close to that of the
Vetus Latina, "Non est opus sanis medicus, sed male habentibus,"
and closer still to St. Ambrose's, "Non opus est sanis medicus, sed
infirmis" (*Apologia Prophetae David, PL* 14:922).

—**C.18.141a** *Claudi Ambulant, leprosi mundantur.* Matt. 11:5, Lk. 7:22;
antiphon sung at vespers on the third Sunday in Advent, *Brev.* 1:cx.

B.16.114 (C.18.144) *Quatriduanus* quelt quyk dide hym walke. Jn.
11:39, "Domine, iam foetet, quatriduanus est enim," quoted in
Nico. 20:3. [C.17.303]

B.16.115 (C.18.145) Ac er he made þe maistrie *mestus cepit esse.* The
words suggest Matt. 26:37, "coepit ... moestus esse," but the
context points to Jn. 11:35, "Et lacrymatus est Iesus." As Pearsall
says, "L has here transferred the words used of the agony of
Christ in the garden to the description of his sorrowing ... before
the miracle of the raising of Lazarus" (299).

B.16.120a (C.18.150a) *Demonium habes &c.* Jn. 7:20, 8:48, 52; cf. Jn.
10:20.

B.16.135a *Domus mea domus oracionis vocabitur.* Matt. 21:13 (cf. Mk. 11:17, Lk. 19:46), quoting Isa. 56:7; said repeatedly at the dedication of a church (*Brev.* 1:mcccclv passim).

—**C.18.157a var.** *Eiecit ementes et vendentes de templo, etc.* (Skeat C.19. 159a). Matt. 21:12, "Et intravit Iesus in templum Dei, et eiiciebat omnes vendentes et ementes in templo...." The word order "ementes et vendentes" occurs in the *Vetus Latina.*

—**C.18.160a var.** *Intra triduum reedificabo illud* (Skeat C.19.162a). Matt. 26:61, "Possum destruere templum Dei, et post triduum reaedificare illud"; cf. Matt. 27:40, Mk. 15:29.

—**C.18.164a** [*Non in die festo,*] *Ne forte tumultus fieret in populo.* Matt. 26:5.

B.16.145 It was hymself sooþly and seide "*tu dicis.*" Matt. 26:25, "Tu dixisti."

B.16.151 (C.18.168) "*Aue, raby,*" quod þat Ribaud, and riȝt to hym he yede. Matt. 26:49. [B.18.50 (C.20.50)]

B.16.157a (C.18.174a) *Necesse est* [*enim*] *vt veniant scandala;* [*Necesse ... scandala* om. C][*verumtamen*] *ve homini illi per quem scandalum venit.* Matt. 18:7. Augustine also omits *verumtamen* (see variants listed in *VL*). [A.11.154a]

—**C.18.179** In inwit and in alle wittes aftur *liberum Arbitrium.* [B.16.16, etc.]

—**C.18.190** And, sondry to se vpon, *solus deus* he hoteth. The phrase is common; e.g., Ps. 85:10, Mk. 2:7, Lk. 5:21, Lk. 18:19. Cf. C.15.135a.

B.16.185 (C.18.192) *Pater* is his propre name, a persone by hymselue.

B.16.186 (C.18.193) The secounde of þat sire is Sothfastnesse *filius.* [B.16.88 (C.18.120), B.17.229 (C.19.195)]

—**C.18.213a** *Celi enarrant gloriam dei &c.* Ps. 18:1.

B.16.214a *Deus meus, Deus meus, vt quid dereliquisti me?* Matt. 27:46 or Mk. 15:34, quoting Ps. 21:2. "Christ's exclamation is taken to signify his humanity as distinct from his Godhead" (Robertson and Huppé 199n46).

B.16.219a (C.18.222a) *Maledictus homo qui non reliquit semen in Israel.* The closest example, and possibly L's source, comes from the *Hereford Breviary* (feast of St. Anne, 26 July): "*Lectio V.* Factum est autem cum appropinquaret dies magnus domini, id est encenio-rum, ruben, qui tunc princeps sacerdotum erat, ioachim inter conciues suos cum oblatione videns, despexit, et munera sua spreuit, dicens Indignum est o ioachim te munera deo offerre, eo quod non fecisti semen in israel, dicente scriptura, *Maledictum esse hominem qui semen non reliquerit in israel*" (ed. W. H. Frere and L.

E. G. Brown, 3 vols. [London: Bradshaw Society, 1904–15], 2:266). The identification comes from M. Teresa Tavormina, who provides a full genealogy of the quotation and a discussion of its relevance here "as a command to spiritual fruitfulness" ("'Maledictus qui non reliquit semen': The Curse on Infertility in *Piers Plowman* B.XVI and C.XVIII," *MAE* 58 [1989]: 117–25).

—**C.18.227** In a *simile* as Eue. Cf. Gen. 2:18, "Dixit quoque Dominus Deus: Non est bonum esse hominem solum: faciamus ei adiutorium simile sibi." M. Teresa Tavormina comments: "The phrase 'in a *simile*,' besides calling attention to the figure of speech underlying the whole passage, has at least two distinct applications to the Father:Son::Adam:Eve correspondence"; see her "Kindly Similitude: Langland's Matrimonial Trinity," *MP* 80 (1982): 124. [C.19.164]

B.16.223a *Spiritus procedens a patre & filio &c.* Athanasian Creed, "Spiritus Sanctus a Patre et Filio: non factus nec creatus nec genitus, sed procedens," *Brev.* 2:47. [cf. C.2.31, C.3.406a, B.10.246a, C.18.51]

—**C.18.238** "Lo! *treys encountre treys*," quod he, "in godhede and in manhede." Pearsall comments: "'Three is set against three.' *treys* is an AN [Anglo-Norman] term from dicing, from the game of hazard (cf. *CT* II.124, VI.653)." M. Teresa Tavormina adds: "An even more attractive possibility is that 'treys' may be the contracted form of *trey-as*, 'three-ace,' a throw of three and one (*OED*, s.v. 'trey' sb., 1c). This word, attested in the fourteenth century, would be an excellent linguistic symbol of tri-unity" ("Kindly Similitude: Langland's Matrimonial Trinity," *MP* 80 [1982]: 126n).

—**C.18.241a** *Tres vidit & vnum adorauit.* Antiphon sung on Quinquagesima Sunday, *Brev.* 1:dxli, dxlvi, and widely quoted as ocular proof of the Trinity (based on Gen. 18:2); see the discussion by Ruth Ames, *The Fulfillment of the Scriptures* (Evanston: Northwestern Univ. Press, 1970), 56–58. Other examples in Alford 1975.

—**C.18.264a** *Fiet vnum ouile & vnus pastor.* Jn. 10:16.

B.16.242a *Quam olim Abrahe promisisti & semini eius.* From the ordinary of the mass, *Missale* 596 (*Brev.* 2:485), and the Mass for the Dead, *Missale* 867* (*Brev.* 2:527); derived from Lk. 1:55, the Magnificat. See also Gen. 12:7, Rom. 4:13, and Gal. 3:16.

B.16.252a (C.18.268a) *Ecce agnus dei* [*qui tollit peccata mundi* added B var.] *&c.* Jn. 1:29, 36; cf. the canon of the mass (*Missale* 623, *Brev.* 2:495). [B.18.324 (C.20.367)]

Passus 17

B.17.1 (C.19.1) I am *spes*, a spie . . . and spire after a Knyght. Allusion to 1 Cor. 13:13, "Nunc autem manet, fides, spes, charitas: tria haec; maior autem horum est charitas." [B.12.29a, B.17.35 (C.19.36), B.17.48 (C.19.46), C.19.53, B.17.84 (C.19.80), C.19.97]

B.17.13 (C.19.14) *Dilige deum & proximum tuum.* [A.11.242, B.13.127 (C.15.134), C.15.140, B.15.584; cf. C.17.140a]

B.17.16 (C.19.17) *In hijs duobus mandatis tota* [*universa* Vulg.] *lex pendet & prophete* [*In hiis duobus pependit tota lex* C var.]. Matt. 22:40. Several early manuscripts of the *VL* read "tota lex pendet"; Hugh gives both *tota* and *universa*; the *Summa Virtutum* reads *tota* (107). *Tota* is also the reading in the Irish MS tradition (Glunz 235).

B.17.35 (C.19.36) And now comseþ *Spes* and spekeþ, þat haþ aspied þe lawe. [B.17.1 (C.19.1), etc.]

B.17.48 (C.19.46) "Go þi gate!" quod I to *Spes*. [B.17.1 (C.19.1), etc.]

B.17.58 (C.19.57) Ne helpe hymself sooþly, for semyvif [*semiuiuus* C var.] he semed. Lk. 10:30.

—C.19.53 Bothe abraham and *spes* and he mette at ones. [B.17.1 (C.19.1), etc.]

B.17.74 And ladde hym so forþ on Lyard to *lex Christi*, a graunge. Gal. 6:2, "Alter alterius onera portate, et sic adimplebitis legem Christi." Commentators gloss the Good Samaritan's action by reference to this verse (e.g., Hugh 6:195). Janet Coleman places L's usage of the phrase in the context of fourteenth-century theology (*Piers Plowman and the Moderni* [Rome: Edizioni de Storia e Letteratura, 1981], 28 and passim. [B.6.221a (C.8.230a), B.11. 211a, C.13.78a]

—C.19.73 And ladde hym forth to *lauacrum lex dei*, a grange. Pearsall notes: "*lavacrum-lex-dei*: 'the bath of the law of God,' i.e. the baptismal font" (309). *Lavacrum* may echo Titus 3:5: "Not by the works of justice, which we have done, but according to his mercy, he saved us, by the laver of regeneration [*per lavacrum regenerationis*]," which Hugh (7:235b) glosses as "per Baptismum."

B.17.84 (C.19.80) And *Spes* spakliche hym spedde. [B.17.1 (C.19.1), etc.]

B.17.91 How þat feiþ fleiʒ awey and *Spes* his felawe boþe. [B.17.1 (C.19.1), etc.]

B.17.103 Saue feiþ and myselue and *Spes* his felawe. [B.17.1 (C.19.1), etc.]

—C.19.97 As faith and his felawe *spes* enfourmede me bothe. [B.17.1 (C.19.1), etc.]

B.17.110 On my Capul þat highte *caro*—of mankynde I took it. Interpretation of the Samaritan's beast as Christ's body is traditional; see Bede's comment, quoted in Robertson and Huppé 205, and Hugh on Lk. 10:34. [B.9.50 (A.10.38)]

B.17.111 He was vnhardy, þat harlot, and hidde hym *in Inferno*. [cf. C.11.22a, B.18.149a (C.20.152a)]

B.17.114a *O mors ero mors tua* [*morsus tuus ero inferne* added B var.] *&c.* Antiphon sung during Holy Week (e.g., *Brev.* 1:dcclxxxii, dccci), based on Osee 13:14 (cf. 1 Cor. 15:55). [B.18.35a]

B.17.151a *Qui conceptus est de spiritu sancto &c.* Apostles' Creed, *Brev.* 2:2.

—**C.19.114a** *Mundum pugillo continens.* From the hymn *Quem terra pontus aethera*, sung at matins in the service of the Blessed Virgin Mary through Advent (*Brev.* 2:286), and in the office of the Annunciation (*Brev.* 2:235).

—**C.19.125a** *Natus est ex maria virgine.* Apostles' Creed, *Brev.* 2:2; cf. line 18 of the hymn above, "Qui natus es de Virgine."

B.17.152a (C.19.127a) [*Et ego si exaltatus fuero a terra*] *Omnia traham ad me ipsum.* [*Hoc autem dicebat, significans qua morte esset moriturus*]. Jn. 12:32–33. Cf. the verse based on this, sung in Holy Week, "Qui expansis in cruce manibus: traxisti omnia ad te secula" (*Brev.* 1:dcclxxxii).

B.17.170a (C.19.134a) *Tu fabricator omnium &c.* From the hymn *Jesu Salvator seculi*, sung in the office for compline (*Brev.* 2:234).

—**C.19.140a** *Dextere dei tu digitus.* From the hymn *Veni creator spiritus*, sung at the beginning of the ordinary of the mass (*Brev.* 2:481) and at Pentecost (*Brev.* 1:mix).

—**C.19.164** Bi this *simile* ... y se an euydence. [C.18.227]

B.17.200a–1 (C.19.166a-67)
Qui peccat in spiritum sanctum &c,
For he prikeþ god as in þe pawme þat *peccat in spiritum sanctum.*
Cf. Matt. 12:32, Mk. 3:29, Lk. 12:10. [B.16.47a]

B.17.212 So dooþ þe Sire and þe sone and also *spiritus sanctus.* [B.16.90 (C.18.123), etc.]

B.17.229 (C.19.195) And þanne flawmeþ he as fir on fader and on *filius.* [B.16.88 (C.18.120), B.16.186 (C.18.193)]

B.17.253a (C.19.219a) *Amen dico vobis, nescio vos &c.* [*vigilate itaque quia nescitis diem neque horam* added B var., from Matt. 25:13]. Matt. 25:12. [B.5.55, B.9.67a]

B.17.257 (C.19.223) And Indulgences ynowe, and be *ingratus* to þi kynde. See above, B.14.169, and the third lesson at matins on Ash Wednesday (*Brev.* 1:dlvi). Schmidt (349) notes Paul's description in 2 Tim. 3:2 ff. "of the *ingrati* who *resistunt veritati* 'resist the truth' (vs. 8)."

B.17.261a (C.19.227a) *Si linguis hominum loquar [& angelorum carita-tem non habuero nichil mihi prodest* added B var.]. 1 Cor. 13:1, "Si linguis . . . charitatem autem non habeam," *capitulum* for Quinqua-gesima Sunday (*Brev.* 1:dxxix, dlii). The reading "caritatem non habuero" appears also in *ME Sermons* 308.

B.17.266a (C.19.232a) *Non omnis qui dicit [mihi* Vulg., B var.] *domine, domine, intrabit [in regnum celorum set qui facit voluntatem* added B var., *in regnum celorum &c.,* C] [*Patris mei, qui in caelis est, ipse intrabit in regnum caelorum*]. Matt. 7:21. The pronoun *mihi* is also lacking in ancient versions of the Bible (see notes to *VL*) and in *ME Sermons* 155.

—**C.19.240a** *Epulabatur splendide & induebatur bisso &c.* Lk. 16:19, "Homo quidam erat dives, qui induebatur purpura et bysso, et epulabatur quotidie splendide." [B.14.123 (C.15.299)]

—**C.19.250a** *Facite vobis amicos de mammona iniquitatis.* Lk. 16:9. [B.6.228a (A.7.212a, C.8.234a)]

B.17.293a (C.19.274a) *Vindica sanguinem iustorum [Vindica domine sanguinem nostrum* B var.]. Apoc. 6:10, ". . . vindicas sanguinem nostrum . . ."; cf. the versicle for Holy Innocents' Day "Vindica sanguinem nostrum" (*Brev.* 1:cccvi) and the antiphon "Vindica, Domine, sanguinem sanctorum tuorum," followed by the versicle "Justorum animae . . ." (*Brev.* 1:ccxxxix).

B.17.310a (C.19.290a) *Numquam dimittitur peccatum &c. [nisi resti-tuatur ablatum* added B var.] [C.6.257a, B.5.273a]

B.17.318a (C.19.298a) *Misericordia eius super omnia opera eius.* [B.5. 281a, B.11.139a (C.12.74a)]

B.17.341a (C.19.321a) [*Sufficit tibi gratia mea: nam*] *virtus in infirmitate perficitur.* 2 Cor. 12:9.

Passus 18

B.18.6 Reste me þere and rutte faste til *Ramis palmarum*. That is, Palm Sunday or *Dominica in ramis palmarum* (*Missale* 253–73).

B.18.7 (C.20.6) Of gerlis and of *Gloria laus* gretly me dremed. Begin-ning of the hymn sung by children in the Palm Sunday procession, "Gloria laus et honor tibi sit, Rex Christe Redemptor" (*Missale* 260).

B.18.8 (C.20.7) And how Osanna by Organye olde folk songen. *Osanna* was sung repeatedly in the antiphons for Palm Sunday: e.g., "Osanna Filio David, benedictus qui venit in nomine Domini, rex Israel: Osanna in excelsis" (*Brev.* 1:dcclx), from Matt. 21:9; cf. Mk. 11:10, Lk. 13:35, Jn. 12:13.

B.18.15 (C.20.13) Thanne was feiþ in a fenestre and cryde "a! *fili dauid!*" Matt. 21:9, "Hosanna filio David: benedictus qui venit in nomine Domini"; cf. Matt. 9:27. [B.19.133 (C.21.133), B.19.136 (C.21.136)]

B.18.17a (C.20.15a) *Benedictus qui venit in nomine domini.* Matt. 21:9 (continued from above), quoting Ps. 117:26; see also Mk. 11:10, Lk. 13:35, Jn. 12:13 (read on Palm Sunday [*Missale* 255]), Nico. 15:6, 24:3. "*Benedictus &c*, which ends the *Sanctus* in every mass, also ends the second Sunday antiphon *Pueri Hebraeorum*" (Schmidt 350). The psalm was said in a variety of other contexts during the Middle Ages, for example, in the ecclesiastical courts (see G. R. Owst, *Literature and Pulpit in Medieval England* [1933; 2d rev. ed., Oxford: Blackwell, 1966], 345) and at royal entries (see Robert Withington, *English Pageantry* [Cambridge, Mass.: Harvard Univ. Press, 1918], 1:134).

—C.20.20 *Liberum dei Arbitrium* for loue hath vndertake. Source unidentified (cf. C.18.118, *libera voluntas dei*).

B.18.23 (C.20.22) In his helm and in his haubergeon, *humana natura.* The source of these words is unidentified, but they may come from a gloss on Eph. 6:13–17, where Paul enjoins his readers to "take unto you the whole armor of God"; e.g., Hugh's comment on the passage contrasts the triple nature of God and the double nature of man ("Nam in natura humana est duplex substantia, sc. anima & corpus").

B.18.24 (C.20.23) That crist be noȝt yknowe here for *consummatus deus.* "There is an allusion here to the doctrine of the impassibility of the godhead, i.e. the insusceptibility to injury or suffering of God in his divine nature, which makes the Incarnation necessary" (Pearsall 320).

B.18.26 (C.20.25) For no dynt shal hym dere as *in deitate patris.* Source unidentified.

B.18.35a (C.20.34a) *O mors ero mors tua* [*O mors, mors tua ero, morsus* C]. [B.17.114a]

B.18.36 (C.20.35) Thanne cam *Pilatus* with muche peple, *sedens pro tribunali.* Matt. 27:19.

B.18.39 (C.20.38) And al þe court on hym cryde "*crucifige!*" sharpe. Jn. 19:6; cf. Jn. 19:15. The cry is used as an example by Gratian of the rule, "Non solum qui manibus occidunt, sed etiam quorum consilio et fraude alii occiduntur, homicidae probantur" (*CIC* 1:1163). [cf. B.18.46–47 (C.20.46–47)]

B.18.46–47 (C.20.46–47)

"*Crucifige!*" quod a Cachepol, "he kan of wicchecraft!"
"*Tolle, tolle!*" quod anoþer, and took of kene þornes.
Jn. 19:15, "Illi autem clamabant: Tolle, tolle, crucifige eum." [cf.
B.18.39 (C.20.38)]

B.18.50 (C.20.50) "*Aue, raby,*" quod þat rybaud and þrew reedes at
hym. Matt. 26:49. [B.16.151 (C.18.168)]

B.18.57 (C.20.57) "*Consummatum est,*" quod crist and comsede for to
swoune. Jn. 19:30.

B.18.68a (C.20.70a) *Vere filius dei erat iste.* Matt. 27:54.

B.18.109a (C.20.112a) *Cum veniat sanctus sanctorum cessabit vnxio
vestra* [*vnxio vestra* om. C]. [B.15.600]

B.18.111 (C.20.114) I drow me in þat derknesse to *descendit ad
inferna*. Apostles' Creed, *Brev.* 2:2; cf. Athanasian Creed, "descendit ad inferos" (*Brev.* 2:48). [cf. C.11.22a]

B.18.112 (C.20.115) And þere I sauȝ sooþly, *secundum scripturas*.
Nicene Creed (*Brev.* 2:484).

B.18.149a (C.20.152a) *Quia in Inferno nulla est redempcio*. Response in
the Office of the Dead (*Brev.* 2:278), originally suggested by Job 7:9
("Sic qui descenderit ad inferos, non ascendet"); cf. *Prick of Conscience* 7248, "Ffor þus says þe haly man Job: *Quia in inferno nulla
est redempcio*" (also 2832); *Hyckescorner* 785–86 (Manly 1:412), "For
Qui est in inferno, nulla est redemptio: / Holy Job spake these wordes
full longe ago." Gray cites numerous examples from the penitential tradition. The saying was common in vernacular literature; e.g.,
Parlement of the Thre Ages 642 (EETS 246 [1959], 31); *Castle of Perseverance* 3096 (EETS 262 [1969], 94); *Ludus Coventriae* (EETS es 120
[1922], 226); *Towneley Plays* (EETS es 71 [1897], 302). [cf. B.17.111]

B.18.162a (C.20.165a) *Ars vt artem falleret*. From the hymn *Pange lingua
gloriosi*, sung on Passion Sunday (*Brev.* 1:dccxvii). [C.20.392a]

B.18.181a (C.20.184a) *Ad vesperum demorabitur fletus & ad matutinum
leticia*. Ps. 29:6.

B.18.186–87 (C.20.191–92)

"Lo! here þe patente," quod Pees, "*In pace in idipsum*,
And þat þis dede shal dure *dormiam & requiescam*."
Ps. 4:9, a prayer at compline; also said in matins on Holy Saturday
(*Brev.* 1:dccxcv), with the verse divided thus as versicle and re-
sponse (Pearsall 327). [B.15.254a]

—C.20.234a *Omnia probate; quod bonum est tenete*. 1 Thess. 5:21.
[B.3.339–43 (C.3.491–95), A.12.50–52, 56–57]

B.18.216 (C.20.225) For til *modicum* mete with vs, I may it wel auowe.
Source, if any, unidentified.

B.18.239 (C.20.248) The oostes in heuene token *stella comata*. The star of Matt. 2 was often interpreted as a comet; for example, *ME Sermons* 227: "For þis stere was no fix stere in heven, noþur no planete, as is mevynge shewed well, but it was a comete, *stella comata*, new made by þe myghty powre of almyȝthy God" (see Alford 1975).

B.18.244a (C.20.253a) [*Domine* added C] *Iube me venire ad te* [*ad te venire* B var.] *super aquas*. Matt. 14:28, "Respondens autem Petrus dixit: Domine, si tu es, iube me ad te venire super aquas." L's word order "venire ad te" is attested by the *Vetus Latina*, Weber, Wordsworth and White, Ambrose (*PL* 14:842), and Hugh of St. Cher.

—C.20.259a *Non visurum se mortem &c.* Lk. 2:26, the promise made to Simeon, "non visurum se mortem, nisi prius videret Christum Domini." For placement of the verse here, see Nico. 18:2.

B.18.252 (C.20.261) For Iesus as a geaunt [*gigas* in numerous MSS] wiþ a gyn comeþ yonde. Allusion to Ps. 18:6, "Exsultavit ut gigas ad currendam viam" (R. E. Kaske, "*Gigas* the Giant in *Piers Plowman*," *JEGP* 56 [1957]: 177–85). The "gyn" by means of which Christ will "bete adoun" his enemies is his dual nature as God-man. See Hugh on Lk. 1:69, "Unde dicit Gigas geminae substantiae, id est, verus Deus, & verus homo" (6:138ᵛ).

B.18.262a (C.20.270a) *Attollite portas*. Nico. 21:1, 3 (the source of the apocryphal Harrowing of Hell), quoting Ps. 23:7; sung in matins on Holy Saturday (*Brev.* 1:dccxcvii).

—C.20.272 [B.18.264] *Principes* of this place, prest vndo this gates. Nico. 21:1, 3 (continued from above), quoting Ps. 23:7.

—C.20.316a *Ve soli!* Eccles. 4:10, "Vae soli, quia cum ceciderit, non habet sublevantem se."

B.18.315a (C.20.349a) *Nunc princeps huius mundi eiicietur foras* [*eiicietur foras* om. C]. Jn. 12:31. [B.9.8 (A.10.8, C.10.135), A.10.62]

—C.20.356a–b
> *Odisti omnes qui operantur iniquitatem;*
> *Perdes omnes qui loquuntur mendacium.*

Ps. 5:7.

B.18.316a, 317a, 318a *Quis est iste? ... Rex glorie ... Dominus virtutum.* Nico. 21:3, quoting Ps. 23:10.

B.18.323 (C.20.366) Patriarkes and prophetes, *populus in tenebris*. Nico. 18:1 ("Populus qui sedet in tenebris"), quoting Isa. 9:2; cf. Matt. 4:16. [B.5.493a (C.7.133a)]

B.18.324 (C.20.367) Songen seint Iohanes song, *Ecce agnus dei*. Nico. 18:3, quoting Jn. 1:29, 1:36. [B.16.252a (C.18.268a)]

B.18.339a (C.20.385a) *Dentem pro dente & oculum pro oculo.* Ex. 21:24, Levit. 24:20, Deut. 19:21, always transposed ("Oculum pro oculo ...").

B.18.340 (C.20.388) *Ergo* soule shal soule quyte and synne to synne wende. [B.8.24 (A.9.20, C.10.28), B.14.62 (C.15.261), B.14.287 (C.16.122a), B.14.292 (C.16.127), B.19.19 (C.21.19)]

—**C.20.392a** *Ars vt Artem falleret.* [B.18.162a (C.20.165a)]

B.18.349a (C.20.395a) *Non veni soluere legem [atque prophecias* added B var.] *set adimplere.* Matt. 5:17, "Nolite putare quoniam veni solvere legem, aut prophetas: non veni solvere, sed adimplere." In quoting only the second half of the verse, L might have thought it necessary to insert the object *legem*; however, his quotation coincides exactly with that of Ambrose in *Liber de Fuga Saeculi* (*PL* 14:607) and other church fathers.

—**C.20.408a** [*Postea sciens Iesus quia omnia consummata sunt, ut consummaretur Scriptura, dixit:*] *Sicio.* Jn. 19:28; the scriptural passage that is fulfilled is Ps. 68:22, "Et dederunt in escam meam fel, Et in siti mea potaverunt me aceto."

B.18.360a *Et cecidit [incidit* Vulg.] *in foueam quam fecit.* Ps. 7:16.

B.18.370 (C.20.412) That I drynke riȝt ripe Must, *Resureccio mortuorum.* Nicene Creed (*Brev.* 2:484); the phrase is common in the NT, e.g., Matt. 22:31, Acts 23:6, passim, Rom. 1:4, 1 Cor. 15:12, passim. [cf. B.18.112 (C.20.115)]

B.18.378a (C.20.420a) *Tibi soli peccaui [et malum coram te feci* C]. Ps. 50:6.

B.18.390a (C.20.433) *Nullum malum impunitum &c [et nullum bonum irremuneratum* added B var., C]. [B.4.143-44 (Z.4.141-42, A.4.126-27, C.4.140-41)]

B.18.392 In my prisone Purgatorie til *parce* it hote. First lesson of the *Dirige* or Office of the Dead for matins, from Job 7:16 (Alford, 1972); for the legal associations, see Alford 1988b. [B.19.295 (C.21.295)]

—**C.20.435a** *Domine ne in furore tuo Arguas me &c.* Ps. 6:2, 37:2 (both "penitential psalms"; see B.13.53). As here, the words are associated with "everelastynge peyne" in *ME Sermons* 29.

B.18.395a (C.20.438a) *Audiui [Audiuit* B var.] *archana verba que non licet homini loqui.* 2 Cor. 12:4, "[Q]uoniam raptus est in paradisum: et audivit arcana verba, quae non licet homini loqui." [A.12.22a]

B.18.399a (C.20.442a) *Non intres in Iudicium cum seruo tuo [domine* added B var.]. Ps. 142:2, "Et non intres in iudicium cum servo tuo." Cf. Matthew of Vendome, *Tobias:* "Non intres in judicium cum paupere, dives, / Cum servo Dominus, cum fluitante potens:

Non in judicium intres cum pulvere fortis" (*PL* 205:941).

B.18.407a (C.20.450a) *Culpat caro, purgat caro, regnat deus dei caro.* From the hymn *Aeterne Rex altissime*, sung on the vigil of Ascension Day (*Brev.* 1:dcccclviii).

B.18.408a-b (C.20.451a-b)
> *Clarior est solito post maxima nebula phebus;*
> *Post inimicicias clarior est et amor.*

Proverbial (Walther 2360c, 2794); *Liber Parabolarum*, "Clarior est solito post maxima nubila phebus; / Post inimicias clarior est et amor" (*Auctores Octo*, sig. O^vii-b); printed in *PL* 210:481–82 as "Clarior est solito, post nubilia plurima, Phoebus, / Post inimicitias, clarior est amor" (Alford 1975, Lindemann).

B.18.421 (C.20.464) Pees, and pees hire, *per secula seculorum.* Formula ending of a prayer, "per omnia secula seculorum" (e.g., *Missale* 30**, 32**, 34**, 3). [cf. B.3.280]

B.18.421a (C.20.464a) *Misericordia & veritas obuiauerunt sibi; Iusticia & pax osculate sunt.* Ps. 84:11. On the development of this verse into the personified Daughters of God, see Hope Traver, "The Four Daughters of God," *PMLA* 40 (1925): 44–92; and G. R. Owst, *Literature and Pulpit in Medieval England*, 2d rev. ed. (Oxford: Blackwell, 1961), 90–92.

B.18.422 (C.20.465) Truþe trumpede þo and song *Te deum laudamus.* Hymn sung at matins on Sundays (*Brev.* 2:27), but identified especially with Easter morning (*Brev.* 1:dcccxiv).

B.18.423a (C.20.466a) *Ecce quam bonum & quam iocundum* [*habitare fratres in vnum* added B var.]. Ps. 132:1, "Ecce quam bonum et quam iucundum, Habitare fratres in unum!" Antiphon (2 ad vesp. in feria 5 per annum); also said in feria 5 in coena Domini (*Missale* 312). The verse is associated consistently by Brinton with *unitas ecclesiae* (1:58, 114). [A.11.192a]

Passus 19

B.19.19 (C.21.19) *Ergo* is no name to þe name of Iesus. [B.8.24 (A.9.20, C.10.28), B.14.62 (C.15.261), B.14.287 (C.16.122a), B.14.292 (C.16.127), B.18.340 (C.20.388)]

B.19.74a (C.21.74a) *Gloria in excelsis deo* [*Et in terra pax hominibus* added B var.] *&c.* [B.3.328, B.12.150 (C.14.94)]

B.19.80a (C.21.80a) *Omnia celestia terrestria flectantur in hoc nomine Iesu.* Philipp. 2:10, "Ut in nomine Iesu omne genu flectatur caelestium, terrestrium et infernorum"; cf. the hymn *Aeterne rex altissimi*, quoted above at B.18.407a (C.20.450a). James Weldon places this verse at the center of a pattern of verbal concordance in the poem ("Gesture of Perception: The Pattern of Kneeling in *Piers Plowman* B.18–19," *YLS* 3 [1989]: 49–66).

B.19.85 (C.21.85) Maistres and lettred men, *Magi* hem callede. Matt. 2:1. [B.12.144 (C.14.88a)]

B.19.118 (C.21.118) A fauntekyn ful of wit, *filius Marie*. Mk. 6:3.

B.19.133 (C.21.133) For þe dedes þat he dide, *Fili dauid, Iesus*. Matt. 9:27. [B.18.15 (C.20.13), B.19.136 (C.21.136)]

B.19.135 (C.21.135) The burdes þo songe, *Saul interfecit mille et dauid decem milia*. 1 Reg. 18:7, "Percussit Saul mille, et David decem millia"; *Brev.* 1:mclxxii, "Saul percussit mille. . . ."

B.19.136 (C.21.136) Forþi þe contree þer Iesu cam called hym *fili dauid*. [B.18.15 (C.20.13), B.19.133 (C.21.133)]

B.19.152 (C.21.152) *Christus rex resurgens* [*a mortuis* added B var.], and it aroos after. Rom. 6:9, "Christus resurgens ex mortuis . . . ," sung as an antiphon during Easter (*Brev.* 1:dccccvii, dccclv; *Missale* 357, 372, 390). The variant *a mortuis* is attested in the writings of Tertullian, Augustine, et al. (see *VL*). [B.19.160 (C.21.160), cf. B.19.161a]

B.19.160 (C.21.160) In ech a compaignie þer she cam, *Christus resurgens*. See above. [B.19.152 (C.21.152)]

B.19.161a (C.21.161a) *Sic oportet Christum pati & intrare &c.* Conflation of Lk. 24:46, "sic oportebat Christum pati, et resurgere . . ." and Lk. 24:26, "et ita intrare in gloriam suam." The verbal concordance between Lk. 24:46 and the previous quotation in B.19.160 (*resurgens / resurgere*) should be noted.

B.19.169 (C.21.169) To Peter and to hise Apostles and seide *pax vobis*. Lk. 24:36, Jn. 20:19, 21, 26; repeated in the first week after Easter (*Brev.* 1:dcccxxx, dcccxxxii, passim; *Missale* 386). [C.17.238]

B.19.172a (C.21.172a) *Dominus meus & deus meus.* Jn. 20:28.

B.19.181a (C.21.181a) *Beati qui non viderunt & crediderunt.* Jn. 20:29.

B.19.187 (C.21.187) To Piers pardon þe Plowman *redde quod debes*. Matt. 18:28, also an antiphon sung on the twenty-second Sunday after Holy Trinity (*Brev.* 1:mccccxlii); the homily preceding the antiphon is a good exposition of the phrase, as is sermon 8 in *ME Sermons* 36–45. See also Augustine, *PL* 38:528–29; Alford 1988b. [B.19.259 (C.21.259), B.19.390 (C.21.390), B.20.308 (C.22.308); cf. B.5.461 (Z.5.131, A.5.233, C.6.315), B.5.467 (A.5.241, C.6.321), B.19.193 (C.21.193)]

B.19.193 (C.21.193) And rewarde hym right wel þat *reddit quod debet*. [see above]

B.19.201 (C.21.201) Oon *Spiritus paraclitus* to Piers and to hise felawes. From the hymn *Beata nobis gaudia*, sung on Pentecost Sunday (*Brev.* 1:mxi); the Holy Spirit, as described in Acts 2:1–4 and prophesied in Jn. 14:16, 26, 15:26.

B.19.206 (C.21.206) *Spiritus paraclitus* ouerspradde hem alle. [B.19.201 (C.21.201)]

B.19.210 (C.21.210) Welcome hym and worshipe hym wiþ *Veni creator Spiritus*. Opening of a hymn sung at Terce on Pentecost Sunday (*Brev.* 1:mviii), and at the beginning of the ordinary of the mass (*Missale* 577; *Brev.* 2:481).

B.19.228a (C.21.228a) *Diuisiones* [*vero*] *graciarum sunt* [*idem autem Spiritus*]. 1 Cor. 12:4; as here *vero* is omitted in Brinton 1:97, and in ancient quotations of the text (e.g., Irenaeus; see notes to *VL*).

B.19.259 (C.21.259) And Registrer to receyue *redde quod debes*. [B.19. 187 (C.21.187), B.19.390 (C.21.390), B.20.308 (C.22.308); cf. B.5.461 (Z.5.131, A.5.233, C.6.315), B.5.467 (A.5.241, C.6.321), B.19.193 (C.21.193)]

B.19.273a (C.21.273a) *Id est vetus testamentum & nouum. Id est* suggests the language of a biblical commentary (cf. B.15.212, "Petrus *id est* Christus").

B.19.276 (C.21.276) *Spiritus prudencie* þe firste seed highte. A specific source has not been identified, but L's use of the four virtues at this point (following Pentecost) may have been inspired by the second lesson, feria 6 after Pentecost (*Brev.* 1:mxxiv). [B.19.455 (C.21.455), B.20.31 (C.22.31)]

B.19.281 (C.21.281) The seconde seed highte *Spiritus temperancie*. See above. [B.20.8, 22, 23 (C.22.8, 22, 23)]

B.19.289 (C.21.289) The þridde seed þat Piers sew was *Spiritus fortitudinis*. Cf. Isa. 11:2, "spiritus consilii et fortitudinis." [B.19.463–64 (C.21.463–64), B.20.24, 25 (C.22.24, 25)]

B.19.295 (C.21.295) And pleieþ al wiþ pacience and *Parce michi domine*. First lesson of the *Dirige* or Office of the Dead for matins, from Job 7:16 (see above, B.18.392); also quoted in the commentary on Cato's distich "Parce laudato" (*Auctores Octo*, sig. C^vi). [B.18.392; cf. C.3.464, C.5.46]

B.19.296a (C.21.296a) *Esto forti animo cum sis dampnatus inique*. Cato 2.14, "Forti animo esto libens, cum sis dampnatus inique: nemo diu gaudet, qui indice vincit iniquo." Loeb edition reads, "Esto animo forti, cum sis damnatus inique: / nemo diu gaudet qui iudice vincit inquo." [cf. C.4.17]

B.19.297, 301, 302, 397, 402, 405, 474 (C.21.297, 301, 302, 397, 402, 405, 474) The ferþe seed þat Piers sew was *Spiritus Iusticie*. [B.20. 24, 29 (C.22.24, 29)]

B.19.390 (C.21.390) To Piers pardon þe Plowman *redde quod debes.*
[B.19.187 (C.21.187), B.19.259 (C.21.259), B.20.308 (C.22.308); cf.
B.5.461 (Z.5.131, A.5.233, C.6.315), B.5.467 (A.5.241, C.6.321),
B.19.193 (C.21.193)]

B.19.394a (C.21.394a) *Et dimitte nobis debita nostra &c.* Matt. 6:12,
from the Lord's Prayer. Other citations from the Paternoster
occur at C.5.46, C.5.87, C.5.88, C.5.107, B.5.341 (A.5.189,
C.6.399), B.5.394 (C.7.10), B.10.468, B.13.396 (C.6.283), B.14.49
(C.15.247), B.14.50 (C.15.249), B.15.179 (C.16.321), C.16.323,
C.16.374a.

B.19.416 (C.21.416) The comune *clamat cotidie,* ech a man til ooþer.
"Cries out daily," a formula used to initiate legal proceedings
against a public enemy; see Alford 1984, 1988b.

B.19.422 (C.21.422) At Auynoun among Iewes—*Cum sancto sanctus
eris &c.* Ps. 17:26. [B.5.278]

B.19.431 (C.21.431) *Qui pluit super Iustos & iniustos* at ones. Matt.
5:45, "ut sitis filii Patris vestri, qui ... pluit super iustos et inu-
stos."

B.19.446a (C.21.446a) *Non occides.* Ex. 20:13, Deut. 5:17, quoted in
Lk. 18:20. [B.10.372 (A.11.254)]

B.19.446a (C.21.446a) *Michi vindictam* [*& ego retribuam* added B var.]
&c. [B.6.226a, B.10.209a, B.10.374 (A.11.255), C.17.235a]

B.19.455 (C.21.455) *Spiritus prudencie.* [B.19.276 (C.21.276), B.20.31
(C.22.31)]

B.19.463 (C.21.463) Wiþ *Spiritus Intellectus* þei toke þe reues rolles.
The phrase may have been inspired by Isa. 11:2, "spiritus sapientiae et intellectus" (cf. B.19.289). More probably, it is a synecdo-
che for *spiritus prudencie,* since *intellectus* is one of the three elements that make up the virtue of prudence; see *FM* 589, "Et ista
prudencia in tribus consistit: in memoria preteritorum, in intelli-
gencia presencium, et in providencia futurorum," and the discussion of the four cardinal virtues in the Proem to *Disticha Catonis*
(*Auctores Octo*).

B.19.464 (C.21.464) And wiþ *Spiritus fortitudinis* fecche it, wole he,
nel he. [B.19.289 (C.21.289), B.20.24, 25 (C.22.24, 25)]

B.19.479a (C.21.479a) *Omnia tua sunt ad defendendum set non ad
deprehendendum.* Analogue in an abbreviated version of Peraldus's
Summa de Vitiis, cited by Siegfried Wenzel, "The Source of Chaucer's Seven Deadly Sins," *Traditio* 30 (1974): 367, "Item si bona
servorum dicantur bona dominorum, hoc intelligitur ad defendendum et non ad depredandum."

Passus 20

B.20.8, 22, 23 (C.22.8, 22, 23) *Spiritus temperancie.* [B.19.281 (C.21.281)]

B.20.24, 29 (C.22.24, 29) *Spiritus Iusticie.* [B.19.297 etc. (C.21.297 etc.)]

B.20.24, 25 (C.22.24, 25) *Spiritus fortitudinis.* [B.19.289 (C.21.289), B.19.464 (C.21.464)]

B.20.31 (C.22.31) *Spiritus prudencie.* [B.19.276 (C.21.276), B.19.455 (C.21.455)]

B.20.33a (C.22.33a) *Homo proponit & deus disponit.* [B.11.37–38 (C.11.303–4)]

B.20.256a (C.22.256a) *Qui numerat multitudinem stellarum et omnibus eis nomina vocat* [*et . . . vocat* om. C]. Ps. 146:4.

B.20.279 (C.22.279) *Non concupisces rem proximi tui.* A maxim of canon law (abbreviated from Ex. 20:17, Deut. 5:21); e.g., Gratian, *Decretum* Dist. 47, and Pennafort 244. Scase observes (24–31) that this quotation "was central to FitzRalph's attack on the friars' claims to jurisdiction."

B.20.308 (C.22.308) And þat Piers pardon were ypayed, *redde quod debes.* [B.19.187 (C.21.187), B.19.259 (C.21.259), B.19.390 (C.21.390a); cf. B.5.461 (Z.5.131, A.5.233, C.6.315), B.5.467 (A.5.241, C.6.321), B.19.193 (C.21.193)]

B.20.340 (C.22.340) "Certes," seide his felawe, "sire *Penetrans domos.*" 2 Tim. 3:6, "Ex his enim sunt qui penetrant domos, et captivas ducunt mulierculas oneratas peccatis, quae ducuntur variis desideriis." A central text in antimendicant writings (e.g., *Upland* 113; Szittya 3–10 and passim; Scase 15, 32–39).

B.20.366 (C.22.366) And make of yow *memoria* in masse and in matyns. A "commemoration," especially of the dead, e.g., *Brev.* 2:90; cf. A.7.87, "And monewe me in his memorie among alle cristene." [B.15.26 (C.16.186), B.15.39a (C.16.201a)]

II
The Biblical Quotations

THIS INDEX REARRANGES THE BIBLICAL QUOTATIONS in the poem according to their order in the Bible; it should be used in conjunction with the previous index. The following entry will serve as an example:

Leviticus 19:18 B.15.584; cf. A.11.242, B.17.13 (C.19.14a)

This indicates that Leviticus 19:18 is quoted at B.15.584, and that similar words from elsewhere in the Bible appear at A.11.242 and at B.17.13 (and correspondingly at C.19.14a).

Genesis

1:26 B.5.486a, B.9.36, B.9.43 (A.10.41a)
1:27 cf. C.18:7
1:31 B.11.398a
2:18 C.18.227
3:16 cf. B.6.233 (A.7.217, C.8.241a)
3:19 B.6.233 (A.7.217, C.8.241a)
6:6 B.9.133a (A.10.162, C.10.222)
6:7 B.9.133a (A.10.162, C.10.222)
9:6 cf. C.18.7
12:7 cf. B.16.242a
18:2 cf. C.18.241a
19:32 B.1.31a (C.1.30a)
30:23 cf. B.16.219a (C.18.222a)

Exodus

20:12 B.5.567a (C.7.216a), C.17.59a
20:13 B.19.446a (C.21.446a)
20:14 B.10.372 (A.11.254)
20:17 B.20.279 (C.22.279)
21:24 B.18.339a (C.20.385a)

Leviticus

19:13 C.3.308a
19:15 cf. B.15.88 (C.16.241a)
19:17 B.11.88, B.11.93 (C.12.34)
19:18 B.15.584; cf. A.11.242, B.17.13 (C.19.14a)
24:20 B.18.339a (C.20.385a)

Numbers

1:50–51 cf. B.12.113 (C.14.58)
3:31 cf. B.12.113 (C.14.58)
18:20 cf. C.5.60a, B.12.189 (C.14.128)
18:20–24 C.5.55, B.15.556 (C.17.219)

Deuteronomy

1:17 cf. B.15.88 (C.16.241a)
5:16 B.5.567a (C.7.216a), C.17.59a
5:17 B.19.446a (C.21.446a)
5:18 B.10.372 (A.11.254)
5:21 B.20.279 (C.22.279)
6:5 B.15.584; cf. A.11.242, B.13.127 (C.15.134), C.15.140, B.17.13
  (C.19.14a)
8:3 cf. C.5.86–87
12:6 B.15.556a (C.17.219a)
19:21 B.18.339a (C.20.385a)
23:25 cf. B.15.530a, C.17.280a
32:35 cf. B.6.226a, B.10.209a, B.10.374 (A.11.255), C.17.235a, B.19.
  446a (C.21.446a)

1 Regum (AV 1 Samuel)

4:6–11 C.Prol.108, 112
4:18 B.10.288; cf. C.Prol.108, 112, B.12.113, 119 (C.14.58)
13:7–14 cf. B.12.113, 119 (C.14.58)
15:9–22 cf. B.12.113, 119 (C.14.58)
18:7 B.19.135 (C.21.135)

24:7 cf. B.12.125a (C.14.69a)

2 Regum (AV 2 Samuel)

6:1–8 cf. B.12.113, 119 (C.14.58)

3 Regum (AV 1 Kings)

3:26 C.11.213a

1 Paralipomenon (AV 1 Chronicles)

15:2 cf. B.12.113, 119 (C.14.58)

2 Paralipomenon (AV 2 Chronicles)

6:30 cf. C.5.32a, B.12.213a (C.14.152a)

Tobias

2:21 C.17.40a
3:6 C.1.143a, C.6.290a, C.17.40a
4:7 cf. B.7.75
4:9 B.10.89a (C.11.69a)

Job

2:10 C.13.17–18
6:5 B.15.318 (C.17.53)
7:9 cf. B.18.149a (C.20.152a)
7:16 B.18.392, B.19.295 (C.21.295)
15:34 B.3.96 (A.3.85, C.3.124)
15:35 B.9.125a (A.10.150, C.10.212a)
19:25 B.11.207 (C.12.115)
21:2 B.13.49 (C.15.55)
21:7 B.10.25a (A.11.23a)
21:13 C.11.22a; cf. B.18.111 (C.20.114)
23:13 cf. B.12.216a (C.14.155a)

Psalms

1:1 B.5.418, B.10.326; cf. B.13.53
4:3 B.15.81b
4:9 B.15.254a, B.18.186–87 (C.20.191–92)
5:7 C.20.356a-b
5:9 C.3.464, C.5.46
6:2 C.20.435a
6:7 B.15.191 (C.16.333)
7:15 B.9.125a (A.10.150, C.10.212a)

7:16 B.18.360a
9b:7 B.13.330a (C.6.76a)
10:4 B.10.29a (C.11.25a)
13:1 B.7.141
13:3 B.4.36a–37a (C.4.36a)
14:1 B.2.39 (C.2.40), B.3.234a, B.7.52a, B.13.127 (C.15.134)
14:2 B.3.237a
14:5 C.2.42, B.3.241a (A.3.221a), B.7.42a (Z.8.47, A.8.46a)
15:5 C.5.60a, B.12.189 (C.14.128)
17:26 B.5.278, B.19.422 (C.21.422)
18:1 C.18.213a
18:6 B.18.252 (C.20.261)   ﹀
19:8–9 B.10.327a (C.5.172a)
21:2 B.16.214a
22:4 B.7.120–21 (Z.8.104, A.8.102–3), A.10.87, B.12.13a, B.12.293a
23:7 B.18.262a (C.20.270a), C.20.272
23:9 B.18.262a (C.20.270a), C.20.272
23:10 B.18.316a, 317a, 318a
25:10 C.3.118a, B.3.249 (A.3.228)
29:6 B.18.181a (C.20.184a)
30:11 C.9.163
31:1 B.5.507 (C.7.152), B.12.177a (C.14.117a), B.13.53, B.13.54a,
    B.14.94
31:2 B.13.53, B.13.54a var.; cf. B.5.418
31:5 B.13.55
31:6 B.13.57 (C.15.60)
32:9 B.9.33a (A.10.34a), C.14.165a, B.14.61a (C.15.260a)
33:11 B.9.109a (C10.202a), B.11.282a
35:7–8 B.5.509 (C.7.154), B.10.416a (C.11.248a)
36:4 C.15.271a
36:24 B.16.25a
36:25 B.7.89 (C.9.163)
37:2 C.20.435a
38:7 C.12.215a
39:6 B.10.45
41:4 B.7.128a (Z.8.111, A.8.110a)
42:1 B.11.286a
42:5 B.11.287 (C.13.101), B.15.180
46:7–8 B.11.311 (C.13.123a), B.11.313 (C.13.125)
48:20 C.11.23a
49:21 B.10.291, B.11.95 (C.12.29a)
50:3 B.5.277, B.13.54

50:6 B.18.378a (C.20.420a)
50:8 B.5.277a (C.6.302)
50:9 C.16.335a
50:19 B.13.58a (C.15.62), B.15.194 (C.16.336a)
52:1 B.7.141
56:5 B.13.330b (C.6.76b)
61:13 cf. C.5.32a, B.12.213a (C.14.152a)
67:7 B.5.490a (C.7.130a)
67:19 B.5.490a (C.7.130a)
68:29 B.6.75–76a (A.7.67–68a, C.8.77–78a)
70:15 A.8.123 (Z.8.125)
72:12 B.10.26a (C.11.23b)
72:20 B.14.131a (C.15.306a)
75:6 B.14.131a (C.15.306)
80:13 B.9.67a (C.10.165a)
84:7 B.5.506 (C.7.151)
84:11 B.18.421a (C.20.464a)
85:10 C.18.190
96:7 B.15.81a
100:7–8 B.13.432a (C.7.92a)
104:15 B.12.125a (C.14.69a)
109:1 C.1.122a
110:3 B.15.327 var., C.17.66a
110:10 B.9.96a (A.10.81a)
111:1 B.5.418, B.10.326, B.13.53
111:3 B.15.327 var., C.17.66a
111:5 B.5.243
111:9 B.15.327, C.17.66a
113b:3 cf. B.12.216a (C.14.155a)
114:9 B.3.311 (C.3.464), C.5.46, B.15.125
118:119 cf. C.10.95
118:158 A.12.19a
118:164 cf. B.8.20a (A.9.16a, C.10.21)
127:1 B.5.418, B.6.250 (A.7.234)
127:2 B.6.252a (A.7.234a, C.8.260a)
131:1 A.11.55 (C.11.49), B.15.490; cf. B.5.466 (Z.5.136, A.5.238, C.6.320)
131:6 B.10.69a (A.11.55a, C.11.49a), B.15.490a
131:17 cf. B.5.506 (C.7.151)
132:1 A.11.192a, B.18.423a (C.20.466a)
134:6 cf. B.12.216a (C.14.155a)
142:2 B.18.399a (C.20.442a)

144:9 B.5.281a, B.11.139a (C.12.74a), B.17.318a (C.19.298a)
144:16 B.14.63a (C.15.262a), C.16.320
146:4 B.20.256a (C.22.256a)
148:5 B.9.33a (A.10.34a), C.14.165a, B.14.61a (C.15.260a)

Proverbs

3:12 cf. B.12.12a
7:26–27 cf. B.9186a–b (C.10.287a–b)
13:24 B.5.39a (C.5.139a)
20:4 B.6.236 (A.7.220, C.8.245a)
20:22 C.5.58a
22:1 B.3.330 (C.3.483)
22:9 B.3.336 (C.3.488), B.3.350 (C.3.498a)
22:10 B.7.143a (Z.8.127, A.8.125a)
24:12 cf. C.5.32a, B.12.213a (C.14.152a)
24:16 B.8.20a (A.9.16a, C.10.21)
24:23 cf. B.15.88 (C.16.241a)
24:29 cf. C.5.32a, B.12.213a (C.14.152a)
25:27 B.15.55 (C.16.217)
29:3 cf. B.9.186a–b (C.10.287a–b)
30:8 B.11.271

Ecclesiastes

4:10 C.20.316a
9:1 B.10.436a (C.11.271a)
10:16 B.Prol.196 (C.Prol.206)
11:6 cf. B.77a–b

Wisdom

10:17 cf. C.5.32a, B.12.213a (C.14.152a)

Ecclesiasticus

1:16 B.9.96a (A.10.81a)
5:5 B.12.207a (C.14.146a)
10:10 B.10.342a
11:9 B.11.395 (C.13.196a)
31:8 B.15.234a (C.16.359a); cf. B.14.104 (C.15.279)
31:9 B.14.104 (C.15.279)
33:19 cf. C.2.187
35:21 cf. C.11.295a (A.11.303a var. Skeat)
38:1 Z.7.267
38:2 cf. Z.7.271, B.7.44a (Z.8.47, A.8.46a), Z.8.61

Isaiah

2:4 B.3.308a (C.3.461a), B.3.324a (C.3.477a)
3:7 B.15.576a
5:22 B.13.61a (C.15.65a)
9:2 B.5.493a (C.7.133a), B.18.323 (C.20.366)
11:2 cf. B.19.289 (C.21.289), B.19.463–64 (C.21.463–64), B.20.24, 25
    (C.22.24, 25)
14:4–6 B.10.333a (C.5.177a)
14:13–14 C.1.113, B.1.119 (C.1.111a), B.15.51a (C.16.213a)
45:22 B.14.180a
55:1 B.11.120a (C.12.55a)
56:7 B.16.135a
56:10 B.10.293a
58:7 C.9.125a, B.10.85a (C.11.65a)

Jeremiah

12:1 A.10.150 var., B.10.25a (A.11.23a)
25:14 cf. C.5.32a, B.12.213a (C.14.152a)
31:34b C.7.147a
50:29 cf. C.5.32a, B.12.213a (C.14.152a)

Ezekiel

16:49 cf. C.15.229a, B.14.77a
18:20 B.9.149 (C.10.236a), B.10.114
18:30 B.13.49 (C.15.55)
33:11 C.14.134a

Daniel

9:24–27 cf. B.15.600, B.18.109a (C.20.112a)

Osee

4:8 cf. B.13.45a (C.15.50a)
13:14 cf. B.17.114a, B.18.35a

Zachariah

13:7 C.9.262

Malachi

3:10 B.15.578

2 Machabees

13:7 cf. C.10.95

Matthew

2:1 B.12.144a (C.14.88a), B.19.85 (C.21.85)
3:2 B.13.49 (C.15.55)
4:4 C.5.86–87, B.14.46b (C.15.244b)
4:16 cf. B.5.493a (C.7.133a), B.18.323 (C.20.366)
5:3 B.14.215a
5:13 B.15.429a, B.15.431a
5:17 B.18.349a (C.20.395a)
5:19 A.11.196a, B.13.118a (C.15.126a)
5:44 cf. B.13.137 (C.15.140)
5:45 B.19.431 (C.21.431)
6:2 A.3.64a, B.3.254a (A.3.233a, C.3.312)
6:3–4 B.3.72a (A.3.54, C.3.74a)
6:5 A.3.64a, B.3.254a (A.3.233a, C.3.312)
6:10 C.5.88, B.14.50 (C.15.249), B.15.179 (C.16.321)
6:11 C.16.374a
6:12 B.19.394a (C.21.394a)
6:16 A.3.64a, B.15.219a (C.16.344a)
6:21 B.13.398a, C.6.285a
6:24 B.13.312a (C.6.60a)
6:25 B.7.131 (Z.8.115, A.8.113), B.14.33a
6:26 B.14.33a
7:1 cf. B.11.90 (C.12.31), B.12.89a, B.14.293 (C.16.128)
7:2 B.1.178a (C.1.174a), C.11.232a, B.11.228
7:3 cf. B.10.268a
7:5 cf. B.10.270a
7:6 B.10.9 (A.11.9, C.11.7)
7:7 C.7.260, B.14.46a var. (C.15.244a), B.15.428a var., B.15.503a
7:12 B.7.60a, C.16.306a
7:16 B.9.155a (C.10.244a)
7:17 B.2.27b (C.2.29a), C.10.244b
7:21 B.17.266a (C.19.232a)
9:4 cf. B.15.200a (C.16.340a)
9:12 B.16.110a
9:13 cf. B.5.498a (C.7.138a)
9:27 B.18.15 (C.20.13), B.19.133 (C.21.133), B.19.136 (C.21.136)
10:17–19 cf. B.10.450a (A.11.296, C.11.275a)
10:22 cf. B.13.50 (C.15.56)

10:28 C.10.99a
11:12 cf. B.10.461 (A.11.305, C.11.287)
11:5 C.18.141a
12:32 B.16.47b, B.17.200a–1 (C.19.166a–67)
12:34 cf. B.12.281 (C.14.203), C.15.118
13:44 C.5.98a
14:28 B.18.244a (C.20.253a)
15:4 B.5.567a (C.7.216a), C.17.59a
15:14 B.10.281a, B.12.185 (C.14.124a)
16:19 B.7.181a (Z.8.164, A.8.159a, C.9.327a)
16:27 cf. C.5.32a, B.12.213a (C.14.152a)
17:19 B.11.281a
18:3 B.15.149a (C.16.298a)
18:7 A.11.154a, B.16.157a (C.18.174a)
18:18 cf. B.7.181a (Z.8.164, A.8.159a, C.9.327a)
18:28 B.19.187 (C.21.187), B.19.193 (C.21.193), B.19.259 (C.21.259), B.19.390 (C.21.390), B.20.308 (C.22.308); cf. B.5.461 (A.5.233, C.6.315), B.5.467(A.5.241, C.6.321)
19:19 B.5.567a (C.7.216a), C.17.59a
19:21 B.11.274a (C.12.167a)
19:23 cf. B.14.212a, C.11.201a
19:29 C.12.160a
20:4 B.10.481a, B.15.500
21:9 B.18.8, 15, 17a (C.20.7, 13, 15a)
21:12 ff. cf. B.15.118 (C.16.273)
21:12 C.18.157a var.
21:13 B.16.135a
22:4 B.15.464a
22:14 B.11.112–14 (C.12.47–49)
22:21 B.1.52–53 (Z.Prol.139–40, A.1.50–51, C.1.48–49)
22:31 cf. B.18.370 (C.20.412)
22:37–40 A.11.242, B.13.127 (C.15.134), C.15.140, B.15.584, B.17.13 (C.19.14); cf. C.17.140a
22:40 B.17.16 (C.19.17)
22:44 C.1.122a
23:2 C.8.86a, A.11.223, B.10.404a (C.11.235a)
23:3 C.8.90a
23:12 A.10.120a; cf. B.15.552a (C.17.215a)
23:27 cf. B.15.115
24:11 B.15.601 (C.17.309)
25:12 B.5.55, B.9.67a, B.17.253a (C.19.219a)
25:23 C.14.214a

26:5 C.18.164a
26:25 B.16.145
26:31 C.9.262
26:37 cf. B.16.115 (C.18.145)
26:41 B.5.442 (Z.5.111, A.5.214, C.7.56), B.5.186 (C.6.168), C.9.259
26:49 B.16.151 (C.18.168), B.18.50 (C.20.50)
26:61 C.18.160a var.
27:19 B.18.36 (C.20.35)
27:40 cf. C.18.160a var.
27:46 B.16.214a
27:54 C.2.31, B.18.68a (C.20.70a)

Mark

2:7 C.18.190
2:17 cf. B.16.110a
3:29 cf. B.16.47a, B.17.200a–1 (C.19.166a–67)
4:24 B.1.178a (C.1.174a), C.11.232a, B.11.228
6:3 B.19.118 (C.21.118)
7:10 B.5.567a (C.7.216a), C.17.59a
10:18 C.15.135a
10:19 B.5.567a (C.7.216a), C.17.59a
10:25 cf. B.14.212a, C.11.201a
11:10 B.18.8 (C.20.7), B.18.17a (C.20.15a)
11:17 cf. B.16.135a
12:30–31 A.11.242, B.13.127 (C.15.134), C.15.140, B.15.584, B.17.13
    (C.19.14); cf. C.17.140a
12:36 C.1.122a
13:9–11 cf. B.10.450a (A.11.296, C.11.275a)
13:33–37 cf. B.5.442 (Z.5.111, A.5.214, C.7.56)
14:27 C.9.262
14:37–38 B.5.442 (A.5.214, C.7.57), C.9.258–59
15:29 cf. C.18.160a var.
15:34 B.16.214a
16:15 B.15.491a (C.17.191)
16:16 A.11.234, B.11.124a (C.12.59a), C.13.87a
16:17–18 B.13.249a (C.15.221a)

Luke

1:25 cf. B.16.219a (C.18.222a)
1:35 cf. B.16.90 (C.18.123)
1:38 B.16.99a (C.18.132a)
1:52 B.15.552a (C.17.215a)

1:55 cf. B.16.242a
1:68 C.15.116a
1:69 cf. B.5.506 (C.7.151)
2:7 B.12.147a
2:14 B.3.328, B.12.150 (C.14.94), B.19.74a (C.21.74a)
2:15 B.12.142a (C.14.86a)
2:26 C.20.259a
5:21 C.18.190
5:31 cf. B.16.110a
5:32 B.5.498a (C.7.138a)
6:20 cf. B.14.215a
6:25 B.13.423a (C.7.83a)
6:27 cf. B.13.137 (C.15.140)
6:31 cf. B.7.60a, C.16.309
6:35 cf. B.14.169, B.17.257 (C.19.223)
6:37 B.11.90 (C.12.31), B.12.89a, B.14.293 (C.16.128)
6:38 B.1.178a (C.1.174a), B.1.201 (Z.1.124, A.1.175, C.1.196),
   C.11.232a, B.11.228, B.12.54a
6:39 cf. B.10.281a, B.12.185 (C.14.124a)
6:41 B.10.268a
6:42 B.10.270a
6:43 B.2.27a (C.2.29a), C.10.244b
6:44 cf. B.9.155a (C.10.244a)
7:22 C.18.141a
7:42 B.5.467 (A.5.241, C.6.321)
7:50 B.11.218
9:8 B.13.195
10:4 C.9.120a, C.9.123a
10:7 B.2.123 (Z.2.95, A.2.86a), B.13.39a (C.15.44a)
10:16 B.13.440a (C.7.100a)
10:27 A.11.242, B.13.127 (C.15.134), C.15.140, B.15.584, B.17.13
   (C.19.14a)
10:30 B.17.58 (C.19.57)
10:40 B.11.252 (C.12.138)
10:42 B.11.255a (C.12.141a)
11:17 B.15.200a (C.16.340a)
12:10 B.16.47a, B.17.200a-1 (C.19.166a-67)
12:20 C.12.215a
12:22 B.7.131 (A.8.113), B.14.33a
12:24 cf. B.14.33a
12:38 cf. B.12.9a
12:47 cf. B.12.56a (C.14.18a)

13:35 B.18.8 (C.20.7), B.18.17a (C.20.15a)
14:10 B.6.47a (C.8.44a)
14:11 A.10.120a; cf. B.15.552a (C.17.215a)
14:12–13 B.11.191a (C.12.103a)
14:18 C.7.292
14:20 B.14.3a (C.7.304a)
14:33 C.12.171a
15:8–10 C.5.98a
16:2 C.9.273
16:3 Z.5.142
16:6 Z.5.143
16:9 B.6.228a (A.7.212a, C.8.234a), C.19.250a
16:19–31 B.14.123 (C.15.299), C.19.240a
18:14 A.10.120a; cf. B.15.552a (C.17.215a)
18:19 C.18.190
18:20 B.5.567a (C.7.216a), B.10.372 (A.11.254), C.17.59a, B.19.446a
   (C.21.446a)
18:25 cf. B.14.212a, C.11.201a
19:8 B.13.195
19:11–28 B.6.239 (A.7.223)
19:23 B.7.83a
19:46 cf. B.16.135a
20:25 B.1.52–53 (Z.Prol.139–40, A.1.50–51, C.1.48–49)
20:42 C.1.122a
21:3 C.13.98a
21:1–4 B.13.197; cf. C.13.98a
22:35 C.9.120a
23:33–43 cf. B.5.476 (Z.5.150, A.5.250, C.6.330)
23:42 B.5.466 (Z.5.136, A.5.238, C.6.320); cf. C.11.49
24:26 B.19.161a (C.21.161a)
24:36 B.19.169 (C.21.169)
24:46 B.19.161a (C.21.161a)

John

1:14 C.3.356, B.5.500a (C.7.140a)
1:29 B.16.252a (C.18.268a), B.18.324 (C.20.367)
1:35 B.16.252a (C.18.268a), B.18.324 (C.20.367)
3:5 B.11.82a
3:8 B.12.63a (C.14.27a), B.12.69a
3:11 B.12.65a, 66, 67
3:13 B.10.382a (A.11.263a, C.11.207a)
5:23 cf. B.13.440a (C.7.100a)

7:20 B.16.120a (C.18.150a)
7:24 B.11.90 (C.12.31)
8:7 C.14.42a
8:34 B.11.204a (C.12.112a); cf. B.Prol.39 (A.Prol.39, C.Prol.40)
8:48 B.16.120a (C.18.150a)
8:52 B.16.120a (C.18.150a)
9:1–3 cf. B.9.149 (C.10.236a), B.10.114
10:11 B.15.497a (C.17.193a), C.17.291a
10:16 C.18.264a
10:20 cf. B.16.120a (C.18.150a)
10:28 cf. B.12.293
10:38 C.16.342a
11:35 cf. B.16.115 (C.18.145)
11:39 C.17.303, B.16.114 (C.18.144)
11:43 B.15.594a
12:13 B.18.8 (C.20.7), B.18.17a (C.20.15a)
12:24 C.12.179a
12:31 B.9.8 (A.10.8, C.10.135), A.10.62, B.18.315a (C.20.349a)
12:32 B.17.152a (C.19.127a)
12:48 cf. B.13.440a (C.7.100a)
13:20 cf. B.13.440a (C.7.100a)
14:6 B.9.164 (C.10.255)
14:9–10 C.7.128a, B.10.252a (C.11.153a)
14:13 C.7.260a, B.14.46a (C.15.244a)
14:30 B.9.8 (A.10.8, C.10.135), A.10.62, B.18.315a (C.20.349a)
16:11 B.9.8 (A.10.8, C.10.135), A.10.62, B.18.315a (C.20.349a)
16:20 C.12.207a
16:24 B.15.428a
17:2 cf. B.12.293
18:38 A.12.28
19:6 B.18.39 (C.20.38)
19:15 B.18.46–47 (C.20.46–47); cf. B.18.39 (C.20.38)
19:28 C.20.408a
19:30 B.18.57 (C.20.57)
20:19, 21, 26 C.17.238, B.19.169 (C.21.169)
20:28 B.19.172a (C.21.172a)
20:29 B.19.181a (C.21.181a)

Acts

2:1–4 B.19.201, 206 (C.21.201, 206); cf. B.12.286a (C.14.208a)
2:3 cf. B.12.286a (C.14.208a)
2:34 C.1.122a

2:38 B.13.49 (C.15.55)
3:6 B.13.254a (C.15.224a)
7:35 cf. B.11.207 (C.12.115)
10:34 cf. B.15.88 (C.16.241a)
20:35 C.14.16a
23:6 ff. cf. B.18.370 (C.20.412), C.20.115

Romans

1:4 cf. C.20.115, B.18.370 (C.20.412)
2:6 C.5.32a, B.12.213a (C.14.152a)
2:23–27 C.10.95
3:16–18 B.4.36a-37a (C.4.36a)
4:13 cf. B.16.242a
6:9 B.19.152 (C.21.152), B.19.160 (C.21.160)
12:3 B.10.121 (A.11.74), B.15.69 (C.16.229–30)
12:15 A.11.193a
12:17 cf. C.5.58a
12:19 B.6.226a, B.10.209a, B.10.374 (A.11.255), C.17.235a, B.19.446a
    (C.21.446a)
13:7 B.5.461 (Z.5.131, A.5.233, C.6.315), B.5.467 (Z.5.137, A.5.241,
    C.6.321); see above, Matt. 18:28

1 Corinthians

1:24 cf. B.16.30 (C.18.34), B.16.36
2:9 cf. C.18.4
3:19 B.12.138a (C.14.83a)
3:18 C.9.127a
7:1–2 B.9.194a (C.10.293a)
7:20 C.5.43a, A.10.112
8:1 B.12.57a
10:4 cf. B.15.212
11:7 cf. C.18.7
12:4 B.19.228a (C.21.228a)
13:1 B.17.261a (C.19.227a)
13:4–5 B.15.157 (C.16.291a)
13:7 C.17.5a
13:12 B.15.162a (C.16.296a)
13:13 B.12.29a; cf. B.17.1 (C.19.1), B.17.35 (C.19.36), B.17.48 (C.19.
    46), C.19.53, B.17.84 (C.19.80), B.17.91, B.17.103, C.19.97
15:12 cf. C.20.115, B.18.370 (C.20.412)
15:55 cf. B.17.114a, B.18.35a
16:13 cf. B.5.442 (Z.5.111, A.5.214, C.7.56)

2 Corinthians

4:4 cf. C.18.7
6:10 C.13.4a
9:9 B.15.327, C.17.66a
11:19 B.8.93 (A.9.83a, C.10.90)
11:24–25 B.13.67a
11:26 cf. B.13.70 (C.15.75a), B.13.73a
11:27 B.13.67 (C.15.73a)
12:4 A.12.22a, B.18.395a (C.20.438a)
12:9 B.17.341a (C.19.321a)

Galatians

1:10 B.13.312a (C.6.60a)
3:16 cf. B.16.242a
4:4 B.16.93 (C.18.126), C.18.138
6:2 B.6.221a (C.8.230a), B.11.211a, C.13.78a, B.17.74
6:5 B.10.116a
6:10 B.10.204a, A.11.245a
6:14 B.15.537a (C.17.198a)

Ephesians

4:1 C.5.43a, A.10.112
4:8 B.5.490a (C.7.130a)
5:3–5 B.Prol.39 (A.Prol.39, C.Prol.40), B.13.456 (C.7.116)
6:2 B.5.567a (C.7.216a), C.17.59a
6:13–17 cf. B.18.23 (C.20.22)

Philippians

2:10 B.19.80a (C.21.80a)
3:19 B.9.62a

Colossians

1:15 cf. C.18.7
3:1 B.10.359a
3:8 cf. B.Prol.39 (A.Prol.39, C.Prol.40)

1 Thessalonians

5:15 cf. C.5.58a
5:21 B.3.339–43 (C.3.491–95), B.3.350 (C.3.498a), A.12.50–52, 56–57,
C.20.234a

1 Timothy

5:18 B.2.123 (Z.2.95, A.2.86a)
6:8 cf. B.7.86a
2 Timothy

3:2 ff B.17.257 (C.19.223)
3:6 B.20.340 (C.22.340)
4:14 cf. C.5.32a, B.12.213a (C.14.152a)

Titus

3:5 cf. C.19.73

Hebrews

10:30 B.6.226a, B.10.209a, B.10.374 (A.11.255), C.17.235a, B.19.446a
   (C.21.446a)
12:4 cf. B.16.47a
12:6 B.12.12a

James

2:1 cf. B.15.88 (C.16.241a)
2:2 cf. B.15.115
2:8 A.11.242, B.15.584, B.17.13 (C.19.14a)
2:9 cf. B.1.96 (Z.1.42, A.1.94, C.1.92)
2:10 B.9.100a, B.11.309 (C.13.122a)
2:11 B.19.446a (C.21.446a)
2:26 B.1.187a (C.1.183a)

1 John

2:15 cf. B.14.60a (C.15.259a)
2:16 B.11.13, 17, 30, 40, 43 (C.11, 172 etc.), C.11.307, 310
3:14 B.11.176a (C.12.99a)
4:8 B.1.86 (Z.1.31, A.1.84, C.1.82)
4:16 B.1.86 (Z.1.31, A.1.84, C.1.82), C.3.403a, B.5.486b, B.9.65a
4:18 B.13.163a, C.15.164a
5:11 cf. B.12.293

1 Peter

2:2 B.11.203 (C.12.111)
2:13 B.11.383a
3:9 cf. C.5.58a
3:20-21 cf. C.11.244
4:18 B.12.281 (C.14.203), B.13.19 (C.15.22); cf. C.15.118

5:8 B.5.186 (C.6.168), B.5.442 (Z.5.111, A.5.214, C.7.56)

Apocalypse

2:5 cf. B.13.49
2:16 cf. B.13.49
3:3 cf. B.13.49
3:19 cf. B.12.12a, B.13.49
6:10 B.17.293a (C.19.274a)
14:13 B.14.213a (C.16.54a)
22:12 cf. C.5.32a, B.12.213a (C.14.152a)

Gospel of Nicodemus (Apocrypha)

3:2 A.12.28
12:1 B.6.226a, B.10.209a, B.10.374 (A.11.255), C.17.235a, B.19.446a
  (C.21.446a)
14:1 B.15.491a (C.17.191)
18:1 B.18.323 (C.20.366)
18:2 C.20.259a
18:3 B.18.324 (C.20.367), C.18.268a
20:3 B.16.114
21:1 B.5.490a (C.7.130a), C.20.264, B.18.262a (C.20.270a)
21:3 B.5.490a (C.7.130a), C.20.264, B.18.262a (C.20.270a)
27:2 cf. C.17.238, B.19.169 (C.21.169)

III
Alphabetical Index

Aperis tu manum tuam B.14.63a (C.15.262a), C.16.320
Appare quod es B.10.261a
Archa dei B.10.288, B.12.113, 119 (C.14.58)
Archa domini C.Prol.108, C.Prol.112
Archa Noe C.11.244
Argentum & aurum non est michi B.13.254a (C.15.224a)
Ars vt artem falleret B.18.162a (C.20.165a)
Atollite portas B.18.262a (C.20.270a)
Audiatis alteram partem C.4.188
Audiui archana uerba A.12.22a, B.18.395a (C.20.438a)
Aue raby B.18.50 (C.20.50)
Auees C.16.323

Beacius est dare C.14.16a
Beati omnes B.5.418, B.6.250 (A.7.234)
Beati pauperes B.14.215a
Beati qui non viderunt B.19.181a (C.21.181a)
Beati quorum remisse sunt iniquitates B.5.507 (C.7.152), B.12.177a
    (C.14.117a), B.13.53
Beati quorum tecta sunt peccata B.12.177a, B.13.54a, B.14.94
Beatus vir B.5.418, B.10.326, B.13.53
Beatus vir cui non imputauit B.13.54a var.
Beatus est diues B.15.234a (C.16.359a)
Beatus est qui scripturas legit B.15.60-61 (C.16.222-23)
Beau fitȝ B.7.168 (Z.8.149, A.8.145, C.9.312)
Beaute sanȝ bounte C.17.163-64
Bele paroles B.15.115
Bele vertue est suffrance B.11.385-86 (C.13.203-4)
Benedicite B.5.390 (C.7.6)
Benedictus qui venit B.18.17a (C.20.15a)
Bona arbor B.2.27a (C.2.29a), C.10.244b
Bonum est vt vnusquisque vxorem suam habeat B.9.194a (C.10.293a)
Bonus pastor animam suam ponit B.15.497a (C.17.193a)
Breuis oratio penetrat celum C.11.295a (A.11.303a Skeat)
Brutorum animalium natura te condempnat B.15.318 (C.17.53)

Canes muti B.10.293a
Cantabit paupertas coram latrone viator B.14.307a
Capias ... Et saluo custodias C.4.164-65
Captiuam duxit captiuitatem B.5.490a (C.7.130a)
Caristiam B.14.73
Caritas B.2.35, C.14.14, C.18.14, C.18.32, C.18.39

Cum sanctus sanctorum veniat B.15.600, B.18.109a (C.20.112a)
Cum veniat sanctus sanctorum (see *Cum sanctus sanctorum*)
Cura animarum B.14.286

Dabo tibi secundum peticionem tuam C.15.271a
Dare histrionibus C.7.118a
Date & dabitur vobis B.1.201 (Z.1.124, A.1.175, C.1.196), B.12.54a
De delicijs ad delicias B.14.144a
De peccato propiciato B.12.207a (C.14.146a)
De re que te non molestat noli B.11.395 (C.13.196a)
Deleantur de libro viuencium B.6.75 (A.7.67, C.8.77)
Demonium habes B.16.120a (C.18.150a)
Dentem pro dente B.18.339a (C.20.385a)
Deposuit potentes de sede B.15.552a (C.17.215a)
Descendit ad inferna B.18.111 (C.20.114)
Deus caritas B.1.86 (Z.1.31, A.84, C.1.82)
Deus dicitur quasi B.12.293
Deus homo C.3.402a
Deus meus . . . vt quid dereliquisti me? B.16.214a
Deus pater, deus filius B.10.246a
Deus tu conuersus B.5.506 (C.7.151)
Dextere dei tu digitus C.19.140a
Dieu saue dame Emme B.Prol.225 (A.Prol.103, C.Prol.226)
Dignus est operarius B.2.123 (Z.2.95, A.2.86a)
Dilige denarium B.10.343a
Dilige deum B.13.127; cf. *Disce, doce, dilige Deum*
Dilige deum & proximum tuum A.11.242, C.15.134, B.17.13 (C.19.14)
Dilige deum propter deum C.17.140a
Dimidium bonorum meorum B.13.195
Dimitte nobis debita nostra (see *Et dimitte*)
Dirige C.3.464
Disce, doce, dilige Deum C.15.140
Disce, doce, dilige inimicos B.13.137
Dispergentur oues C.9.262
Dispersit, dedit pauperibus? B.15.327
Diu perseuerans B.13.50 (C.15.56)
Diuicias nec paupertates B.11.271
Diuisiones graciarum sunt B.19.228a (C.21.228a)
Dixi & confitebor tibi B.13.55
Dixit dominus domino meo C.1.122a
Dixit & facta sunt B.9.33a (A.10.34a, C.14.165a), B.14.61a (C.15.260a)
Dixit insipiens B.7.141

142 ALPHABETICAL INDEX

(C.16.122a), B.14.292 (C.16.127), B.18.340 (C.20.388), B.19.19 (C.21.19)
Ergo saluabitur B.12.282 (C.14.204)
Esto forti animo B.19.296a (C.21.296a)
Esto sobrius B.5.186 (C.6.168)
Et cecidit in foueam B.18.360a
Et dimisi eos secundum desideria eorum B.9.67a (C.10.165a)
Et dimitte nobis debita nostra B.19.394a (C.21.394a)
Et egenos vagosque induc (see *Frange esurient*)
Et qui bona egerunt B.7.113-14 (Z.8.96, A.8.95-96, C.9.287-88), C.12.119a
Et quorum tecta sunt peccata (see *Beati quorum tecta*)
Et si sal euanuerit B.15.431a
Et vidit deus cogitaciones eorum B.15.200a (C.16.340a)
Et vidit deus cuncta que fecerat B.11.398a
Et visitauit & fecit redempcionem C.15.116a
Ex vi transicionis B.13.151
Existimasti inique B.10.291, B.11.95 (C.12.29a)

Faciamus hominem ad ymaginem B.5.486a, B.9.36, B.9.43 (A.10.41a)
Facite vobis amicos de mammona B.6.288a (A.7.212a, C.8.234a), C.19.250a
Fiat voluntas C.5.88, B.14.50 (C.15.249), B.15.179 (C.16.321)
Fides non habet meritum B.10.256a (C.11.157a)
Fides sine operibus B.1.187a (C.1.183a)
Fides, spes, caritas B.12.29a
Fides sua B.11.218
Fiet vnum ouile C.18.264a
Fili dauid B.18.15 (C.20.13), B.19.133 (C.21.133), B.19.136 (C.21.136)
Filij hominum dentes eorum B.13.330b (C.6.76b)
Filius B.16.88 (C.18.120), B.16.186 (C.18.193), B.17.229 (C.19.195)
Filius dei C.2.31, B.10.246a
Filius Marie B.19.118 (C.21.118)
Filius non portabit B.9.149 (C.10.236a), B.10.114
Fodere non valeo Z.5.142
Fornicatores B.2.181 (C.2.194)
Frange esurienti panem tuum C.9.125a, B.10.85a (C.11.65a)
Fuerunt michi lacrime mee B.7.128a (Z.8.111, A.8.110a)

Gazophilacium B.13.197
Gaudere cum gaudentibus A.11.193a
Gigas B.18.252 (C.20.261)

Inebriemus eum vino B.1.31a (C.1.30a)
Infamis B.5.168
Inferte omnes decimas B.15.578
Infirmata est vertus C.9.163
Ingrati B.14.169
Ingratus B.17.257 (C.19.223)
Inicium sapiencie B.9.96a (A.10.81a)
Inquirentes autem dominum B.9.109a (C.10.202a), B.11.282a
Intencio iudicat hominem A.10.90
Interpone tuis interdum gaudia curis B.12.22a
Intra triduum reedificabo illud C.18.160a var.
Ita [in]possibile est diuiti C.11.201a, B.14.212a
Ite in vniuersum mundum B.15.491a (C.17.191)
Ite missa est B.5.412
Ite vos in vineam meam B.10.481a, B.15.500
Iube me venire ad te B.18.244a (C.20.253a)
Iudica me B.11.286a
Iunior fui etenim senui B.7.89 (C.9.163)
Iusticia eius manet B.15.327, C.17.66a

Laȝare veni foras B.15.594a
Laboraui in gemitu meo B.15.191 (C.16.333)
Labores manuum tuarum B.6.252a (A.7.234a, C.8.260a)
Latro B.5.476 (Z.5.150, A.5.250, C.6.330)
Lauabis me C.16.335a
Lauacrum-lex-dei C.19.73
Legenda Sanctorum B.11.161, B.11.220, B.15.269, C.17.157
Leuyticy C.5.55, B.15.556 (C.17.219)
Lex Christi B.17.74
Libenter suffertis insipientes B.8.93 (A.9.83a, C.10.90)
Libera voluntas dei C.18.118
Liberum Arbitrium C.16.158, 162, 165, 173, 182, 194; C.18.1, 3, 104; B.16.16, 46, 50; C.18.137, 179
Liberum dei arbitrium C.20.20
Licitum B.11.96
Locutum me aliquando penituit C.13.224b

Magi (see *Ibant magi*)
Maledictus homo qui non reliquit semen B.16.219a (C.18.222a)
Maria optimam partem elegit B.11.255a (C.12.141a)
Mea culpa C.6.64 (B.5.77 Skeat)
Melius est bonum nomen B.3.330 (C.3.483)

Melius est mori C.1.143a, C.6.290a, C.17.40a
Melius est scrutari B.11.231
Memento [Domine] A.11.55 (C.11.49), B.15.490
Memento [mei] B.5.466 (Z.5.136, A.5.238, C.6.320)
Memoria B.15.26 (C.16.186), B.20.366 (C.22.366)
Mens B.15.25 (C.16.185)
Mercedem Z.8.61
Mestus cepit esse B.16.115 (C.18.145)
Metropolitanus B.15.42 (C.16.204), B.15.516 (C.17.267)
Michi vindictam B.6.226a, B.10.209a, B.10.374 (A.11.255), C.17.235a,
    B.19.446a (C.21.446a)
Miserere mei deus B.5.277, B.13.54
Miseretur & commodat B.5.243
Misericordia eius super omnia opera eius B.5.281a, B.11.139a (C.12.74a),
    B.17.318a (C.19.298a)
Misericordia & veritas obuiauerunt sibi B.18.421a (C.20.464a)
Modicum B.18.216 (C.20.225)
Monache, si indiges B.15.343a
Mulier que inuenit dragmam C.5.98a
Multa fecit deus B.10.45
Multi multa sciunt C.11.163, B.11.3
Multi [sunt vocati] B.11.112 (C.12.47)
Mundum pugillo continens C.19.114a

Natus est ex maria virgine C.19.125a
Ne forte tumultus C.18.164a
Ne sitis personarum acceptores B.15.88 (C.16.241a)
Ne soliciti sitis B.7.131 (Z.8.115, A.8.113), B.14.33a
Nec michi nec tibi C.11.213a
Necesse est vt veniant scandala A.11.154a, B.16.157a (C.18.174a)
Necessitas non habet legem C.13.44a
Negocium sine dampno B.14.315a (C.16.149a)
Nemini salutaueritis C.9.123a
Nemo ascendit ad celum B.10.382a (A.11.263a, C.11.207a)
Nemo bonus C.15.135a
Nemo potest duobus dominis seruire B.13.312a (C.6.60a)
Nemo sine crimine viuit B.11.404 (C.13.212)
Nesciat sinistra B.3.72a (A.3.54, C.3.74a)
Nescit aliquis vnde venit B.12.69a
Nichil iniquius quam amare pecuniam B.10.342a
Nichil inpossibile volenti B.11.281a
Nisi granum frumenti C.12.179a

Nisi quis renatus fuerit B.11.82a
Nisi renunciaueritis omnia C.12.171a
Nisi sicut paruuli B.15.149a (C.16.298a)
Nolite fieri sicut ypocrite tristes B.15.219a (C.16.344a)
Nolite iudicare B.11.90 (C.12.31), B.12.89a, B.14.293 (C.16.128)
Nolite mittere B.10.9 (A.11.9, C.11.7)
Nolite mittere falsem B.15.530a
Nolite tangere christos meos B.12.125a (C.14.69a)
Nolite timere eos C.10.99a
Nolo mortem peccatoris C.14.134a
Nominatiuo, pater & filius C.3.406a
Non concupisces rem proximi tui B.20.279 (C.22.279)
Non de solo . . . vivit homo C.5.86–87, B.14.46b (C.15.244b)
Non dimittitur peccatum (see *Numquam dimittitur peccatum*)
Non eligas cui miserearis B.7.77a–b
Non est sanis opus medicus B.16.110a
Non est timor dei B.4.37a
Non habitabit in medio domus mee B.13.432a (C.7.92a)
Non inflatur B.15.157 (C.16.291a)
Non in solo pane (see *Non de solo*)
Non intres in Iudicium B.18.399a (C.20.442a)
Non leuabit gens B.3.324a (C.3.477a)
Non licet uobis legem voluntati C.9.213a
Non mecaberis B.10.372 (A.11.254)
Non morabitur opus C.3.308a
Non occides B.19.446a (C.21.446a)
Non oderis fratres B.11.88, B.11.93 (C.12.34)
Non omnis qui dicit domine B.17.266a (C.19.232a)
Non plus sapere B.10.121 (A.11.74), B.15.69 (C.16.229–30)
Non reddas malum C.5.58a
Non veni soluere legem B.18.349a (C.20.395a)
Non veni vocare iustos B.5.498a (C.7.138a)
Non visurum se mortem C.20.259a
Nullum malum inpunitum B.4.143–44 (Z.4.141–42, A.4.126–27, C.4.
    140–41); B.18.390a (C.20.433)
Numquam colligunt de spinas B.9.155a (C.10.244a)
Numquam dimittitur peccatum C.6.257a, B.5.273a, B.17.310a
    (C.19.290a)
Numquid, dicit Iob, rugiet onager B.15.318 (C.17.52a)
Nunc princeps huius mundi (see *Princeps huius mundi*)

O felix culpa B.5.483a (C.7.125a)

O mors ero mors tua B.17.114a, B.18.35a
O stulte C.12.215a
O vos omnes sicientes B.11.120a (C.12.55a)
Ociositas & habundancia panis B.14.77a
Odisti omnes qui operantur iniquitatem C.20.356a-b
Omnia celestia terrestria flectantur B.19.80a (C.21.80a)
Omnia probate B.3.339-43 (C.3.491-95), A.12.50-52, A.12.56-57, C.20.234a
Omnia que dicunt facite C.8.90a
Omnia traham ad me ipsum B.17.152a (C.19.127a)
Omnia tua sunt ad defendendum B.19.479a (C.21.479a)
Omnis iniquitas quantum ad misericordiam dei B.5.283a (C.6.338a)
Opera enim illorum sequuntur illos B.14.213a (C.16.54a)
Operibus credite C.16.342a
Osanna B.18.8 (C.20.7)

Pacientes vincunt B.13.135a (C.15.137), B.13.171a (C.15.156a), B.14.33c, B.14.54 (C.15.253), B.15.268, B.15.598a
Panem nostrum cotidianum C.16.374a
Parce B.18.392
Parce michi domine B.19.295 (C.21.295)
Parum lauda B.11.106a (C.12.40a)
Pastor B.15.43 (C.16.205)
Pastores loquebantur ad inuicem B.12.142 (C.14.86a)
Pateat B.14.190a
Pater B.16.185 (C.18.192)
Pater Abbas B.5.171 (C.6.153)
Paternoster C.5.46, C.5.87, C.5.107, B.5.341 (A.5.189, C.6.399), B.5.394 (C.7.10), B.10.468, B.13.396 (C.6.283), B.14.49 (C.15.247), C.16.323
Pauci [electi] B.11.114 (C.12.49)
Pauper ego ludo B.11.269a (C.12.154a)
Pauper non habet diuersorium B.12.147a
Paupertas est absque sollicitudine semita B.14.309a (C.16.143a)
Paupertas est odibile bonum B.14.276 (C.16.116), B.14.286a (C.16.123)
Paupertatis onus B.6.315 (C.8.336a)
Pax vobis C.17.238, B.19.169 (C.21.169)
Peccatoribus dare B.15.343a
Pecuniosus B.11.58 (C.12.10)
Pena pecuniaria non sufficit B.11.58a (C.12.10a)
Penetrans domos B.20.340 (C.22.340)
Penitencia B.5.474 (Z.5.148, A.5.248, C.6.328)

Penitet me fecisse hominem B.9.133a (A.10.162, C.10.222)
Per confessionem peccata occiduntur B.14.92
Per Euam cunctis B.5.603a (C.7.250a)
Per passionem domini B.14.190b
Per primicias & decimas B.15.556a (C.17.219a)
Per seculum seculorum B.18.421 (C.20.464); cf. *culorum*
Periculum est in falsis fratribus B.13.70 (C.15.75a) (see also *Vnusquisque a fratre*)
Perniciosus dispensator B.9.94a
Petite & accipietis B.15.428a
Petrus id est christus B.15.212
Philosophus esses si tacuisses B.11.416a (C.13.224a)
Piger propter frigus B.6.236 (A.7.220, C.8.245a)
Pilatus ... sedens pro tribunali B.18.36 (C.20.35)
Placebo B.3.311 (C.3.464), C.5.46, B.15.125
Plenitudo temporis B.16.93 (C.18.126), C.18.138
Ponam pedem in aquilone B.1.119 (C.1.111a), B.15.51a (C.16.213a)
Pontifex B.15.42 (C.17.204)
Populus (qui ambulabat) in tenebris B.5.493a (C.7.133a), B.18.323 (C.20.366)
Porro non indiget monachus B.15.343a
Possessio sine calumpnia B.14.296a (C.16.132a)
Post mortem B.13.44 (C.15.49)
Potencia dei patris B.16.30 (C.18.34)
Pre manibus C.3.300, C.9.45
Precepta Regis B.Prol.145
Presul ... Pontifex ... Metropolitanus B.15.42–43 (C.16.204–5)
Preuaricatores legis C.10.95
Primus heremita B.15.286 (C.17.13)
Princeps huius mundi B.9.8 (A.10.8, C.10.135), A.10.62, B.18.315a (C.20.349a)
Principes C.20.272
Pro dei pietate B.7.46
Pro hac orabit ad te B.13.57 (C.15.60)
Proditor est prelatus B.9.94a
Propter deum subiecti estote B.11.383a
Psallite deo nostro B.11.311 (C.13.123a)
Pseudopropheta B.15.601 (C.17.309)
Pur charite C.8.169, A.7.182 (Z.7.180), B.6.253 (Z.7.239, A.7.237, C.8.265), B.8.11 (A.9.11, C.10.11), B.13.30 (C.15.32)

Quadriduanus C.17.303, B.16.114 (C.18.144)

Qualis pater talis filius B.2.27a (C.2.27a)
Quam olim Abrahe promisisti B.16.242a
Quando misi vos sine pane C.9.120a
Quandocumque ingemuerit peccator C.7.147a
Quant oportet vient B.10.445
Quare impij viuunt? B.10.25a
Quare non dedisti pecuniam B.7.83a
Quare placuit? B.12.216a (C.14.155a)
Quare via impiorum prosperatur? A.11.23a
Quasi dormit C.9.258
Quasi modo geniti B.11.203 (C.12.111)
Que perfecisti destruxerunt B.10.29a (C.11.25a)
Quem diligo castigo B.12.12a
Querite & inuenietis B.15.503a
Qui agit contra conscientiam A.10.94a
Qui bona egerunt (see *Et qui bona*)
Qui circuit omne genus A.10.108a
Qui conceptus est de spiritu sancto B.17.151a
Qui crediderit et baptizatus fuerit A.11.234, B.11.124a (C.12.59a),
  C.13.87a
Qui cum patre & filio B.5.58 (Z.5.72, A.5.42, C.5.199)
Qui facit & docuerit A.11.196a, B.13.118a (C.15.126a)
Qui facit peccatum B.11.204a (C.12.112a)
Qui in caritate manet C.3.403a, B.5.486b, B.9.65a
Qui ingreditur sine macula B.3.237a
Qui loquitur turpiloquium B.Prol.39 (A.Prol.39, C.Prol.40)
Qui manet in caritate (see *Qui in carite manet*)
Qui non diligit B.11.176a (C.12.99a)
Qui numerat multitudinem stellarum B.20.256a (C.22.256a)
Qui offendit in vno B.9.100a, B.11.309 (C.13.122a)
Qui parcit virge B.5.39a (C.5.139a)
Qui peccat in spiritum sanctum (see *Videatis qui peccat*)
Qui pecuniam suam non dedit B.3.241a (A.3.221a)
Qui pluit super Iustos B.19.431 (C.21.431)
Qui sapiunt nugas C.11.18a–b
Qui se exaltabit (see *Qui se humiliat*)
Qui se humiliat A.10.120a
Qui simulat verbis B.10.195-96 (A.11.147-48)
Qui vero non crediderit condempnabitur A.11.234 var.
Qui vos spernit B.13.440a (C.7.100a)
Quia antelate rei C.3.344a
Quia cum iustis non scribantur B.6.76a (A.7.68a, C.8.78a)

Quia in Inferno nulla est redempcio B.18.149a (C.20.152a)
Quia reddit vnicuique iuxta opera sua C.5.32a, B.12.213a (C.14.152a)
Quia sacrilegium est res pauperum B.15.343a
Quia super pauca fuisti fidelis C.14.214a
Quicumque reliquerit patrem C.12.160a
Quid consideras festucam B.10.268a
Quid est ueritas? A.12.28
Quis est ille B.14.104 (C.15.279)
Quis est iste? B.18.316a, 317a, 318a
Quis vestrum sine peccato est C.14.42a
Quodlibet B.15.382
Quodcumque ligaueris super terram B.7.181a (Z.8.164, A.8.159a, C.9. 327a)
Quodcumque pecieritis (a patre) in nomine meo C.7.260a, B.14.46a (C.15.244a)
Quodcumque vultis B.7.60a, C.16.309
Quod scimus loquimur B.12.65a, 66, 67
Quomodo cessauit exactor B.10.333a (C.5.177a)
Quoniam literaturam non cognoui A.8.123 (Z.8.125)
Quorum deus venter est B.9.62a
Quorum tecta sunt peccata (see *Beati quorum*)

Racio B.15.28 (C.16.188)
Ramis palmarum B.18.6
Recordare B.4.120
Redde racionem villicacionis C.9.273
Redde quod debes B.19.187 (C.21.187), B.19.259 (C.21.259), B.19.390 (C.21.390a), B.20.308 (C.22.308)
Reddere B.5.467 (Z.5.137, A.5.241, C.6.321)
Reddet vnicuique iuxta opera sua (see *Quia reddit vnicuique*)
Reddit quod debet B.19.193 (C.21.193)
Reddite B.5.461 (Z.5.131, A.5.233, C.6.315)
Reddite Cesari B.1.52-53 (Z.Prol.139-40, A.1.50-51, C.1.48-49)
Redemptor B.11.207 (C.12.115)
Regum C.3.407, B.3.259 (A.3.238, C.3.413)
Remocio curarum B.14.293a (C.16.128a)
Resureccio mortuorum B.18.370 (C.20.412)
Retribuere dignare domine C.3.340a

Saluabitur vix B.12.281 (C.14.203), B.13.19 (C.15.22)
Sanctorum C.17.157
Sanitatis mater B.14.303a (C.16.138a)

Sapience C.3.485, C.3.496
Sapiencia dei patris B.16.36 (C.18.40)
Sapiencia huius mundi B.12.138a (C.14.83a)
Sapiencia inflat B.12.57a
Sapiencie temperatrix B.14.312a (C.16.146a)
Sapienter B.11.313 (C.13.125)
Satis diues est B.7.86a
Saul interfecit mille B.19.135 (C.21.135)
Sciant presentes & futuri B.2.74a (C.2.81)
Sciencie appetitus hominem B.15.63a (C.16.225a)
Scientes et non facientes B.12.56a (C.14.18a)
Secundum scripturas B.18.112 (C.20.115)
Semiuiuus B.17.58 (C.19.57)
Sensus B.15.29 (C.16.189)
Sepcies in die cadit Iustus B.8.20a (A.9.16a, C.10.21)
Serus est alterius B.5.269a-b (C.6.293a-b)
Seruus nequam B.6.239 (A.7.223)
Set non erat ei locus B.12.147a
Si C.3.327
Si ambulauero in medio vmbre mortis B.7.120-21 (Z.8.104, A.8.102-3, B.12.293a)
Si bona accepimus a domino C.13.17-18
Si culpare velis B.10.266a-b
Si cum christo surrexistis B.10.359a
Si hominibus placerem christi B.13.312a (C.6.60a)
Si indiges & accipis (see *Monache, si indiges*)
Si linguis hominum loquar B.17.261a (C.19.227a)
Si non in prima vigilia B.12.9a
Si quis amat christum B.14.60a (C.15.259a)
Si quis videtur sapiens C.9.127a
Si tibi sit copia B.10.89a (C.11.69a)
Si vis perfectus B.11.274a (C.12.167a)
Sic oportet Christum pati B.19.161a (C.21.161a)
Sicio C.20.408a
Sicut de templo omne bonum progreditur B.15.118 (C.16.273)
Sicut qui mel comedit B.15.55 (C.16.217)
Simile C.18.227, C.19.164
Simile est regnum celorum C.5.98a
Sine restitucione C.6.257
Sit elemosina tua B.7.75
Sola contricio delet peccatum B.11.81a
Sola fides sufficit B.15.389 (C.17.121)

Sompnia ne cures B.7.156 (Z.8.138, A.8.134a)
Spera in deo B.11.287 (C.13.101), B.15.180
Spes B.17.1 (C.19.1), B.17.35 (C.19.36), B.17.48 (C.19.46), C.19.53,
    B.17.84 (C.19.80), B.17.91, B.17.103, C.19.97
Spiritus B.15.36 (C.16.198)
Spiritus fortitudinis B.19.289 (C.21.289), B.19.464 (C.21.464), B.20.24-
    25 (C.22.24-25)
Spiritus Intellectus B.19.463 (C.21.463)
Spiritus Iusticie B.19.297, 301, 302, 397, 402, 405, 474 (C.21.297, 301,
    302, 397, 405, 474)
Spiritus paraclitus B.19.201, 206 (C.21.201, 206)
Spiritus procedens a partre B.16.223a
Spiritus prudencie B.19.276 (C.21.276), B.19.455 (C.21.455), B.20.31
    (C.22.31)
Spiritus sanctus B.16.88 (C.18.120), B.16.90 (C.18.123), B.17.212
Spiritus temperancie B.19.281 (C.21.281), B.20.8, 22, 23 (C.22.8, 22,
    23)
Spiritus vbi vult spirat B.12.63a (C.14.27a)
Stella comata B.18.239 (C.20.248)
Sub molli pastore C.9.265a
Sum Rex, sum princeps B.Prol.132-38 (C.Prol.150-56)
Sunt homines nequam B.12.50a
Sunt infelices quia matres sunt meretrices C.3.190a
Sunt iusti atque sapientes B.10.436a (C.11.271a)
Super cathedram moysi C.8.86a, A.11.223, B.10.404a (C.11.235a)
Super innocentem munera non accepit C.2.42, B.7.42a (Z.8.47, A.8.46a)
Supersedeas C.2.190, C.4.190, C.9.264

Tanquam nichil habentes C.13.4a
Te deum laudamus B.18.422 (C.20.465)
Ter cesus sum B.13.67a
Tezaurisat & ignorat C.12.215a
Tibi soli peccaui B.18.378a (C.20.420a)
Tolle, tolle B.18.47 (C.20.47)
Transgressores B.1.96 (Z.1.42, A.1.94, C.1.92)
Tres vidit & vnum adorauit C.18.241a
Treys encountre treys C.18.238
Trinitas vnus deus C.3.406
Tristicia vestra vertetur in gaudium C.12.207a
Tu dicis B.16.145
Tu fabricator omnium B.17.170a (C.19.134a)
Turpiloquio B.13.456 (C.7.116)

Vbi thesaurus tuus C.6.285a, B.13.398a
Ve soli C.20.316a
Ve terre vbi puer Rex est B.Prol.196 (C.Prol.206)
Ve vobis qui potentes estis B.13.61a (C.15.65a)
Ve vobis qui ridetis B.13.423a (C.7.83a)
Velud sompnium surgencium domine B.14.131b (C.15.306b)
Veni creator Spiritus B.19.210 (C.21.210)
Verbum caro factum est C.3.356, B.5.500a (C.7.140a)
Vere filius dei erat iste B.18.68a (C.20.70a)
Via & veritas B.9.164 (C.10.255)
Videatis qui peccat in spiritum sanctum B.16.47a, B.17.200a–1 (C.19.166a–67)
Videte ne furtum sit C.17.40a
Vidi preuaricantes & tabescebam A.12.19a
Vidit deus (see *Et vidit deus*)
Vigilare C.9.259
Vigilate B.5.442 (Z.5.111, A.5.214, C.7.56)
Vigilate itaque quia nescitis B.17.253a var.
Villam emi C.7.292
Vindica sanguinem iustorum B.17.293a (C.19.274a)
Virga tua & baculus tuus A.10.87, B.12.13a
Virtus in infirmate perficitur B.17.341a (C.19.321a)
Visitauit & fecit (see *Et visitauit*)
Vnusquisque a fratre B.13.73a (see also *Periculum est*)
Vnusquisque portabit onus suum B.10.116a
Volucres celi deus pascit B.14.33b
Vos estis sal terre B.15.429a
Vos qui peccata hominum comeditis B.13.45a (C.15.50a)
Vt quid diligitis vanitatem B.15.81b
Vultus huius seculi C.14.32a
Vxorem duxi C.7.304a, B.14.3a

Ymago dei C.18.7

Piers Plowman: A Guide to the Quotations consolidates—and adds to—what is known about the nearly 600 different quotations in Latin and French (counting repeated instances, nearly 1,200 in all) in Langland's poem. With the translations and commentary, the quotations account for nearly half the poem's substance and, perhaps, much of its form as well. While Langland's poem is, of course, much more than the sum of its borrowings, no study—whether of its author, audience, or art—can afford to ignore the borrowings.

The volume begins with an introductory essay which analyzes the various lines of transmission of the quotations. The quotations are then presented in three ways: Index One lists them in text order and provides extensive information on sources and analogues. Index Two arranges the biblical quotations in biblical order. And Index Three arranges all the quotations in alphabetical order.

This first comprehensive guide to the Latin and French quotations in all three versions (Athlone edition) will facilitate access to Langland's quotations and their sources and will serve as an invaluable research tool and the foundation for further study of their artistic function.

John A. Alford, Professor of English at Michigan State University, is the author of *Piers Plowman: A Glossary of Legal Diction* (1988) and has published numerous articles in *Speculum, Medium Aevum,* and *Chaucer Review*. He also edited *A Companion to Piers Plowman* (1988), co-authored *Literature and Law in the Middle Ages: A Bibliography of Scholarship* (1984), and has been co-editor of *Yearbook of Langland Studies* since 1987. Mr. Alford is a 1988 Guggenheim Fellow and has also received two Fellowships from the National Endowment for the Humanities.

mrts

medieval & renaissance texts & studies
is the publishing program of the
Center for Medieval and Early Renaissance Studies
at the State University of New York at Binghamton.

mrts emphasizes books that are needed —
texts, translations, and major research tools.

mrts aims to publish the highest quality scholarship
in attractive and durable format at modest cost.